SHOCK TROOPS

SHOCK TROOPS

THE HISTORY OF ELITE CORPS AND SPECIAL FORCES

DAVID C. KNIGHT

This edition published by
Bison Books Corporation
17 Sherwood Place
Greenwich CT 06830
USA

Copyright © 1983 Bison Books Corp.

ISBN 0 86124 126 6

Printed in Hong Kong

Page 1: Members of a Waffen SS unit wait for the moment to make an
attack from trenches around Leningrad.
Page 2-3: LVTP-7 amphibious assault vehicles of the US Marines
advance during an exercise in 1977.
Below: The Marines storm ashore at Inchon, 15 September 1950,
during the Korean War.

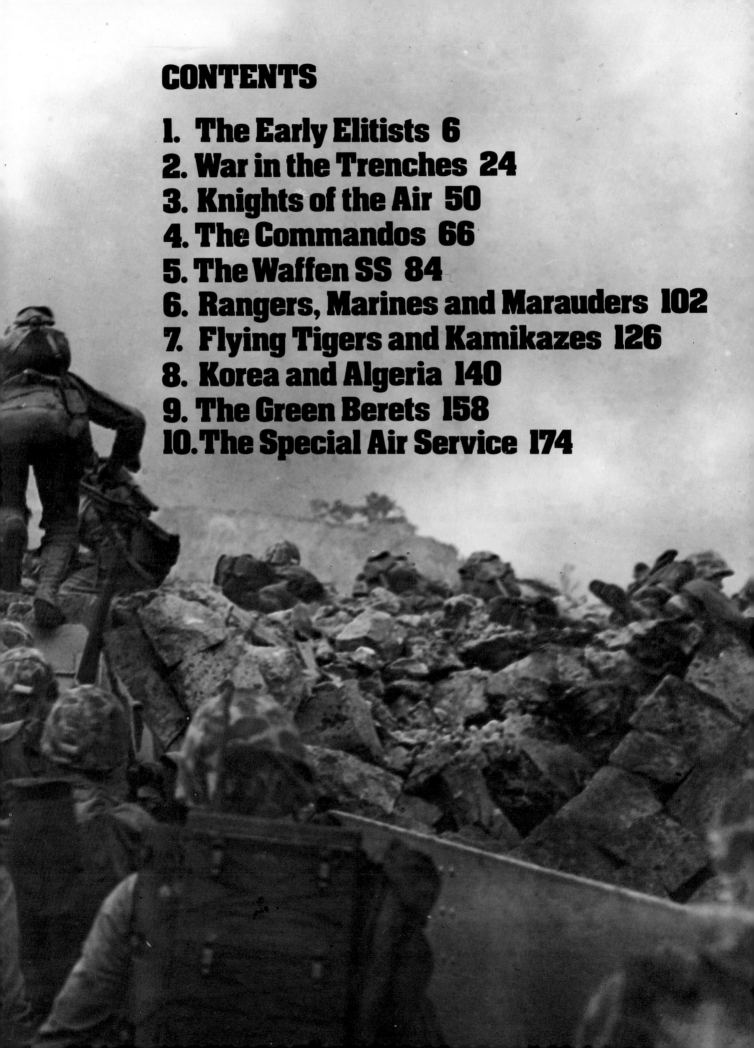

CONTENTS

The Early Elitists

In their early years the US Marines and the French Foreign Legion both fought all around the world – 'From the Halls of Montezuma to the shores of Tripoli.' Battles in Mexico and North Africa are among those proudly remembered by both corps and have helped form their distinguished traditions.

The military services of many nations have forged iron-tough elite shock troops of special men whose deeds transcended those of their brothers-in-arms. Theirs has been the duty that went beyond ordinary soldiering. These 'mission impossible' elitists were picked because their nerves wouldn't break, their guts wouldn't spill and their dedication to their outfits wouldn't let them quit. In comparatively modern times – within the last 200 years – two such military organizations broke new ground and truly earned their laurels as superior shock troops: the French Foreign Legion and the United States Marine Corps.

The French Foreign Legion

As one of the first modern elite shock-troop organizations, none could surpass the courage, fighting ability and magnificent *espirit de corps* of the crack French Foreign Legion. Between its inception in 1831 and World War I, the Legion, with its men proudly wearing its distinctive *kepi blanc* (white headdress) with *nuque couvre* (neck cover), served in North Africa, Spain, the Crimea, Italy, Mexico, West Africa, the Far East and Madagascar. As their fighting fame increased, a mystique of invincibility and reckless valor began to grow up around these hardbitten 'forgotten men' with their faces deeply tanned by the African sun.

This legend of invincibility influenced many of the Legion's foes. The mere presence of a single battalion of Legionnaires attached to larger units of other troops was often enough to turn the tide of battle. This aura was due largely to the fact that the Legionnaire, despite being led by French officers and serving in a special part of the French Army, paid no allegiance to France whatever. His loyalty was to the Legion itself, to its flag and, of course, to his fellow Legionnaires. Once enlisted, he had no home or family but the Legion, no identity in the outside world that he had renounced for the Legion. The Legion – at least for the term of his enlistment – became his world.

Thus when the Legionnaire fought, he did so tenaciously, jealously and absolutely. Whatever diminished the Legion diminished him. That is why the Legion's *Salle d'Honneur* (Hall of Honor)

Opposite: Two Foreign Legion soldiers in the uniforms worn during the Crimean War. On the left a sergeant of grenadiers and on the right a fusilier private.

contains long lists of Legionnaires decorated for such acts as bringing in their dead under enemy fire and shielding their wounded officers with their own bodies. Furthermore, all too frequently in the Legion's history its men have realized – as many did in Mexico – that they were probably dying for a worthless cause, *un sacrifice inutile*. But always their fierce and consuming pride in the Legion kept these men at their guns when lesser troops broke and ran.

While the Legion is actually a highly disciplined professional army of mercenaries that has been in almost continuous combat since 1831, it

Below: A Legionnaire in the official uniform of 1831. The high shako, blue coat and red trousers are basically similar to those worn by most contemporary French infantry units.

has often been romanticized by writers as a haven for criminals, forlorn lovers and unhappy noblemen. While the Legion has had more than its share of these types, its members were more likely to be European professional soldiers who preferred fighting with the Legion to garrison duty with their own armies. From the 1830s until today, the countries of Europe have yielded an unbroken stream of men who, forced or eager to leave their homes for an alien flag, have accepted the challenge *Marcher ou crêver* – 'March or die.'

Misconceptions about the Legion were perpetuated by such 19th-century popular novelists as Percival Wren, author of *Beau Geste* and *Beau Sabreur*, and Ouida (Louise de la Ramée) who wrote *Under Two Flags*. In these tales the characters have invariably committed some crime and enlist in the Legion to avoid arrest. In fact, however, recruits were fingerprinted and subject to the laws of extradition enforceable in French territory, and the Legion itself was under the military laws of France. In some stories the character was arrested in France and given the choice of imprisonment or joining the Legion. Here the authors had confused the Legion with the notorious *Battalion d'Afrique*, which was composed entirely of criminals who were given that option. Actually, the Legionnaires regarded the *Bat' d'Af,* as it was nicknamed, with vast contempt and would fight on the spot if confused or compared with it.

From the beginning, most of the Europeans 'between the ages of 18 and 40, at least five feet tall, but with a physique permitting them to campaign in North Africa or the Far East' who went to enlist were of four types. First were those men who needed to flee from their own countries for political reasons and who, in many cases, were former officers or soldiers. Next in frequency, according to reports by Legion officers who judged the applicants, were the adventure seekers: men who were 'disgusted by petty good fortune, sick of Northern fogs or smoky industrial cities.' Many of these joined *pour aller vers le pays du soleil* – to go to the countries of the sun.

The third group consisted of petty delinquents who thought the Legion would be better than eventual prison, but actual and known criminals were always returned to justice and not permitted to enlist. The men in this third group had to be judged capable of rehabilitation or, in the French phrase, finding *leur équilibre*. The fourth group joined the Legion to try to forget, in a soldier's life, their domestic or romantic disappointments. In the later days of the Legion, there were also men who joined because it had become a family tradition to do so. Among these were many Swiss whose fathers, uncles and even grandfathers had preceded them.

A prospective recruit, who had to enlist in French territory and travel at his own expense to the recruiting office, could join under his true name or under one of his own devising. It was not uncommon to see a recruit, stripped for his

identity papers were not demanded, but if he had them he was encouraged to produce them; the Legion preferred to know whom it was covering with anonymity. The recruit was, in fact, expected to reveal his true identity in confidence when he gave the false name under which he wished to serve. As the Legion officially put it: 'The Legion asks sincerity in exhange for an incognito and no Legionnaire has ever regretted complying.'

At Sidi-bel-Abbès, the recruit underwent several months of hard training; the Legion's objective was to 'cut off all thoughts of the past.' Drill and instruction were in the French language, with explanation where necessary in the Legionnaire's own tongue. At other times, he could speak any language he wished to anyone who could understand it. On his second night at Sidi-bel-Abbès he was initiated into the mysteries of the heroic battle at Camerone – a name sacred to all Legionnaires. This story, which was read aloud, recounted the fight made by three officers and 60 Legionnaires against 8000 Mexicans at Camerone, Mexico, on 30 April 1863. The revered tale is read not only to recruits, but to all members of the Legion every year – wherever they are on the anniversary of that day.

As to the Legion's officers, only the top cadets at St. Cyr (the French West Point) were permitted to choose the Foreign Legion or, if they did not wish service abroad, the *Chasseurs Alpins*. Thus the newly enlisted expatriate met in his officer a Frenchman to whom the glory of France and the tradition of gallantry were realities. Moreover, these young officers were constantly reminded by their superiors that 'You are commanding men who are probably as well educated as yourselves and of as good a family.' A case in point was that of one young officer who joined the Legion shortly after World War I to find that his

Left: A soldier of the Swiss Hohenlohe Regiment which was incorporated into the Legion in March 1831.

Below: Captain Danjou inspires his men during the early stages of their defense of the farm buildings at Camerone, the Legion's most famous battle.

physical, holding a scrap of paper with his new name on it at which he sneaked a last glance as he stepped before the recruiting board. This would be the name he would live with – and perhaps die with – while in the Legion.

If the medical officer found him satisfactory, the board would give him the brief verdict: *'Bon pour le service* (fit for service).' The recruit then signed his name to the provisional enlistment binding him for five years. He also took an oath to serve the Legion (not France). The Legion's unofficial motto, *Legio Patria Nostra* (The Legion is our Fatherland), also told the recruit where his first loyalty lay. All ties now cut with the outside world, alone, and often penniless, he was shipped across the Mediterranean to the famous Maison-Mère – the Mother House – of Legion headquarters at Sidi-bel-Abbès, Algeria. He had thus 'accepted to serve with honor and fidelity in all places the Government of the French Republic wishes to send me.'

It is a common myth that the Legion asked no questions of a recruit. This is not strictly true. His

company commander was Prince Aage of Denmark, and that men included a Bourbon prince and the German Kaiser's nephew.

In the aftermath of the Napoleonic Wars, a time of revolts and revolutions, many displaced and desperate young men were pouring into France: German students and professors, Poles who had escaped execution or Siberian exile from their partitioned country, veterans of Swiss Hohenlohe regiments, discontented Slavs and many others, including deserters from foreign armies. Louis-Philippe, the new King of the French, decided to take advantage of all this idle and potentially dangerous manpower by establishing the Foreign Legion on 10 March 1831. The royal edict announcing its creation stated: 'A legion composed of foreigners shall be formed. This legion shall be called the Foreign Legion [*La Légion Etrangère*].' The edict also decreed that the Legion was to serve only outside France, thus ridding the country of these young *éléments troublés* while creating a powerful instrument of French policy in her newly acquired colonies.

Hundreds of these displaced and hopeless young men flocked to the new Legion – the first of a continuous line of adventurers, deserters, fugitives and other expatriates who have filled its ranks. For the first few years only, Legionnaires were divided up by nationality. The first battalion comprised the Swiss Hohenlohe veterans and the other six were, respectively, Swiss, German, Spanish, Italian and Sardinian, Belgian and Dutch, and Polish. (In the Legion's history it has numbered among its ranks men of over 60 nations.) Their first flag was a tricolor bearing a bronze rooster, one talon on a glove marked *France*, with the inscription 'The King of the French to the Foreign Legion.'

In the name of eliminating Arab anarchy and barbarity, France had begun its conquest of Algeria, North Africa, in 1830 by landing troops just west of Algiers. But there they were confined until the Legion was sent out in 1832. The Legionnaires had been shipped to Africa in the uniform of the French Infantry – red trousers and a high-collared blue tunic – in which they were expected to march and fight in the sands of the desert. They did so, too, until the uniform was gradually modified to the familiar white trousers bloused over tightly-laced boots, a nearly swallow-tailed blue tunic and, of course, the *kepi blanc* with *nuque couvre*. With the arrival of the Legion, Algiers was occupied, as well as Oran to the west and Bône to the east. Then, in the first of their remarkable achievements of building roads as they fought, the Legionnaires of the 2nd Battalion constructed the *Chaussee de la Légion* south of Algiers to Bouffarick.

Below: The Emperor Napoleon III urges his men into the attack at the Battle of Solferino, June 1858. The plight of the wounded after Solferino, many of them Legionnaires, inspired a civilian onlooker, Henri Dunant, to work to establish what eventually became the Red Cross.

The Arab peoples fighting the invading French were fanatical, brave, and staunch believers in their Islamic faith, which assured them of eternal Paradise if they died fighting their enemies. The Arab leader of this resistance – and the arch-enemy of the Legion for 16 years – was Abd-El-Kader. Only in his early 20s in 1832, he was handsome and learned, a poet and a horseman, and a direct descendant of the prophet Moham-med himself. Finally captured in 1848, he was imprisoned in a French castle and eventually died, aged over 80, in Damascus, wearing, ironi-cally enough, the Grand Cross of the Legion of Honor and leaving five wives to mourn him.

When Kader threatened Tlemcen in western Algeria, one of the great Legion leaders, Colonel Bugeaud, marched out to meet and check him. Under Bugeaud, the Legion began its great epic. Later the 4th and 5th Battalions, comprising 2500 men, were sent to attack Kader in the foot-hills of the Atlas Mountains south of Oran. The Arab leader held the hills with some 12,000 men. Attacking up the rough slopes, the Legionnaires were stopped and had to turn back. When the fierce Arab cavalrymen counterattacked, Bugeaud's men were shot and hacked down with swords by the hundreds. Only the French Army's artillery saved them from complete annihilation.

Then in 1835, in an odd move of European diplomacy, the entire Legion was pulled out of Africa and 'ceded' to Spain to help the infant Queen Isabella and her Regent Mother hold the

Above: Allied artillery help repel a Russian sortie against the besiegers of Sebastopol.

Left: A Foreign Legion rifleman of about 1857, wearing medals and long-service badges.

A corporal of a light infantry company of the Legion and a rifleman in the dress worn during the Mexican campaign. The traditional kepi and neck cover can be seen.

after a harsh winter of frozen hands and feet, with many amputations. At this point Louis-Philippe saw the hopelessness of the situation and refused to send reinforcements. The toll of combat and disease decreased the Legion from five battalions to three, later to two, and at last to only one.

Their final action in Spain was an assault on a large Carlist force at Barbastro in which their commander, Colonel Conrad, was killed. Thus of the 4100 Legionnaires of the 'Old Legion' who landed in Spain, only 63 officers and 159 men were left, abandoned by the king who had put his name on their flag, and by their Spanish allies. Once back in France, a new Legion was formed and men were assured of a sergeant's rank if they reenlisted. In fact, 63 of the 'Old Legion' did sign up again – marking the lowest strength to which the Legion has ever dwindled in its history. And they were immediately shipped back to Africa to take up the cudgels once more against Kader.

In their new campaign to wrest Algeria from the Arabs, the Legion's first objective was to storm and capture the city of Constantine, east of Algiers. This formidable citadel stood on a sheer precipice a thousand feet high and was held by an ally of Kader's named Ahmed Bey who, it was said, had blinded the musicians who played for his nude dancing girls. The assault column was 1200 strong and consisted of Legionnaires, Zouaves, Grenadiers and light infantry. Some of the great names in their history led the Legionnaires that day – Combes, Bedeau and young Saint-Armand. In penetrating the outer wall on their first rush, the French had not been aware that there was a second wall, from which they were met with sheets of fire loosed by turbaned Arabs at windows in the town above. When French sappers arrived to blow up the wall with powder sacks, the Arabs forestalled them by toppling the wall over onto them.

In the Constantine mêlée, it was Captain Saint-Armand who shouted the now-famous battle cry 'A moi, la Légion!' Having finally gained the town proper, they struggled on in house-to-house fighting, with Combes falling mortally wounded just as the Arabs surrendered. After the savage battle, Saint-Armand, inspecting his bleeding, dusty and exhausted men, declared, 'Our Legion has become immortal.'

Even so, Kader's forces, except in the coastal cities, held Algeria south of Blidah in an arc extending nearly to the gates of Oran and carried on constant guerrilla warfare against the French. While his men might run from a Legion bayonet charge, they would slip away over the Atlas foothills, re-form and attack at other points. Thus the Legion under Colonel Bugeaud fought almost every day, their numbers stretched pitifully thin. Sentinels were paired and every second man in the command was on guard all night. After sticking out two weeks of combat in the hills, units were given two weeks' rest in the coast towns on the Mediterranean.

Spanish throne against the forces of the pretender Don Carlos, brother of the former king. Landing in the Balearic Islands in August, the Legion's commander, Colonel Bernelle, made the wise move of integrating the battalions as they have remained ever since – without regard for nationality.

Soon the Legion, some 4000 strong, was ferried across to Tarragona, near Barcelona, on the mainland. The partisan, though powerful, Carlists were based along the Arga and Ega Rivers in the mountainous Basque area. The Royalist Army was moving northeast against them to try to push them out of their hilly retreats and up against the Pyrenees, behind which French Army troops were waiting. But the Carlists were among their own hill people who fed and sheltered them, and they refused to fight an open battle with the larger Royalist Army. Only the Legion was fit for the guerrilla warfare which had to be waged.

Advancing north into Catalonia in the fall of 1835, the Legion succeeded in wiping out the Carlist bands in fighting as fierce as that against Abd-El-Kader. By Christmas they were ordered to join the Royalist Army, which had had bad reverses near Estella. Their shoes and uniforms were now in tatters, and they had not been paid since landing in Spain, but bribes by the Carlists to join them were scorned. In February a thousand of them beat off six times their own number in a day-long action, while the Royalist troops stood by as virtual onlookers. Even the Legion was unable to break the Carlist strength

By 1841 there were two full regiments of the Legion, one in Oran and Algiers and the other holding the province of Constantine. Their columns were constantly pressing on Kader, trying to force him into infantry action and to encircle his main forces outside Blidah, which the Legionnaires held fast despite the fierce charges of the formidable Kabyle warriors. One Legionnaire wrote home about the gruesome custom of affixing the severed heads of fallen Kabyles to the gateposts of Blidah, a practice borrowed from the enemy.

The slow encircling of Kader's forces proceeded, and at last some of his camps were surprised and every male slain by the French. Just before the Legion attacked at Zhigeli, one Legionnaire saw Kader himself riding with his men, 'his dark and bearded countenance standing out.' In one of the all-out battles of the Algerian campaign, the Legionnaires charged with bayonets fixed, driving the Arabs over the cliffs and into the Mediterranean, where many swam swiftly offshore and got away to fight another day. Then in May 1841, at Duera, Kader stormed a Legion post with over 2000 tribesmen, butchering 450 of the French garrison of 750. When relief parties finally arrived, even the toughest Legionnaires were shaken by what they saw. In reprisal, the Legion moved out in force to take Kader in his stronghold at Thaza. But the Arab leader had already flown to Morocco. His castle, largely undefended, was looted and blown up by the Legionnaires.

Colonel Bugeaud then had his Legionnaires start the other work for which they were so noted, constructing roads, bridges and canals along the trackless coast. Permanent fortifications were also started at such points as Maccara, Kader's home town, and the Legion's permanent home city of Sidi-bel-Abbès. Over the years it became a beautiful modern city, site of the Legion's Mother House with its shrines and monuments to its heroes.

In 1846 Kader left the sanctuary of Morocco, regathered his forces and took up the struggle against the French. In this fighting, the 2nd and 3rd Battalions of the Legion under Colonel Pelissier bottled up an Arab force in the caves of the Atlas Mountains. But their position was too strong to storm, and an officer who was sent to demand their surrender was murdered. In a prelude to modern flamethrowers, Pelissier fired the caves to drive the enemy out to negotiate, but the sun-dried grass, bush and manure flared up so fiercely that 500 Arabs were suffocated before the rest could surrender.

Thanks in large part to the roads they had built, the Legion now succeeded in driving Kader south to the high plateau and the snows of the Grand Atlas. Thus his communications were cut and his satellite tribes to the north were reduced. Unable to sustain his forces without his gunrunners of European arms and ammunition, Kader once again headed for Morocco. However, the

Moroccans threw him out of their country and he was forced at last to surrender to the French, whereupon he was sent off to his long exile in the castle at Pau.

With the conquest of Algeria completed, things were comparatively quiet for the Legion for a few years – until in 1854 the bugles at Sidi-bel-Abbès blew assembly for the Crimean War.

On 27 March 1854 an Anglo-French-Turkish alliance was signed against Russia, which was moving troops down through the Balkans into Turkish territory. Soon Anglo-French divisions began to embark for the Crimean Peninsula. The Legion's 1st Regiment went ashore at Gallipoli on 14 June carrying flags embroidered with the Bonaparte eagles of the new Emperor, Napoleon III. They also brought cholera with them, losing some 200 Legionnaires to the disease, including the heroic young Captain Saint-Armand of the Constantine assault. On 14 September the Legion's regiments, fighting as a brigade, crossed the Black Sea to land at Eupatoria on the Crimean Peninsula. This put them north of the big arsenal and naval base at Sebastopol where the Russian fleet was moored. Four days later, with British and Turkish units, the Legion was marching south for Alma and Balaclava, where they engaged the Russian forces on the 20th.

Here, for the first time, the Legion was not up against untrained Arab tribesmen or Spanish revolutionaries, but disciplined soldiers of the biggest army in Europe. Indeed, many Russian

A drummer and sergeant of the Legion in the uniform worn in 1872.

Legionnaries were staring down the gunbarrels of their own countrymen. The Allies began their attack with great fury but units became entangled in the first rush. Trying to keep them evenly aligned, a French officer, seeing a Legion battalion moving with parade precision, yelled to them: 'Legionnaires, serve as an example to the others!' And they did. The Legion commander, Colonel Viénot, then turned his guns on the stubborn Russian right wing, which suddenly gave way, and the entire enemy line began streaming off toward Sebastopol. By 1 October the Allied batteries and entrenchments had hemmed in the peninsula.

As usual, the Legion was ill-clothed for such a campaign; it was bitter cold and constant rain was falling, with winter fast approaching. The tanned veterans of Africa found firewood scarce and in their miserable trenches they had to make chimneys for their campstoves from cans. On 5 November the Russians broke out in a fierce attack on the British lines and in pea-soup fog overran four outpost companies of Legionnaires in a shallow ravine. But the discipline for which they were now famous enabled them to re-form and hold the position until the whole Legion brigade came to their relief and drove off the Russians.

All winter both sides attacked and counterattacked, and at last the besieged Russians grew weaker. In the cruel mud and snow they were driven back down into Sebastopol. In May Legion units charged across the Russian parapets almost daily, only to be repulsed by the tenacious enemy. On one of these forays, Colonel Viénot fell dead with a bullet in his head. Looking at his still warm body, his men were struck by the fact that there was no blood on his milk-white beard. The gate of the 1st Regiment Headquarters at Sidi-bel-Abbès would later bear his name.

On 6 September, after 11 months of bitter siege, the famous Malakoff Redoubt fell to the Allies, with the entire 1st Regiment of the Legion having volunteered to spearhead the attack. That night, their fleet in flames, the Russians evacuated Sebastopol. The Legionnaires moved into a tent city until March of the following year, when peace was signed in Paris. Embarking again for Algeria, the Legion paused only at the Golden Horn to receive medals and honors from the Turkish sultan to add to the ever-growing list of victories for their flag.

Back at Sidi-bel-Abbès, the battered Legion, with fresh recruits, was reorganized into two new regiments. Their next problem was a new revolt of the fanatical Kabyle warriors of the high plateau. The veterans of the Crimea moved out against them, with Colonel MacMahon (of the subsequent tragedy at Sedan in 1871) among their commanders. It took until July of the next year to subdue the Kabyles. One captured tribesman confided to a Legionnaire that it was the movement of the Legionnaires' great capes that had caused them to give up. 'When we saw those big capes coming up to take our entrenchments from the rear without even returning our fire, then we went away.' Meanwhile, in support of the fighting Legion, the 1st Battalion was irrigating fever-stricken land, draining swamps and building new roads.

In the trumped-up war arranged by Napoleon III and Prime Minister Cavour of Sardinia in the name of uniting Italy under King Victor Emmanuel II, the men of the Legion were sent to fight the Austrians in Northern Italy. Hearing the bugles blow again at Sidi-bel-Abbès, they embarked for the third time to fight in Europe – from which they were exiles by choice. But by then many of the long-time veterans among them had become too hardened to care where or against whom they fought.

Landing at Genoa on 26 April 1858, the Legion was brigaded with the Zouaves as a division of the 2nd Corps under a famous Legionnaire leader, General Épinasse. On 4 June the 2nd Corps, as the advance body of the main Army, crossed the Ticino River and headed for Magenta and the Austrian Army four miles away in Lombardy. Halfway there, the Legionnaires had to cross a swiftly flowing canal; on the opposite bank white-coated Austrian soldiers poured slashing point-blank fire into their ranks. With their famous ax-bearing sappers cutting a path, the Legion crossed and gained a tenuous foothold on the other bank. Re-forming, the Legionnaires executed a bayonet charge that drove the Austrians back to the railroad west of Magenta. But there they held firm.

After a short rest, the Legion renewed its attack across the tracks in the van of the entire Corps. As so often, one of their colonels, De Chabrière, was shot dead. In the Legionnaires' wake the whole 2nd Corps poured into Magenta. As night came on, the Legionnaires found themselves fighting from house to house, as they had at Constantine. At nine o'clock the beaten Austrians withdrew to the west of Milan and that night the exhausted Legionnaires slept in the streets of Magenta – a name that would soon be emblazoned on their flag.

Three days later the Legion led the 2nd Corps into cheering Milan. However, the wounded, with no anesthetics available and lacking even stretcherbearers, were 'in all stages of agony and pain, only half clad, torn, dirty, and muddy in their own blood.' Nor was this the end of the campaign for the Legion. The Austrian Army by mid-June had taken up strong defense positions near Lake Garda below the snow-capped foothills of the Italian Alps. The dusty, sweltering French pursuing columns arrived in the Solferino Heights on the evening of 23 June – and were attacked the next morning by the Austrians. An observation balloon was sent aloft which revealed that the central heights of Solferino were lightly held; if taken, the Austrian forces would be cut in half.

Napoleon III himself finally determined that

the 1st Brigade of the Legion would spearhead the attack. Storming their way upward, the Legionnaires captured the hill known as the Spy of Italy and planted their flag on it, whereupon the French artillery poured their fire into the retreating Austrians until a sudden summer storm broke off the fighting in the late afternoon. Thousands of men on both sides fell in this mighty battle and, next morning, on the Spy of Italy alone, there lay the bodies of 1600 French regulars and Legionnaires.

Before they sailed back to Africa, the Legion was paraded through Paris before wildly cheering crowds. In Algiers trouble was brewing again, as usual. For the Legionnaires who had helped win a European war in 20 days, it took 30 to compel Sheik Beni-Suassen to sue for peace.

From 1863 to 1867 the Legion fought the senseless Mexican campaign to place and maintain the Hapsburg Archduke Maximilian on the throne of Mexico as emperor. After four years of almost constant combat, this unrighteous cause – supported wholeheartedly by Napoleon III – would end in failure, with the Legion retreating to its ships for passage back to Sidi-bel-Abbès. Yet it was here, at a small village marked on few maps, that the valor of a few dozen Legionnaires created for the Legion its most imperishable legend.

Early in 1862 French troops landed at Veracruz with the object of marching to Mexico City where Maximilian would be installed as emperor. However, this expeditionary force, ravaged by yellow fever, got no farther than Puebla, from which it was beaten back by the armies of Benito Juárez. It was only with great difficulty that they rallied and held at Orizaba. When word of this reached Algeria, Legion officers begged their Emperor to send them to Mexico, unaware that Napoleon, hoping to gain control of all Mexico, had already promised Maximilian to commit the Legion there for ten years to protect French interests. Since the American Civil War was then at its height, Napoleon correctly calculated that neither Union nor Confederate forces would interfere with his Mexican designs.

On 9 February 1863 two battalions of the Legion under Colonel Jeanningros embarked from Africa and 40 days later they were laying siege to 18,000 Juaristas in Puebla. They soon found that North Africa at its worst was not as bad as the steamy plains around Puebla. A great many fell ill from yellow fever or typhus. Vultures waiting to feed on their dead were nothing new to the Legion, but there was a peculiar horror about the Mexican variety; they did not circle over the corpses, but squatted around them in menacing circles, waiting to tear at the dead flesh.

It was on 30 April 1863, at Camerone, that a few members of the Legion did the deed that no Legionnaire would ever forget. The 3rd Company of the 1st Battalion moved out from Chiquihuite at one o'clock in the morning to clear the road for a convoy coming from Soledad to Puebla. They numbered 60 men under Captain Danjou and Lieutenants Vilain and Maudet. About daybreak they were to reach the waterhole at Palo Verde, by a road that took them through the devastated hamlet of Camerone, where the only building standing was a ruined ranchhouse with a corral.

About seven o'clock they halted in the heavy woods at Palo Verde and started to cut firewood to brew coffee. Suddenly, out of the hill passes and across the plain behind them, poured a horde of charging horsemen. At first the Legionnaires thought they were French – until they saw the tall Mexican saddles and heard the firing. Soon the riders had ringed the woods and crossed the access roads. Danjou, with two files on either side of the road, started back toward Camerone. The Mexican horsemen were coming at them from all sides now, and the 3rd Company formed up in a hollow square to take – and break – the first mass attack. Somehow they fought their way to within a few hundred yards of the red-roofed hacienda, where they thought they could hold out until relief came.

By the time they reached it, however, the Mexicans had taken the big ranchhouse and only the corral with its open sheds was available to the French. By nine o'clock Danjou had barricaded his Legionnaires in the northwest side of the corral. An hour and a half later, Mexican bugles blew for a parley and in good French the enemy officers called to Danjou to surrender, pointing out that his situation was hopeless and that their own strength was over 2000. They also assured him that no harm would come to him or his remaining men. Danjou refused and then went from one post to another, calling the name of each man to swear that he would fight to the death with him. He had just obtained the word of the last man when he was struck by Mexican bullets. Two Legionnaires sprang forward to protect his body with their own – firing as they did so – until Danjou died five minutes later.

The small band held on until noon, with Vilain in command, when the entire hacienda fell into Mexican hands. Suddenly they heard trumpets blaring and thought for a moment that relief had come at last. But then they heard the roll of the small Mexican drums and realized that new enemy infantry was coming up. From the roofs of the sheds they saw three fresh battalions advancing on them, and knew then that there could be no other ending but death. Even so, none complained when Vilain turned down another offer to surrender.

They fought on under the blistering sun. Their canteens were empty and they wet their lips with wine or urine. Around two o'clock Vilain fell dead of slugs taken at almost point-blank range. When Maudet took charge, he again refused an offer to surrender, even when the enemy set fire to the sheds' roofs and the choking smoke added to their gnawing thirst. At last only Maudet, Corporal Maine and Legionnaires Katau, Wenzel, Constantin and Leonhart were still on their feet

Juaristas, driving them north toward the Rio Grande. By late spring of 1864, the Legion in Mexico had lost in combat and from disease over 800 of its original strength of 1400. As for Maximilian, the first year of his regime made it evident that there was no popular support for it and that his authority rested solely on French bayonets. Indeed, by 1865 most of France wanted to break off the Mexican adventure, and to these wishes Napoleon began to yield.

Once back in its African home, the Legion resumed its running fight with the unruly Arab leaders. But not for long. When France declared war on Prussia in July 1870, a badly-dispersed and disorganized French Army soon suffered severe reverses at the hands of the well-trained German Army. In a few short weeks, French forces were bottled up in the fortress at Metz and General MacMahon surrendered his army at Sédan, with Napoleon III himself among the prisoners. The siege of Paris began on 19 September. Once again the Legion was needed – this time in France itself – to aid the army of the new French leader, Léon Gambetta, who was trying to organize defense lines south of the Loire.

Before the Legion embarked from Oran for Toulon, its commanders thought it wise to leave behind its German Legionnaires – so far as they could be identified – in Algeria. In early November they helped retake Orléans, but then the German forces proved too strong the Army of the Loire and the Legion began to retreat south and east. By 6 December the Legion, fighting savage rearguard actions and now down to a mere 1000 men, reached St. Florent. Here they were given 2000 untrained recruits and by January had joined the Eastern Army around Besançon. On the 14th they stormed the heights above Sainte-Suzanne with great vigor, whereupon a French general reported: 'The Legion has just done, alone, the work of a whole division.' But it proved impossible to hold the heights without supplies, and one night they struggled down through deep snows to Besançon to await the inevitable French defeat.

There the Legion waited two weeks in misery until the surrender of Paris. In their ranks was Peter I of Serbia, then still a prince. After the Peace of Versailles, with its cession to Prussia of Alsace-Lorraine, the Legion wondered what its own fate would be as a fighting unit of a defeated nation. Fortunately for them, Chancellor Bismarck had no interest in France's colonies in Africa; after being sent to suppress the terrible street-wars of the Commune in Paris, they were allowed to embark for their African home.

No sooner had the Legion returned than the worst revolt since the first French landings broke out. Once again the Legion's columns went out against the Arabs, led this time by the fierce Ouled Sidi Cherih. Alongside the men of these Arab tribes fought their women, who were particularly skillful in knifing and killing the French wounded. However, the Legion was able to press

firing. At three o'clock, the six of them charged crazily out of their barricades with bayonets fixed. When Maudet fell, Katau flung himself on his body and was killed in the act. Now completely surrounded, Wenzel, Constantin and Maine were overpowered. Legionnaire Maine, badly wounded at Sebastopol, was miraculously not even scratched at Camerone.

Half of the 63 Legionnaires already lay dead and a dozen others were dying of their wounds. Yet the Mexicans, brave men themselves, treated the enemy wounded well. Although 300 Mexicans had been killed, their commander allowed one of the three survivors to send his famous message to his colonel: 'The 3rd Company of the 1st is dead, my Colonel, but it did enough to make those who speak of it say, "It had nothing but good soldiers."' Oddly, Danjou's body was never found, but his wooden hand (he had lost a hand at Sebastopol) was recovered and taken to repose in the Hall of Honor at Sidi-bel-Abbès; today it can still be seen at the Museum of the Foreign Legion at Aubagne near Marseilles, the Legion's headquarters since 1962. Thirty years after the battle, the Mexican government permitted a monument to be erected at the foot of a tall tree in Camerone.

On 19 May the city of Puebla surrendered to the French and on 7 June the Legion entered Mexico City, with Napoleon ordering it reinforced with new men from Africa. With the capital city as their headquarters, the Legion and other French forces kept up their attacks on the

Cherih toward the Moroccan frontier and finally defeated his forces.

Not until 28 September 1883 were conditions in Africa such that the Legion could be sent for pacification purposes to the Far East, where France had acquired the new colonies of Indochina (Vietnam) and Cambodia. That day the famous 1st Battalion, 600 men strong under Colonel Donnier, embarked to sail east of Suez. In mid-November they reached Hanoi to begin their warfare against the *Pavilions Noirs*, the Black Flags, of China. The Legion would be fighting these and other Oriental forces who claimed sovereignty over the new French protectorates until 1887.

Despite the risks of death and torture, service in the *Extrême Orient* (the Far East) came to be eagerly sought after. Far East pay was the highest the Legion offered and the rate of exchange was quite favorable. Another inducement was the women of Tonkin, Annam, Cambodia and Cochin-China, who were neither veiled nor otherwise taboo. A pseudo-domestic arrangement was frequently possible to which apparently no one – including the officers – objected.

After some isolated adventures in French West Africa and against the Hova natives in Madagascar – France's great island protectorate – in the 1890s, the Legion devoted itself to the continuing problems of North Africa until World War I. Chief among these was maintaining order in Morocco, across whose frontiers Arab tribes had been raiding into the valleys of South Oran. These raids were generally hit-and-run affairs in which the Legion saw much action in chasing the aggressors back across the border.

French officers who had long been fighting in the desert were convinced that these dissidents could not be put down unless all of the caravan routes were in French hands. Accordingly, the Legion was beefed up with additional men, and columns, often several hundred strong, were constantly sent out to patrol these routes. One of them went on an astounding 1100-mile march of 70 days through blistering heat of 125 degrees. On the plains of El Moungar stands a monument inscribed:

Here Fought during 8 Hours against Moroccan Dissidents 113 Legionnaires of the 22nd Mounted Company of the 2nd Foreign Regiment. Two officers . . . were mortally wounded. 34 Killed and 47 Wounded.

This action just preceded the arrival of one of the great heroes of the Legion, Colonel Lyautey. He joined the Legion at Ain Sifra in South Oran shortly after some 500 Legionnaires held the oasis of Taghit to the southwest for eight days against thousands of dissidents – one of the greatest glories of the Foreign Legion. When he inspected the survivors and the garrison at Ain Sifra, Lyautey asked the men: 'Have any of you served with me before?' Legionnaire after Legionnaire stepped forward to say: 'I brought you word at . . . I was with you at Pac Luong . . . I was in your escort at Tananariva. . . .' From Ain Sifra, where Lyautey lived in splendor like a great lord to impress the Arab dissidents, ceaseless patrols continued to police the caravan routes to deny them to the Arabs.

Under Lyautey, the Legion seemed to pride itself on the hardships it was called upon to endure. 'It was a heroic period,' wrote one officer later. 'We marched unceasingly . . . revictualling was conspicuous by its absense; no supply trains; it was the regime of *Kessara* (rice and grease), watered with whatever water could be found. Wine? We did not know its color. . . .' Lyautey often accompanied these columns. At this time, out of the depths of the Sahara, there appeared again the dissident leader Bou-Ammama off to the southwest in Mauretania. It was there that the Legion crushed him.

Major French operations against Morocco began with the occupation of Oudjda on the Algerian frontier. However, it was soon apparent that the lack of roads west from Oudjda would prevent a real thrust against the dissidents. Accordingly, on 7 August 1907, an expeditionary force – including the 6th Battalion of the Legion's 1st Regiment – was landed at Casablanca. So fierce was the resistance that it took French forces well into the New Year to subjugate the area around Casablanca. A punitive expedition to Marrakesh followed on the news that a French doctor there had been murdered by Arab dissidents. Later, Marrakesh was occupied and the French now felt sure they were masters of the deserts of North Africa. However, in Fez in 1911 the new Sultan of Morocco was attacked by a force of Berber dissidents but the Legion was sent to his relief and occupied the city.

On 13 July Colonel Lyautey made a triumphal entry into Fez, founded when the great Arab leader Haroun-al-Raschid was in his glory. It was in this city that the Moroccan Protectorate was proclaimed and from Tripoli to Tangiers, south to the Ivory Coast and Dahomey and east to Chad, the power of the French seemed inviolate after 80 years of struggle – thanks in large part to the Foreign Legion. In the years following, the Legion also became mechanized, with the first desert troop trucks hauling Legionnaires across the wastes. In the beginning, the old veterans deplored them, but in time they were to become as much as part of the Legion as the *kepi blanc*.

In May 1914, near Meknès, columns of the Legion from the west and east joined, and at Taza, east of Fez, there was a grand review on the 18th before Lyautey, the resident general. One month later, a nephew of Maximilian, the Archduke Franz Ferdinand, was assassinated. Soon the assembly bugles were to blow again at Sidi-bel-Abbès, and the men of the Legion would be summoned to the Western Front for combat in World War I.

The US Marine Corps

Older than the French Foreign Legion by 56 years, the United States Marine Corps did not at first function primarily as ground shock troops. Rather, as one of their sobriquets so aptly describes them, they were essentially 'soldiers of the sea' aboard naval vessels.

The first US Marines, called Continental Marines, were formed at the outbreak of the American War of Independence. The Continental Congress, on 10 November 1775, passed a resolution prescribing two Marine battalions. No one, this resolution stipulated, could be a Marine except '. . . such as are good seamen, or so acquainted with maritime affairs as to be able to serve to advantage by sea. . . .' And indeed, it was no accident that the American Colonies enlisted Marines even prior to the Declaration of Independence on 4 July 1776. George Washington, John Adams and others of the Founding Fathers were convinced that the sea was the chief defense of North America. And in fact, the Atlantic and Pacific Oceans are still one of the continent's main barriers of defense – which is why the United States today possesses one of the world's most powerful navies and certainly the world's most efficient corps of Marines.

When the Marine Corps was first organized, and for almost a century thereafter, it closely resembled the British Royal Marine. This was only natural, since the organization of the Continental Marines, like that of the Continental Navy itself, was modeled after the Mother Country's. England provided the sole familiar pattern on which the Continental Congress could create

armed forces. However, the US Marine Corps eventually developed independently to become a world-renowed body of seagoing soldiers.

During its first 125 years, service on the Navy's major ships was the primary function of the Corps. Marines served as captain's orderlies, performed guard duty, enforced discipline and participated in boarding and landing parties. Ashore, Marine detachments provided security at naval stations and bases. As the Navy replaced sails with steam power, this mission gradually changed. In 1894 Congress directed the Corps to provide forces to take and defend naval bases near operational areas. During the 1920s and 1930s, the Corps developed the doctrine, techni-

Above: The first US Marine recruits are berated by their sergeant, establishing a long tradition. Looking on are Captain Nicholas and Lieutenant Parke, two of the Corps' first officers.

Below: Marines from the sloop *Ranger* (Captain John Paul Jones) set out to raid the English coastal town of Whitehaven in 1778, during the War of Independence.

ques, organization and equipment needed for the amphibious assaults of World War II and the Korean War.

The first action in which the Continental Marines took part was a raid on New Providence Island in the Bahamas, where the British had stockpiled large supplies of cannon and gunpowder. On 3 March 1776 the Marines landed, captured two British forts and took away 88 guns, 14 mortars and much ammunition. These were delivered to General Washington's Continental Army and aided him in carrying on the Revolution. The officer who commanded the Marines at New Providence was Captain Samuel Nicolas. Later promoted, he was senior Marine officer during the Revolution and was thus the Corps' first commandant.

Continental marines fought in several land battles of the Revolution, including those at Fort Mifflin and Princeton in 1777. They also took part in all the major naval actions of the war. But in 1784, after the peace with Great Britain, both the Navy and Continental Marines were disbanded. For the next 14 years, the United States actually had no federal Navy or Marine Corps.

In 1798, with attacks on American shipping by the Barbary pirates (North African raiders from Tripoli, Tunis and Algiers, then called the Barbary States) and by French privateers, the United States was forced to reactivate the Navy. On 11 July 1798 Congress established a permanent Marine Corps. Its strength was 33 officers and 848 enlisted men.

In the Quasi or Naval War with France of 1798-1801, Marines saw combat in many actions, especially in boarding and taking French privateers and merchantmen. In 1800 they also made the only two landings of the war, at Santo Domingo and at Curaçao, West Indies. In Tripoli in 1805, a small band of Marines under Lieutenant Presley Neville O'Bannon captured the fortress at Derna in a daring raid. It was the first time the American flag was raised over a fortress in the Old World. This action inspired the phrase '. . . to the shores of Tripoli' in 'The Marines' Hymn.'

In the 19th century US Marines landed and fought everywhere the Navy did, including the Falkland Islands, Haiti, West Africa, China, Okinawa, Formosa, Sumatra, Hawaii, Egypt and the Arctic. This roster of farflung places justifies the claim: 'We have fought in every clime and place/Where we could take a gun.'

In the 19th century Marines also served ashore in self-contained units. For example, marine companies and battalions fought in the War of 1812. In August of 1814, when the British marched on Washington, DC, Marines and sailors put up the only resistance. Outside Washington, at Bladensburg, a large American army of militia and regulars panicked and ran before the Redcoats. But the outnumbered Marines, with Navy gunners in support, fought the British off for two hours before they were overwhelmed.

Marine companies and/or battalions also fought in the Creek and Seminole Wars (1836-1842) and in the Mexican War (1846-1848). In the latter conflict, a Marine battalion served with

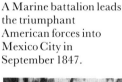

A Marine battalion leads the triumphant American forces into Mexico City in September 1847.

Above: A Marine guard formed up before an inspection aboard the USS *Portsmouth* in 1895.

Left: Part of the Marine contingent of the Allied relief force which was sent to Peking during the Chinese Boxer Rebellion.

Above: Marines hike into the Philippine jungle during the fighting there in the early 1900s.

Below: Marines in full equipment get ready for a march in the streets of Veracruz in 1914.

General Winfield Scott's army and helped capture Mexico City. This explains the reference to the Halls of Montezuma in 'The Marines' Hymn,' as that city had been the capital of King Montezuma's great Aztec Empire.

As the Civil War approached, Marines were called out in 1859 to quell the rebellion that John Brown had tried to stir up by seizing the United States Arsenal at Harper's Ferry, Virginia. Since the Marines at Washington were the nearest troops to Harper's Ferry, they were ordered to recapture the arsenal and take Brown into custody. In a matter of hours the marines and a small force of soldiers, under the command of the then Colonel Robert E. Lee, had accomplished their mission. In the Civil War, detachments of Marines fought at the first Battle of Bull Run in July 1861, on the Mississippi River and in the Navy's landings on the Confederate coast.

In 1898 the Spanish-American War brought important developments for the Marine Corps. As soon as the war was declared, a strong battalion of marines was attached to the Atlantic Fleet. In June of 1898 these men landed at Guantanamo Bay, Cuba, and swiftly captured this strategic site as a base for the Navy. It is still a US Naval Base at this writing. Guantanamo Bay was the first landing by American troops in Cuba and the first time since the Civil War that a separate Marine expeditionary force had been organized and committed. US Marines also saw combat in Guam and Puerto Rico. From 1898 on the Corps worked to keep such expeditionary forces ready for immediate deployment overseas.

In the years after the Spanish-American War, the Marine Corps saw much active service. Since many of these actions took place in tropical countries, they are popularly called the 'Banana Wars.' Marines fought against the fierce Moro tribesmen in the Philippine Insurrection of 1899-1902. To protect US citizens and property, the Marines were sent to China during the Boxer Rebellion in 1900; there they fought valiantly at the American Legation in Peking. They also served in Cuba, Nicaragua, Veracruz, Haiti and Santo Domingo.

Prior to World War I, the Corps grew in strength from 4800 in 1898 to over 10,000 officers and men in 1916, chiefly because it had become a national force-in-readiness. When trouble threatened US bases or citizens anywhere in the world, the Navy and Marines were usually called upon to protect them. Because of these numerous expeditions in the years between 1898 and 1916, the Marine Corps was well prepared to serve in World War I.

Above: A Marine artillery unit fires at insurgents during the 1916 intervention in the Dominican Republic.

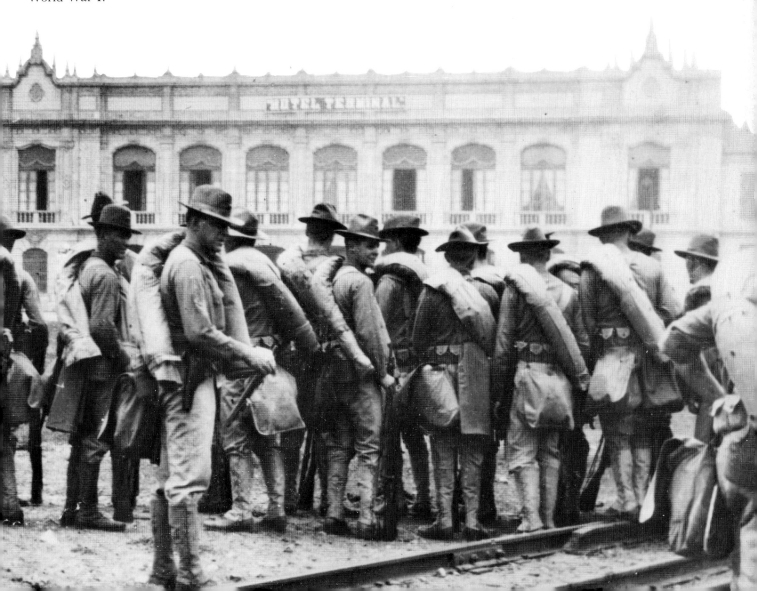

War in the Trenches

Each army came to terms with the grim realities of trench warfare in World War I in its own way but the aggressive 'can do' attitude of the elite forces gave them a status and importance far beyond their numbers.

While most of the truly elite shock troops of World War I fought on the side of the Allies, Germany had done some experimenting with them late in 1915. Used first in the fighting around Mulhausen, these units were composed of soldiers under the age of 25, who had been specially trained in hand-to-hand fighting. As did the *Waffen* SS a few years later, they took the Totenkopf, or death's head, as their insignia and were rewarded with extra rations. Comradeship between officers and enlisted men was encouraged, with the men given the privilege of addressing their superiors by the familiar *du*. Also taught infiltration tactics, these *Stosstruppen* (literally, "troops that strike") were later used with good success against the Russians at Riga and the Italians at Caporetto in 1917. But it was in the last great spring offensives of the war that the *Stosstruppen* were used in more numbers than before and they were, in fact, the backbone of this final German effort.

Prior to this, the ranks of the German forces in the west were combed for the best volunteers to fill the ranks of these strike battalions; they were then trained in independent action and the handling of light automatic weapons and flamethrowers. Emphasis was also placed on using individual initiative and by-passing strongpoints. The *Stosstruppen*'s main mission was to lead other units through breaks in the enemy front. Their officers were told not to stop to reassemble, but always to keep going so that the force of their momentum would not be lost. Lengthy artillery preparations were not used before their attacks because the element of surprise would be thrown away thereby. Instead, short, incisive barrages were pinpointed against critical headquarters, opposing batteries, and road junctions. Further, smoke and gas shells rather than high-explosive ones were fired in pre-attack bombardment of front line positions. The reason for this was to avoid the churning up of terrain that had previously impeded so many attacks. When the order to attack was given, the storm troops went forward and either isolated or bypassed strong points. Later, in the second phase of the storm assault, these were either reduced by light artillery or eventually taken by conventional infantry.

Opposite: Marines man an anti-aircraft machine gun position in France in 1918.

WAR IN THE TRENCHES

Right: General Oskar von Hutier who played a large part in developing the tactics employed by German storm troops in World War I.

Left: Colonel Georg Bruchmüller who planned the artillery barrages which preceded the advance of the storm troops in France in 1918.

Below: Laden down with bundles of grenades German storm troops nonetheless keep up a rapid advance.

Actually, these storm attacks had the effect of lengthening the flanks on the bulges caused by the assaults and soon required more men to man them, thus producing higher casualties than expected. In addition, because the Allied blockade had denied these troops many of their creature comforts, the *Stosstruppen* often turned into little more than looting gangs when they ran across British supply dumps containing cigarettes and liquor. Leaders were frequently scacrificed to no purpose and by mid-April the German offensive was bogged down in the British Fifth Army sector. From late March to June the Germans, using up what remaining shock troops they had, pounded away at the Allied lines and, indeed, gained much ground. But in the end the Allied wall failed to crack. By summer, with the loss of its leadership cadres, the German Army began to lose cohesion and eventually collapsed in November.

On the advent of World War I, the Allied side boasted most of the seasoned shock-troop outfits. The French had, as always, the Foreign Legion and its crack mountain battalions of the *Chasseurs Alpins*. The Italians had their celebrated *Arditi*, who battled gallantly against the Austrians in the Dolomites and Alps of Northern Italy. And in 1917 the United States sent units of the Marine Corps to be brigaded with Army divisions on the Western Front.

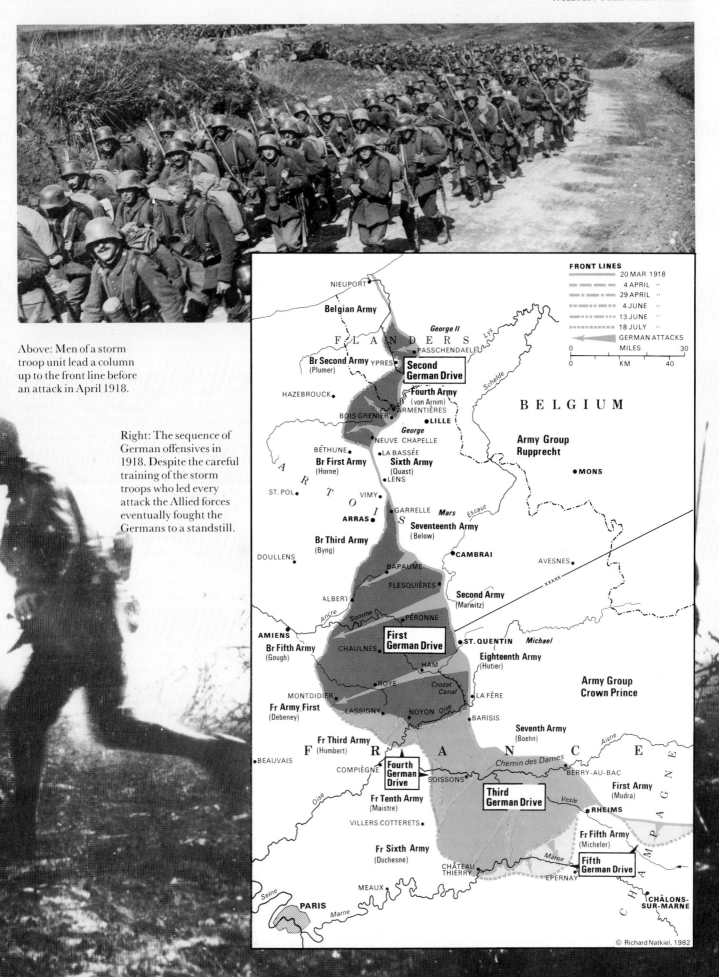

Above: Men of a storm troop unit lead a column up to the front line before an attack in April 1918.

Right: The sequence of German offensives in 1918. Despite the careful training of the storm troops who led every attack the Allied forces eventually fought the Germans to a standstill.

FRONT LINES

	20 MAR 1918
	4 APRIL "
	29 APRIL "
	4 JUNE "
	13 JUNE "
	18 JULY "
	GERMAN ATTACKS

MILES 0 — 30

KM 0 — 40

NIEUPORT

Belgian Army

F L A N D E R S

George II

Lys

PASSCHENDAELE

Br Second Army
(Plumer)

YPRES

Second German Drive

Fourth Army
(von Arnim)

ARMENTIÈRES

BOIS GRENIER

LILLE

Schelde

B E L G I U M

HAZEBROUCK

George

NEUVE CHAPELLE

BÉTHUNE

LA BASSÉE

Br First Army
(Horne)

Sixth Army
(Quast)

LENS

Army Group Rupprecht

•MONS

ST. POL

VIMY

GARRELLE

Mars

Escaut

ARRAS

Seventeenth Army
(Below)

Br Third Army
(Byng)

CAMBRAI

AVESNES

DOULLENS

BAPAUME

FLESQUIÈRES

Second Army
(Marwitz)

xxxx

ALBERT

Ancre

Somme

PÉRONNE

First German Drive

CHAULNES

ST. QUENTIN

Michael

Br Fifth Army
(Gough)

HAM

Eighteenth Army
(Hutier)

ROYE

Crozat Canal

LA FÈRE

Army Group Crown Prince

MONTDIDIER

NOYON

Oise

BARISIS

Fr Army First
(Debeney)

LASSIGNY

Seventh Army
(Boehn)

Fr Third Army
(Humbert)

F R A N C E

Aisne

•BEAUVAIS

COMPIÈGNE

Fourth German Drive

SOISSONS

Chemin des Dames

BERRY-AU-BAC

Third German Drive

Vesle

First Army
(Mudra)

Fr Tenth Army
(Maistre)

RHEIMS

VILLERS COTTERETS

Fr Fifth Army
(Micheler)

Oise

Fr Sixth Army
(Duchesne)

Marne

Fifth German Drive

C H A M P A G N E

CHÂTEAU THIERRY

EPERNAY

CHÂLONS-SUR-MARNE

MEAUX

Seine

PARIS

Marne

© Richard Natkiel, 1982

Right: General Paul Rollet, 'The Father of the Legion', pictured toward the end of his service. Rollet was one of the most decorated officers in the French Army and commanded the Legion for the latter part of World War I.

Above: Legionnaires work to emplace an old 155mm gun some time shortly after the outbreak of World War I. Many obsolete weapons were pressed into service to make good in part the need for heavy artillery.

The Foreign Legion

When mobilization orders reached Africa in 1914, units of the Legion holding Fez in Morocco consisted largely of Central Europeans, while those at Sidi-bel-Abbès were 'Western' or Russian. A few days after war was declared, the Moroccans launched a savage attack at Taza, near Fez. So well did the Central European Legionnaires acquit themselves in checking this attack that French authorities felt that the loyalty of units in Morocco – whatever their origin – was unquestioned. Hence, these veterans could be sent to France as training cadres for a new Legion which would see action on the Western Front.

Thus the famous Moroccan Division from Sidi-bel-Abbès departed for France, and recruiting offices for foreigners opened in Paris and other cities in August 1914. At this time, there

were many American expatriates living in France and these young men – fired with dreams of glory in the new war – proved to be fresh and eager material for the ranks of the Legion, since it was impossible for a foreigner to enter the French Army except as a Legionnaire.

Among these Americans was the poet Alan Seeger who wrote home that 'It is for glory alone that I engaged.' Others who joined 'for the duration' were Bill Thaw of Pittsburgh and late of Yale University (later to be killed in air combat when he transferred to the Lafayette Escadrille); Rene Phelizot of Chicago; Jules Bach of St. Louis; James Stewart Carstairs and a number of others then in Paris. Perhaps the best-known of these young men were Alan Seeger, Paul Rockwell and John Jay Chapman. There was also Edmund Gênet, a descendant of the famous Citizen Gênet, Minister to America from the French Revolution faction, who had settled in America and married into a prominent family. Gênet, who also left the Legion for the Flying Corps, would become one of the first Americans killed in air action.

These Americans began their training by drilling in the garden of the Palais Royale with Charles Sweeney, a West Pointer, as their instructor. On 25 August a large group of them left for training camp at Rouen. They had come from Boston, New Orleans, Mobile, San Francisco, Cleveland, New York and other cities and towns. Among them was a Columbia professor, a jeweler, a black barber, a boxer, a textile salesman, a fruit peddler, actors, artists, adventurers and rich young men.

In mid-September there was a call at Rouen for volunteers who had had military experience to go to the front. Almost every American stepped forward, claiming to have seen action in various revolutions in Mexico and Central America. When their French officers pointed out their clumsiness in drill, they simply replied that their combat had been largely of the guerrilla type. Up they went to the fierce fighting around Cambrai. Chapman found himself the only American in a company of Polish Legionnaires. Other Americans found themselves fighting alongside Spaniards, Turks, Africans, Chinese, Greeks and Russian Jews. Rockwell paired off with an exotic new comrade – a Fiji prince who had been educated at Oxford. The Americans found that the South American Legionnaires were very popular and were 'good shots, generous, and not afraid to risk their skins.' When Rockwell's platoon attacked Hill 140 at Arras, no North Americans were killed, but a Columbian, an Ecuadorean and three Argentinians lost their lives.

A few of the Americans turned out to be *mauvais types* who either deserted or were court-martialed. But the winter fighting of 1915, wrote Seeger, 'pretty well weeded out the objectionable specimens,' and their replacements were 'men it is an honor to fight beside.' The Legion distinguished itself in the Champagne action, with green recruits learning fast from veterans. And the

French officers disappointed no one in living up to the Legion's reputation. Attacking at Rheims on 19 May, as part of Marshal Pétain's 33rd Corps, the Legion regiment lost three successive commanders and five company commanders. After they had taken their objective within an hour, the Legion's flag was decorated with the Croix de Guerre. Writing home, John Chapman reported that a German prisoner said his unit had not attacked because 'Though the Legion were not very good shots, their fame with the bayonet was such that we feared a hand-to-hand conflict.' Only a few days before this action, the 52nd anniversary of Camerone had been celebrated with the traditional reading of the time-honored account to entrenched Legionnaires.

Meanwhile, a month before Camerone on 28 March, a battalion of the Legion from Sidi-bel-Abbès took part in the great Gallipoli landing at Sed-ul-Bahr. It took five days of slaughter to secure the beachhead. Every French officer of this battalion and all but some hundred men lay dead by 2 April. The command fell to Sergeant-Major Léon, who managed to hold the narrow perimeter line until more troops landed. For his fearless leadership, he was awarded the Légion d'Honneur and made an officer. After the Dardanelles misadventure, units of the Legion were shifted to Serbia to cover the tragic retreat from Nish before Bulgarian troops. Last to retreat, the Legionnaires had their revenge a year later when they entered Monastir with the first patrols of Serbian cavalry.

Only a few days before the fall offensive of 1915 in Champagne, there was, wrote Seeger, 'great and unexpected news. All American volunteers in the Legion are to be given the privilege of entering a French regiment. I [however] have always been loyal to the Legion.' Most Americans did make the change – some going to the Flying Corps – but Seeger stayed. A few weeks later, the Legion was in combat in Champagne, fighting furiously but suffering grievous losses. By October the remnants of two regiments had to be joined into a single *Régiment de Marche de la Légion Etrangère*, considered elite shock troops of the first stripe. Seeger, in his boyish way, 'remained true to the Legion where I am content and have good comrades. We are *troups d'attaque* now and so will assist in all the big *coups*.'

In October 1915 the Legionnaires, Seeger and Gênet among them, were paraded in a review before King George V of England and President Poincaré. Gênet wrote that he was 'on the very side rank' as they passed and 'Believe me, I held my chin up and kept my eyes open.' A year later Gênet left the Legion for the Flying Corps and met his death soon afterward.

After the review the newly consolidated regiment was shifted to the Front along the Somme River. At Belloy-en-Santerre, it fought from one ruined house to another until the town fell. Seeger was soon to publish his best-known poem, 'I have a Rendezvous with Death.' It was to be

prophetic, for it was in that same flaming town, during the summer offensive of 1916, that Alan Seeger fell. On that day his decimated company was commanded at the last by a corporal.

By 1917 only ten of the original 70-odd Americans were left in the Legion on the Western Front. Thirty-eight had died of wounds, and the rest had either succumbed to disease or been discharged or transferred. Of the final survivors, most had been wounded from one to four times. Eight of the American volunteers had won the Légion d'Honneur and 52 the Croix de Guerre.

From the spring of 1917 until the end of the war, the Legion on the Western Front was commanded by one of its most celebrated officers, Lieutenant-Colonel Paul Rollet, and it became the most decorated regiment in the French Army. Rollet was immensely popular with his men, who called him 'The Father of the Legion.' He, in turn, honored them by consistently refusing promotions away from his troops. In 1916 Rollet led his Legionnaires through Paris with five new citations and the *fourragère* of the Croix de Guerre on their flags beside their other honors. After their courageous fighting around Verdun that

Like every other unit in the French Army the Legion went to war in 1914 wearing a uniform that had changed little since the early nineteenth century.

29

Below: A French charge early in World War I. All too often the bravery and *esprit de corps* of the men of the Legion was wasted in tactically naive frontal attacks.

year, Marshal Pétain awarded them the Cross of the Legion of Honor.

Oddly enough, the Germans opposing the Legion often posted signs on their trenches exhorting it to disband and go home, adding that 'Germany has no corps of foreign volunteers and France should not have one either.' When these signs had no effect, the Germans resorted to leaflets which read: 'Men of the Foreign Legion: Hereafter when we capture one of you, we will hang you instead of shoot you. You are not worth a bullet.'

Such threats, however, only caused the Legion to fight harder. On 20 August 1917 the Legion led a dawn attack on the east side of Camière Wood, so successful that their bugles were sounding one of their favorite combat tunes, 'Madelon,' as they pushed into the town of Forges. As 1918 began, their brigade commander said of his men that they had 'that power and confidence . . . which is incomparable and without equal.' But this last year of the Great War inflicted sickening losses on the Legion. Around Soissons in May and June

they lost 1250 men – a fifth of their strength. Yet on 13 September the Legion captured the entire headquarters staff of Crown Prince Wilhelm's elite *Totenkopf* (Death's Head) Regiment and 500 of its rank and file. Fewer than 60 days later the war ended, and by that time over 5000 Legionnaires had been killed in action in France.

After the Armistice, when the French Army was paraded through Paris, the Legion, led by Rollet, was the first to march under the Arc de Triomphe. Soon after Legion recruiting stations along the Rhine, ironically, did a brisk business in bringing the Legion up to strength again. Here many a dispirited German ex-soldier, who not long before had threatened to hang Legionnaires, sought refuge and anonymity in the ranks of the Foreign Legion. Once again, the Legion's mystique worked wonders, for so strong and infectious were its traditions that the German volunteers were soon at one with them.

In August 1919 President Poincaré awarded the *Médaille Militaire* to Colonel Rollet to be emblazoned on the Legion's flag. Then veterans and recruits alike were shipped back to Fez, where Legionnaires who had not seen service in France were still in combat against Arab dissidents. All during the European war, General Lyautey had maintained the status quo with only five Legion battalions and three mounted companies. In November 1914, in the middle of the Atlas Mountains, there had been a French disaster at El-Herri where an entire Legion column was almost wiped out. Encouraged by this, the fierce Berber tribesmen had launched a long series of raids and forays, led by Abd-El-Malete, a grandson of that old Legion foe, Abd-El-Kader himself. Not until 1917 was he driven into sanctuary after suffering many casualties. Yet the following year had seen a savage action at Gaouz in which several Legionnaires had died of fatigue and their leader, Captain Timn, severely wounded, had had to carry on tied to his horse.

In the years between the two World Wars, the few surviving Legionnaires did most of their fighting in Morocco and Syria. French authorities were worried that a 'new' Foreign Legion could not be brought up to the standard of the old

on account of the depletion of French manhood. And in the light of her increased imperial commitments, France depended on the Legion more than ever.

This fear proved groundless, as a steady supply of new recruits began to enlist. They were drawn from the White Russian Armies brought to Constantinople in dreadful plight, from German Sparticists and other extremists, from homeless Bulgarians and Balts – from all those who had been on the wrong side in the Great War or who had nothing for which to go home. These, as usual, the Legion welcomed as lost sons, molding desperate, diverse and often mutually hostile men into proud Legionnaires. As one officer put it: 'There is no *new* Legion. There is only *the* French Foreign Legion.'

Above: Legion veterans on parade in Paris on Bastille Day 1939, shortly before service in another European war.

The Chasseurs Alpins

The elite *Chasseurs Alpins*, or Alpine light infantry battalions of the French Army, were known as the 'Blue Devils' (*Les Diables Bleus*) because of their dark blue uniforms and their valor. They were actually modeled on the first Italian Alpine companies, which were formed in 1872. In 1888 the Triple Alliance of Italy, Germany and Austria renewed itself and the French general staff – still smarting from the humiliating defeats of the Franco-Prussian War – decided that special mountain units would be necessary in the event of hostile Italian units on the frontier.

Thus 12 of the existing 30 chasseur, or light infantry, and cavalry battalions were retrained into Alpine chasseurs and posted to the Franco-Italian border. Simultaneously, 12 mountain pack-batteries of artillery were created for their use. Since there were six Italian Alpine regiments at this time, the French and Italian forces were more or less well matched.

The *Chasseurs Alpins* retained the dark blue uniform of the regular chasseurs. However, the *kepi* was replaced by the beret, and the dark blue tail coat that buttoned at the back (reminiscent of the old Legionnaires' tunic) was replaced by a short tunic and cape of the same color. Retained were the white buttons and braid, the jacket frogging (looped ornamental braiding), the trouser facing and the yellow braiding – all characteristic of the chasseur uniform.

These new French mountain battalions were never organized into regiments, but remained corps battalions for greater mobility – a typical system in the French Army. Yet they were loosely formed into 'Alpine Groups' supported not only by their mountain batteries, but also by units of customs men and forest rangers. These chasseur battalions were remarkable for their continuity and homogeneity. In 1914 the 31 battalions numbered more than 20,000 men. They were easily mobilized, being recruited exclusively among the mountain districts where they made their homes and usually served as well. Moreover, they had top officers drawn from those graduates of St. Cyr who were given their choice of either the Legion or the Chasseurs for command duty.

Assigned to the difficult snow-covered Vosges, the Chasseurs would dare any danger, sometimes dashing down the steep slopes on their skis and landing with terrifying suddenness in the enemy trenches, wielding their bayonets. On one occasion in 1915, a small band of them were entrenched atop Jartmannsweiler Kopf when they were surrounded and cut off from their base by Germans. After several days about 40 of them attempted to make a sortie by glissanding on their skis down into the midst of the enemy, shouting *'Vive la France!'* The rest stood their ground until overpowered and taken prisoner. In June of that year, another company of Chasseurs became isolated on a hill. They made camp and

Opposite: *Chasseurs Alpins* moving up a glacier during a training exercise. Such training was intended to produce soldiers who could carry out every military maneuver in the most severe conditions.

Below: A nineteenth century illustration depicting a chasseur in full equipment and showing the chasseurs defending a typical mountain position.

LIEBIG'S FLEISCH-EXTRACT.

Geschützbeförderung auf einen
Bergkamm.

Left: An advertising poster for a meat concentrate showing chasseurs hauling an artillery piece to a mountain position. In the years before World War I the chasseurs became famous throughout Europe for their mountaineering exploits. The scene depicted was repeated many times during World War I. Manhandling an artillery piece weighing several tons to a mountain top and then keeping it supplied with ammunition must indeed have been a gruelling struggle.

Below: As well as problems of rough terrain the chasseurs had to learn to fight in typical inclement mountain weather.

there defended themselves, with the aid of artillery shells from their distant batteries, for three days until they were rescued. When their ammunition ran low, they rolled rocks down onto their assailants.

Typically strong, daring and spirited, the Blue Devils won wide admiration for their deeds in the fighting on the hilly borders of Alsace. At Badonviller, through which they fought the Bavarians and other German troops, the sound of their voices raised in their well-known bugle march heartened the villagers hiding in cellars beneath the feet of the fighters.

On the day when ill-fated Gerbeviller was first attacked, about 70 determined Chasseurs defended it for hours against a force some 4000 strong. In the Champagne sector, several battalions of the Chasseurs were instrumental in breaking through enemy lines of the left center. Later in the war, Chasseur battalions made the Germans pay dearly for every foot of ground taken at the Caures Woods around Verdun, at Fort Vaux and along the Somme.

After the war the *Chasseurs Alpins* units returned to their garrisons and were reduced to nine battalions. Strengthened again for World War II, they first fought in northeastern France. When France fell, most of the Chasseurs turned to guerrilla warfare, and their activities made notable contributions to the Resistance.

Below: A group of chasseurs rest on a hill after a training climb.

Below: Marines on parade at Quantico with the Lewis machine guns which they had to exchange for unreliable French designs before they were sent to France.

The US Marine Corps' 4th Brigade

In early 1917, as the United States drifted toward war, the US Marine Corps was larger, better trained and organized, more experienced and better led than at any time in its history. The 1916 Naval Personnel Bill had enlarged the Corps by nearly 50 percent, and President Wilson had subsequently authorized another enlargement to nearly 700 officers and 17,400 enlisted men. Marine Corps recruiting, spurred into high gear by the electric effect of the slogan 'First to Fight,' was more successful than ever before.

By capitalizing on the general desire to get overseas, the Corps soon found itself swamped by top-quality recruits. Mare and Parris Islands were overwhelmed, and temporary training stations had to be set up at the Norfolk and Philadelphia Navy Yards. Parris Island handled most of the recruits and was destined to train no fewer than 46,000 of them before the end of the war. When Congress authorized the Corps to go

as high as 30,000 men in May, there were already nearly 22,000 Marines. So many high-spirited young Americans volunteered that by early June General George Barnett, the Corps Commandant, closed down officers' appointments from civilian life and, for the duration, filled the officer corps from the ranks. But the Corps badly needed an East Coast base for training and organizing new Marines into tactical units. A new site at Quantico, Virginia, seemed to provide all the facilities needed – training areas, deep-water approaches for transport ships and a good railroad line. In May 6000 acres were leased by the Navy and Quantico was soon in business.

With his new recruiting and training program in full swing, General Barnett had no intention of using his expanded Corps merely for such naval service duties as guarding ship and shore installation. The Wilson administration and the War Department inadvertently gave Barnett the chance to commit the Corps to the ground war in Europe, thus allowing it to make good its boast

'First to Fight.' Barnett, of course, was well aware that the Corps had to send troops to France if it were to justify its expansion, its recruiting appeals and its claims to elitism. The General Staff, however, was not enthusiastic about sending an expeditionary force until it could organize a national army of millions.

In April 1917 the British and French sent special missions to Washington to plead for at least a token commitment to bolster flagging Allied morale. While Congress toiled over selective service legislation, the General Staff planned to send one regular Army division to France – probably the 1st Division. By the end of May, President Wilson had named Major General John J. Pershing to command the American Expeditionary Force. In the confusion, Barnett shrewdly persuaded the War Department to include a Marine regiment in the first contingent. Aided by Navy Secretary Josephus Daniels and William Benson, Chief of Naval Operations, Barnett cajoled the War Department into accepting his offer of one

Above: A group of recruits being sworn in at the Marine Corps' receiving station at Parris Island, South Carolina.

Above: An American artillery unit moves through a ruined village in the painting 'Village of the Dead' by George Harding.

Left: American forces on the attack with armor support in heavily wooded country near Chateau Thierry.

Right: A Marine recruiting poster of the World War I period.

Marine regiment immediately and another to follow, thus forming a full infantry brigade of more than 6000 men organized like the Army's.

Pershing, never enthusiastic about the idea, had no choice in the matter, which was decided by War Secretary Newton D. Baker and Army Chief of Staff Tasker H. Bliss. The War Department promised to provide any weapons and equipment the Marines needed to bring the regiments up to Army tables of organization if the Corps would furnish the original regiments and adequate replacements, to which Barnett agreed. Pershing himself promised to treat the Marines equally in all supply and personnel matters, and

Secretary Baker went so far as to pledge that the Marine brigade would be assigned to a combat division.

The first regiment to be raised for action was the 5th Marines. Assembled in Philadelphia, the 5th was hurriedly formed by merging barracks companies, ships' detachments, small companies drawn from the Caribbean and recruit drafts. In each company, only the commander and senior lieutenant were prewar officers; the rest were new officers from military schools like Virginia Military Institute, or ROTC graduates from land-grant universities and Eastern colleges. The enlisted men were about half prewar veterans and half new recruits – mostly city toughs and farm boys. Among the non-coms and older privates there were, wrote one officer:

> . . . a number of diverse people who ran curiously to type, with drilled shoulders and bone-deep sunburn, and a tolerant scorn of nearly everything on earth. Their speech was flavored with Navy words, and words culled from all the folk who live on the seas

and the ports where warships go. . . . Rifles were high and holy things to them, and they knew five-inch broadside guns. They talked patronizingly of war, and were concerned about rations. They were the Leathernecks, the Old Timers.

The new 3600-man Marine infantry regiments were bigger and different from anything of the kind in the past. The new companies had six officers and 250 enlisted men. However, the Arabic numbering of companies in Marine style served to confuse Army officers who had anything to do with them. The 5th Marines had three infantry battalions of Army size – more than 1000 officers and men – but the companies retained their Marine Corps designations; in the 1st Battalion the companies were the 17th, 49th, 66th and 67th. Moreover, the 5th was composed of the finest junior officers and enlisted men ever to serve in the Corps, leavened by hardened majors, captains and sergeants. Although the 5th Marines had little time to train as a unit before sailing in June 1917, it was nevertheless a high-spirited, self-confident unit deeply imbued with the Corps esprit and conscious of its mission to enhance the Corps' reputation for valor.

By early June the 5th Marines, commanded by Colonel C.A. Doyen, was ready to embark for France with the first convoy. But then came a hitch. A day before they were scheduled to go aboard ship, Barnett opened a message from Secretary Baker which began: 'I am very sorry to have to tell you that it will be utterly impossible for the War Dept. to furnish transportation for a Marine regiment with the first outfit sailing. . . .'

To a less determined man than Barnett, these words would have meant the end of the Corps' hopes of getting to France. But the Commandant, who had foreseen such an eventuality, simply replied: 'Please give yourself no further trouble in this matter, as transportation for the Marines has been arranged.'

And so, in fact, it had. Barnett's friend, Admiral Benson, had reserved the Navy transports *Henderson*, *Hancock* and *DeKalb* for the 5th Marines. Thus it was that the regiment sailed for Europe on 13 June 1917, rendezvoused with the first convoy at sea and went ashore at St. Nazaire on 27 June, with all hands eager to get to the war.

Once arrived 'Over There', the 5th was supposed to go into intensive training for trench warfare with the 1st Infantry Division (Big Red One). However, this plan was frustrated by General Pershing, whose main problem at the moment was creating a system of training camps and logistical installations to support both the 1st Division and those being trained in the States. Since the 5th Marines was excess in the 1st Division, Pershing assigned them all over France as security detachments and labor troops.

His action was not based on any lack of confidence in the Marines, whose discipline and soldierly appearance he actually admired, but on the pressing need to provide men for the AEF's support system. His decision was supported by the General Staff, which believed the Marines would make perfect provost guards. As a result, seldom did more than one battalion of the 5th take part in the 1st Division's training in the summer and fall of 1917. The Marines themselves griped and bemoaned these security duties. One of them confided to Pershing's press

Marine recruits receiving musketry training at a Stateside training camp in 1918.

Above: General Pershing (right) and Marshal Foch pose for a photograph after a conference in July 1918.

Top right: Marines storm a German machine-gun position during the final advances of 1918. The German machine gunners usually provided the most tenacious element of the German defense despite the demoralization of many of their supporting infantry units.

Bottom right: 'On the Trail of the Hun on the St. Mihiel Drive' by W J Alward. While the combat troops like the Marines quickly adapted to the demands of trench warfare their supply services often found difficulty in keeping up with the fighting.

secretary that at least such duty would help prepare him for a postwar job: 'I can wear a striped waistcoat and brass buttons and open cab doors in front of a New York hotel.'

Angry at this treatment of the 5th Marines, Commandant Barnett, who with others in the Corps was beginning to suspect an Army conspiracy to deny the Marines a combat role in the war, vigorously stated in American newspapers that the Corps would soon see action. In fact, however, AEF headquarters planned to release the 5th for training as soon as it had enough units to create another Marine regiment. But, as Barnett was well aware, as long as the Corps had only one regiment in France, it was likely to remain something of an unwanted child in the combat scheme of things.

In the light of this, General Barnett had already begun organizing another regiment at Quantico – the 6th Marines, together with the 6th Machine Gun Battalion – to complete the full Marine Brigade for the AEF. Trained hard by its commanding officer, Colonel Albertus W. Catlin, the 6th boasted only a few veteran officers and sergeants, but it had the pick of the new wartime lieutenants and recruits. Catlin proudly proclaimed that some 60 percent of the troops were college men. Although not entirely trained, the 6th soon satisfied Catlin and Barnett and was shipped off to Europe in late 1917, landing in France in February 1918.

Early that year, the two regiments were combined into a brigade, which AEF headquarters designated the '4th Infantry Brigade,' but which the Corps self-styled the 4th Marine Brigade; it was commanded by Doyen, now a brigadier general. Pershing's staff did not object to this

special designation, thus ensuring that the brigade would retain its Marine Corps identity not only in official reports but in the newspapers as well. The 4th Marine Brigade then started intensive trench warfare training assigned to the newly assembled 2nd (Indian Head) Division, which was destined to become the top fighting infantry division of the AEF. Acting as instructors to the new Marine Brigade were several dozen members of the *Chasseurs Alpins*.

The 4th, with its 280 officers and 9164 enlisted men, was the largest formation of Marines ever fielded up to this time. The enlisted Marines saw to it that no one confused them with Army soldiers. When their distinctive forest-green uniforms unravelled and wore thin, they sewed their Marine buttons onto Army khakis and wore their revered globe-and-anchor insignia on their overseas hats, helmets and breast pockets. Some unidentified lover of the Corps sent literally hundreds of these insignia to the 4th so that the men never ran short of them.

During the muddy and frigid winter of 1917-18, the 4th Brigade trained with their French instructors and soldiers of the 2nd Division. The Marines had to learn Army drill, which they despised, and to turn in their trusted Lewis machine guns for French Chauchat automatic rifles and Hotchkiss machine guns, both heavy and unreliable weapons that used ammunition different from the Marines' Springfields, thus complicating supply problems which were already sufficiently snarled. They dug trenches, fired weapons, threw grenades, fought lice and colds in their billets in French barns and cottages, went on backbreaking hikes in the snow and sleet and griped about the food. One sergeant commented that his company had become 'so damned mean they'd have fought their own grandmothers.' Yet withal, morale remained high, and the Marines took to playing football with such wild abandon that General Doyen had to prohibit it as too dangerous.

By early spring of 1918, the 4th was ready to complete its training with a tour of of trench warfare in the front lines. As was customary for unblooded troops, a relatively stable sector with well-established defensive positions was selected – the Toulon sector on the heights of the Meuse southeast of Verdun where, on St. Patrick's Day, first the 5th and then the 6th Marines relieved French units in the line. After four days sandwiched between experienced French battalions, the Marines were pulled out of this quiet sector to help plug a dangerous gap the Germans had opened in their great Aisne offensive launched on 21 March. The enemy was trying to drive a wedge between the British and French Armies.

In the trenches the Marines rapidly settled into a life of night patrols, box barrages, raids, carrying parties through the mud, gas alarms, cooties and rats. One night the unlucky 74th Company suffered a night bombardment by gas shells which caught the men asleep in billets; one shell alone, bursting inside a building occupied by a platoon, killed 39 Marines. During the week of 9 May, with 128 killed and 744 wounded during 53 days in the trenches, and having played an honorable though minor role in the Aisne offensive, the 4th Brigade was relieved, to join its parent 2nd Infantry Division for final training at Chaumon-en-Vexin, between Paris and Beauvais.

Now two significant events befell the 4th Brigade. The first was the replacement of General Doyen, who had fallen sick, by an Army commander, Brigadier General James G. Harbord, who had been Pershing's chief of staff. Pershing had warned Harbord, 'Young man, I'm giving you the best brigade in France – if anything goes wrong I'll know whom to blame.' Although not a Marine but a veteran cavalryman, Harbord was an excellent choice: between him and the 4th, it was love at first sight. Later, Harbord would write: '. . . They never failed me. I look back on my service with the Marine Brigade with more pride and satisfaction than on any other equal period in my long Army career.'

The second important event was that of 27 May 1918, when General Erich von Ludendorff

kicked off his powerful Chemin-des-Dames offensive against the Aisne Heights, severed the northern front and nearly reached Paris. Four days later, the 2nd Division was on the Paris-Metz road slogging eastward toward the Marne. On the night of 5 June, the Brigade found itself astride this main highway only a few kilometers northeast of the place where Marshal Gallieni, with his Paris taxi cabs, had checked General von Kluck's advance on Paris in 1914. Here the Marines observed retreating French Army stragglers who advised the Americans to join them. 'Retreat, hell,' snorted a Marine captain. 'We just got here.'

On the left of the highway in the 5th Marines' sector was a rolling wheat field, behind which squatted a forbidding square mile of woods, rocks and hunters' trails – the Bois de Belleau. In Belleau Wood there was marshalled a well-organized center of resistance held by the 461st Imperial German Infantry – the biggest single body of veteran regular troops that the Marines had been up against since they had faced the Redcoats at Bladensburg in 1814. Belleau Wood and the neighboring hamlet of Boursches just to the east of it was a bristling island of weaponry.

In the preceding two days, the Marines and soldiers of the 2nd Division had dug in across the Paris-Metz road and, as the French were retreating, the first Germans hit the American line, only to be driven off by the massed bursts of the Marines' 6th Machine Gun Battalion. Then, on 6 June, the 4th got ready for a counterattack of its own. The first assault was executed by the 1st Battalion, 5th Marines, commanded by Major Julius Turrill. At dawn they surged through the wheat fields toward a hill half a mile north. By noon, Hill 142 was in the hands of surviving Marines of the 49th and 67th Companies. In this, its first attack, the 1st Battalion had suffered 410 casualties since daybreak.

The second phase of the day's attack took the Marines into Belleau Wood itself. These were the men of the 3rd Battalion, 5th Marines (Major B.S. Berry) and also the 2nd and 3rd Battalions of the 6th Marines (Majors Thomas Holcomb

and B.W. Sibley). In exchange for a toehold on the edge of the Wood and for the little town of Boursches, the Corps paid the high price of 1087 casualties in this late afternoon assault.

Boursches would not have remained in Marine hands had it not been for the valor of two lieutenants, J.F. Robertson and C.B. Cates (later to become a Corps Commandant), who held on to their positions in spite of searing German counterattacks. Sergeant Major John H. Quick, already a Medal of Honor man, was also responsible for the gallant holding action. That day he won the Army's Distinguished Service Cross for driving a Model T Ford truck loaded with small arms ammunition and grenades through heavy enemy fire to resupply fragments of Holcomb's battalion clinging precariously to the ruins of Boursches.

Another Marine, also a Medal of Honor man, distinguished himself that day and wrote a colorful chapter in Corps history. This was Gunnery Sergeant Daniel Daly. In the fields of waving wheat and oats, rifle and machine-gun fire delivered by German veterans from well-dug-in positions was pouring through the grain in sheets, clipping off sprigs and plowing into the chests and helmets of pinned-down Marines. Any forward movement seemed suicidal. Suddenly, Daly swung his bayoneted '03 rifle over his head with a forward sweep, motioning his platoon to advance, as he screamed at his men: 'Come on, you sons of bitches! Do you want to live forever?'

Among the hundreds of casualties on 6 June, Major Berry of the 3rd Battalion fell wounded and Colonel Catlin of the 6th Marines was shot through the right lung as he led his regiment forward. It would not be until 20 November 1943, on the beaches of Tarawa, that the Corps would suffer such heavy losses in a single day's assault.

On the 8th, 9th and 11th of June, battalions of the 5th and 6th Marines – notably Lieutenant Colonel F.M. Wise's 2nd Battalion, 5th Marines – fought their perilous way up the long axis of the Bois de Belleau. By dusk of the 12th, Wise had assaulted and penetrated the third and final German defense line. Save for some hotly-contested ground around an abandoned hunting lodge in the extreme northern edge of the Wood, the Marines finally held the Bois. At dawn on the the 13th, however, the German IVth Corps counterattacked behind a fierce barrage of artillery and mustard gas. As this assault rolled in, smashing first at Boursches and then at the line of Marines defending the rising ground at the edge of the Bois, the enemy met a new experience – well-aimed fire from Marine '03s, which at 300 and 400 yards began dropping their pot-helmeted soldiers like flies. But the Germans still pressed on in ragged ranks. For a short while it was thought by higher command that Boursches must be given up for lost. Yet the 1st Battalion, 6th Marines, commanded by Major John (John-

Marine riflemen fire from a hastily constructed position to beat off a German patrol during the last stages of the German advance in the summer of 1918.

ny the Hard) Hughes, despite 450 gas casualties, held fast. That day a happy General Harbord could report to Division: 'There is nothing but US Marines in the town of Bourches.'

Yet the final mop-up of the Wood proved to be slow and stubborn, for the Germans still held the far tip of the Bois. From the 15th to the 22nd, the 7th Infantry took over from the Marines, who were depleted and exhausted. When the Marines returned to Belleau, they found the front lines as they were when they had been relieved. After dark on 23 June, the 3rd Battalion, 5th Marines, made an effort to root out the tenacious enemy, but the results were discouraging. The following day – all day long – the artillery of the 2nd Division pounded and plastered the Germans' positions until they could stand no more of the holocaust. This did the trick, and a final assault by the 3rd Battalion, 5th Marines, commanded by Major Maurice Shearer, overran the tip of the Bois.

One abiding legacy of the action at Belleau Wood was a term that was to become part of the military lexicon. As the Marines and soldiers scratched out their shallow rifle pits in the shell-churned mud of the Bois, someone called them 'fox-holes'; this nickname caught on and a correspondent heard and used it in his dispatches. Another byproduct of the action was the publicity explosion over the deeds of the 4th Marine Brigade, aided by the flowery prose of Floyd Gibbons, the news correspondent. His stories gained additional impact from the fact that he was wounded not once but three times, losing his left eye in the wheat field on 6 June. 'I am up front and entering Belleau Wood with the US Marines,' opened one of his reports. To the news-hungry folks at home, the 4th Marine Brigade became the heroes of the hour. Yet it also caused resentment in Army circles, for the soldiers of the 2nd Division had fought just as bravely and well.

Nevertheless, among those who accorded the 4th unstinting praise for its superb showing at the Bois were two of its superiors – Assistant Secretary of the Navy Franklin D. Roosevelt and French General Joseph Degoutte, under whose 6th Army the 2nd Division had gone into combat. In August Roosevelt inspected the Brigade at Nancy after visiting Belleau Wood. Forthwith, the future president directed that Marine Corps regulations be changed to permit Marine enlisted men to wear the globe and anchor on their collars (previously only officers had done so). And General Degoutte, in a citation, proclaimed that henceforth Belleau Wood would bear the name 'Bois de la Brigade de Marine.'

After Belleau Wood the 4th went to the rest areas along the Marne River – but it was pitifully reduced, with 4677 of its former members killed or wounded. On 14 July Harbord was promoted to Major General and assumed overall command of the 2nd Division. Colonel Wendell C. Neville, senior regimental commander, was given his first star and became the 4th's commander. In less

than a month, the 2nd Division was sent into action for the second time.

On 15 July 1918 Ludendorff's German Army began its last great push of the war. This was a thrust by a dozen German divisions under General Hutier to jump off from the Aisne, capture Rheims and then advance swiftly on Paris. All that resulted was a salient, or bulge, between Soissons on the Aisne and Chateau-Thierry on the Marne. To cut down this salient, Marshal Foch (at Pershing's insistence) decided to counterattack in the Soissons area. The American 1st and 2nd Divisions were then attached to the French 20th Corps, which was composed of Moroccans, Senegalese and the Foreign Legion. Thus it was that in the savage battle at Soissons, US Marines and Legionnaires were in some sectors fighting almost shoulder to shoulder.

On 16 July the 20th Corps began to concentrate and gather strength for its initial attack. The Indian Head Division was slated to launch its spearhead from the forest preserve at Villiers-Coterets, with the 5th Marines carrying the point and the 6th Marines in Corps reserve. On the black and stormy night of 17 July, the 28,000-man 2nd Division marched through the darkened Retz Forest on its most miserable trek of the war. All night it rained, with the Marine Brigade staggering forward through deep clinging mud, their transports collapsed and their stomachs empty and growling. For the dawn H-hour, rifle

American machine gunners prepare to fire their Chauchat light machine gun from an improvised firing position. The French-made Chauchat has been described as one of the worst designed firearms ever and was universally unpopular with the Marines and other troops to whom it was issued.

Opposite: A wounded
Marine receives first aid
before being taken to a
hospital in the rear, 22
March 1918. Even at this
stage when the Marines
were being introduced to
trench warfare in quiet
sectors there was always
a stready drain of
casualties.

companies had to double-time to reach their line of departure at the appointed time. Mules toting machine guns plunged and fell in the mire, columns slowed and jammed up, guns and caissons slid sideways across the files and men slipped into deep ditches and broke arms and legs. Hour after hour, cold, famished and soaked to the skin, the Marines slogged forward, each man carrying a 45-pound pack.

Without having eaten or slept, the 5th Marines jumped off before dawn behind a rolling barrage opened up by the 20th Corps. They pressed forward like zombies, alongside the Moroccans, whom they soon outdistanced, and by noon they had taken the Beauepaire Farm two miles beyond their departure point. When dusk came, they had advanced three more miles, driving the Germans before them.

The hero of the assault proved to be a feisty Serbian-born gunnery sergeant named Louis Cukela of the 66th Company, 5th Marines. He made a series of headlong rushes on three machine-gun nests in the Foret de Retz, the last of which he wiped out with German potato-masher grenades he had captured. For these deeds, Cukela won both the Army and Navy Medals of Honor and was later commissioned. A character who frequently doubled up his comrades with his own special brand of English, he once reprimanded a young Marine for a job poorly done by exclaiming 'Next time I send a goddam fool, I go myself!'

The following morning at Soissons, the 6th Marines, under Colonel Harry Lee, advanced another mile and a half against stiffening German resistance and devastating sheets of well-aimed artillery fire. Without realizing it, the regiment had run smack into a massed enemy counterattack. Marines were falling like ninepins and the push was fast becoming suicidal. One officer had only two men left in his entire company. When the 6th Marines' casualties hit 50 percent and Major Sibley's 3rd Battalion (originally in reserve) had melted into Hughes' and Holcomb's 1st and 2nd Battalions, the Marines at last dug in within rifle range of the Soissons-Chateau-Thierry road – the main artery of General Hutier's salient. When night fell, the 2nd Division was relieved by a fresh division. Final casualties of the 4th Marine Brigade in the Battle of Soissons were 1972 killed or wounded.

Based on the questioning of a few Marines taken prisoner, German intelligence had arrived at some interesting conclusions about the American Marine Corps:

The Marines are considered a sort of elite corps, designed to go into action outside the US. The high percentage of Marksmen, Sharpshooters, and Expert Riflemen, as perceived among our prisoners, allows a conclusion to be drawn as to the quality of the training in rifle marksmanship the Marines receive. The prisoners are mostly of a better class, and they consider their membership in the Marine Corps to be something of an honor. They proudly resent any attempts to place their regiments on a par with other infantry regiments.

Meanwhile, General Harbord was promoted and relieved of his command of the 2nd Division. Marine Corps General John A. Lejeune, who had been sent from the States to command the 4th Brigade, was then elevated to command the 2nd Division – the first and only Marine officer ever to command an Army division in combat. When Lejeune reached France in June, he brought with him proposals to Pershing from Barnett that the Corps be allowed to provide one or more divisions for the AEF. Pershing dismissed these recommendations; he was willing to accept another Marine Brigade in France, but not as combat troops. He still felt that they were needed for rear-area jobs, such as provost guard. Although Pershing admired the Marines, he and the General Staff were inclined to think that while they were excellent for minor operations, for real war, leave it to the Army.

After two fights like Belleau Wood and Soissons, the 2nd Division deserved and got a breather with a ten-day assignment to a quiet sector with headquarters at Marbache on the Moselle River. The next month, September, would bring another big push by the Allies. But this one was to be primarily an all-American show in which two US corps were to reduce the St. Mihiel salient along the Meuse. This time the Marines were to be the divisional reserve.

After their depleting summer battles, the Brigade was still some 2500 men understrength. General Lejeune's chief problem was to get it up to strength without having to accept Army replacements – a situation repugnant to him as 'disastrous to the esprit de corps of the 4th Brigade.' at once appealed to the Marines' old friend General Harbord, who now had the job of reorganizing the Service of Supply, or 'SOS.' Since many Marines in France had ended up in SOS, Harbord was in a position to help. After Lejeune's appeal, he looked the other way as small detachments of Marines – guards, orderlies, chauffeurs, clerks – were quietly sent to the 4th Brigade.

Soon the replacement problem was solved and the Brigade trained, rehearsed and finally rolled their packs for the next action. On the dark and rainy night of 11 September, the Marines, now led by General Neville, moved into their reserve positions for the attack toward the Meuse. At one o'clock the following morning, the American artillery unleashed the opening salvos of a four-hour preparation bombardment, after which the artillery lifted and the 2nd Division jumped off behind a rolling barrage. The Marine Brigde followed the advancing Army units, who acquitted themselves admirably. By dusk, the doughboys had rounded up over 3000 prisoners.

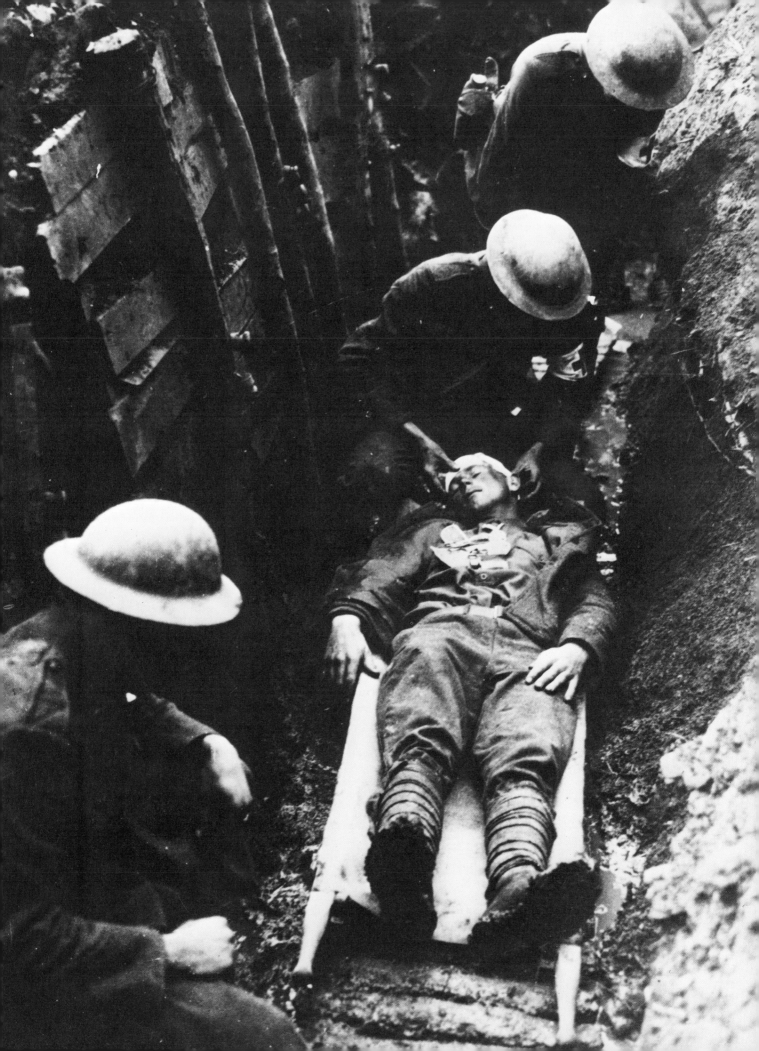

The day after the Army's leap forward, the Marines passed through the soldiers and began the task of eliminating the many German outposts that guarded the formidable Hindenburg Line. Many of these were thick concrete structures and others were deep underground dugouts. Even so, Colonel Logan Feland's 5th Marines, on the right, succeeded in knocking many of them out; by 15 September he and his men had reached their objectives. They dug in immediately for the expected enemy counterattack – which came at once and was repulsed.

Much stiffer resistance was encountered by

Marines rest in a French village before marching to the front to join the Battle of Belleau Wood.

Colonel Harry Lee's 6th Marines. In the Bois de la Montagne, the 2nd Battalion found tenacious tenants in several dugouts. When they were finally evicted, the Germans, using gas and artillery, counterattacked four times – only to be thrown back. At nightfall on the 15th, when the 2nd Division was relieved, the 2nd Battalion, 6th Marines, was still there.

For the Marine Brigade, the Battle of St. Mihiel was a relatively light action; even so, they had lost 132 dead and 574 wounded, mostly from the 6th Regiment.

When Lejeune's 2nd Division left the St. Mihiel lines, it was temporarily detached from American command and assigned to the French 4th Army under General Henri Gouraud, a one-armed veteran of Gallipoli. Gouraud told Lejeune that the 2nd would be in temporary reserve, but promised him it would see plenty of action soon. On 26 September the Meuse-Argonne offensive was kicked off, with the American 1st Army advancing beside Gouraud's troops. By the end of the month, the French forces had slowed to a stop in the Champagne sector near Somme-Py before the outer works of the Hindenburg Line. The key tactical feature in this landscape was a small mountain ridge named Blanc Mont Ridge. Here the Kaiser himself had witnessed the launching of Ludendorff's July push. The battered terrain before Blanc Mont was a putrid morass created by four years of shelling. 'It was a place,' as one Marine put it, 'just built for calamities.'

As spent French battalions clung to hard-won enemy trenches, the French staff cast envious glances at Lejeune's intact division. Suggestions were made to dismember it and use the big American brigades to replace their own losses in the lines. Appalled, Lejeune appealed desperately to Gouraud, promising that if the 2nd were kept whole, he could and would take Blanc Mont. Gouraud complied and on 29 September the 2nd received its orders to attack on 3 October.

The plan was for the Marine Brigade to press forward on the left and seize the Ridge itself. The 3rd Infantry Brigade would angle in from the right. As the Marine Brigade advanced, the French would renew their attack along the Brigade's left on a battered German position called the Essen Trench. In less than three hours, the assault companies of these battalions were firing Very shells, meaning 'Objective Taken.' One company, the 17th of the 5th Marines, had fought a war all its own on the left to capture the machine-gun-studded Essen position, which the French had been unable to take. Ultimately, however, it was in vain, for the Germans counterattacked and regained it. Elements of the 5th Marines then had to capture it all over again.

During the advance of the Marines, two men performed feats that won them the Medal of Honor. Private John Kelly spotted a machine-gun nest whose fire was raking and killing many of his fellow Marines. He darted ahead through a withering American artillery barrage, slew two machine gunners and herded back eight prisoners through the same barrage. Corporal J.H. Pruitt succeeded in knocking out two German machine guns and capturing 40 prisoners, only to be shot dead a few minutes later.

So rapid was the Marines' advance that soon they had carried their colors to the summit of Blanc Mont. However, its western slopes were still in German hands, because the French had not been able to keep pace with the Marines. Thus the Marine Brigade had an exposed left flank all the way back to the Essen Trench. To plug this alarming gap and deal with the stubborn German machine gunners, the 5th Marines stepped in.

The next day at dawn, the 5th Marines in a column of battalions passed through the 6th Marines and pressed forward toward the small town of St. Étienne, three miles beyond Blanc Mont. Meanwhile, the 6th Marines took over the left-flank gap and went to work on some six dozen enemy machine guns still holding down the French on Blanc Mont's west slopes. By noon Major H.J. Larsen's 3rd Batalion, 5th Marines, had pushed within 1000 yards of St. Etienne, but here the Germans made a spirited counterattack – probing deep into the weak left flank of the Brigade. The rear battalion of the 5th Marines was the 1st, commanded by Major George Hamilton. Seeing the Germans attacking the Brigade's flank, he swung his people half-left and counterattacked. It was a mere thousand

Marines against the whole German 149th Infantry. Without any artillery support, the four companies pressed on against searing fire for a distance of 800 yards up a low slope called Ludwig's Rücken. One survivor recalled:

> Singing balls and jagged bits of steel spattered on the hard ground like hail; the line writhed and staggered, steadied and went on, closing toward the center as the shells bit into it. High explosive shells came with the shrapnel, and where they fell geysers of torn earth and black smoke roared up to mingle with the devilish yellow in the air. A foul murky cloud of dust and smoke formed and went with the thinning companies. . . .

What was left of the 1st Battalion, scarcely more than 100 Marines, fought their way up the Ludwig's Rücken, tore into the Germans and pushed them back onto St. Etienne.

For three more days, the splintered Brigade fought on toward St. Étienne. Because the 5th Marines were spent, the 6th – hardly in much better shape – mounted the final assault. At last the French 11th Corps, long behind on the murderous left, came forward as the Germans either gave way or were killed. On 8 October the 75th and 76th Companies, 6th Marines, entered the town. Facing a last bitter counterattack, the two companies – one commanded by a sergeant as the senior Marine still on his feet – hung on until relieved by Army troops on the 10th.

The taking and securing of Blanc Mont cost the Corps dearly – 2538 men killed or wounded. Rifle battalions that went into this action more than 1000 strong marched out of it with 300 or fewer. In one 5th Marines company, as the battle was ending, 230 rations came forward for the company's last reported strength: only 22 officers and men remained to eat them. They used the extra cans of corned beef for revetments against German fire.

On 24 October, the First (American) Army Headquarters summoned General Lejeune for what was to be the 4th's last fight of the war. He was informed that the US Meuse-Argonne push was bogged down. His 2nd Division was needed to shatter the Brünhilde and Freya *Stellungen* (positions named after Wagnerian heroines) in the Hindenburg Line. The 2nd was to be the point of this assault wedge.

At 5:20 AM on D-day, the 4th Brigade jumped off behind a creeping barrage, their objective to capture Barricourt and force the Germans beyond the Meuse. Unnerved by the massive artillery preparation and sensing defeat at this late stage of the war, the Germans slowly gave way before the Marine advance. At eight o'clock, the initial *Stellung* had been taken and the assault companies were being leapfrogged by fresh units so as to maintain the momentum of the attack. Around noon the heights at Barricourt were reached and a few hours later Marines were digging in on the crucial high ground. That night a fresh Army brigade relieved them.

In the following week, rapid advances were made by the 2nd Division and on 9 November it reached the Meuse River to regroup for a forced crossing. Once again the 4th was to spearhead the assault. On the 10th, the last day of the war, the 5th Marines's lead battalions under Major Hamilton launched a desperate attack under vicious shelling across the fire-swept footbridges built by Army engineers. Within hours, both units were across and consolidating.

Next morning, the 11th of November, the 5th Marines struck out against lessening enemy resistance. At last, 'A few minutes after 11 o'clock,' recalled General Lejeune, 'there were tremendous bursts of fire from the two antagonists and then – suddenly – there was complete silence.'

World War I was over. Since their initial entry into combat in March 1918, Marine units had sustained more battle casualties in eight months' fighting than the entire Corps in its preceding 142 years of existence. The total was 11,366 officers and men, of whom 2459 were killed or missing in action. Only 25 Marines became prisoners of war. 'Surrendering,' reflected one Marine officer, 'wasn't popular at the time, and the only way to capture a Marine was to knock him senseless first.'

Red Cross ladies present flowers to men of the 2nd Marine Division on their triumphant return to New York, 8 August 1919.

49

Knights of the Air

The fighter pilots of World War I soon became public heroes but their glamorous image belied the demanding and deadly nature of their work and the truly elite-force skills they developed.

When World I broke out in 1914, aviation was still in its infancy. Only a dozen years before the Wrights had achieved mankind's first powered flight. Louis Bleriot, in his frail monoplane, had flown the English Channel just five years before the big guns began to speak along the Western Front. Yet by 1914 all the major armies had aircraft units for scouting purposes and very soon aggressive and daring aviators were firing on each other with pistols, carbines or rifles. Purpose-built fighting machines, armed with machine guns, very quickly made an appearance but this game of death in the air was primarily personal – one man against his opponent.

As the bitter war years passed, the planes got better and faster and the casualty lists grew longer. Among both those aviators who died and those who survived were the most glamorous heroes of World War I – the aces. Some of them belonged to two famous squadrons, one German and the other on the Allied side. The pilots of these units – Richthofen's Flying Circus and the *Escadrille Lafayette* – became the acknowledged air elitists of The Great War.

Von Richthofen's Flying Circus

In mid-1917, German Imperial Headquarters acted to change the structure of the Air Service. The individual *Jastas*, or Chaser Squadrons, were combined, four at a time, into single, highly-mobile units. The first such unit would be known as *Jagdgeschwader 1*, or JG 1, and the 25-year-old ace, Freiherr (Baron) Manfred Albrecht von Richthofen, was named its commanding officer. Although Richthofen's old Jasta had received this popular nickname earlier, JG 1 was now to become known officially as *Richthofen's Fliegende Zirkus*, with headquarters at Courtai in Belgium, as of June 1917. But the story of its commander as a fledgling air ace had begun two years before its creation.

A former career cavalry officer, Richthofen had volunteered for the Air Service in 1915 and – ironically, with some difficulty – had finally qualified as a pilot at the end of that year. While serving on the Russian front in 1916, he came under the influence of the colorful German ace, Captain Oswald Boelcke. A natural candidate for hero worship, Boelcke, with his battered nose

Opposite: Oberleutnant Lothar von Richtofen, brother of the Red Baron and a noted ace in his own right, being assisted from the cockpit of his Albatros DIII scout plane. After long patrols in open cockpits pilots could often hardly move with the effects of the cold.

The ace Carl Schäfer poses in the cockpit of his Albatros fighter. Schäfer was killed in action in June 1917 after recording 30 victories in combat.

and easy charm, was then known as the world's greatest fighter pilot, with 19 kills to his credit. He wore Germany's highest and most unusual decoration, the *Ordre pour le Mérite*, known popularly as 'The Blue Max,' and boasted that in his earlier battles 'I shot down an Englishman every morning before breakfast.'

Boelcke was looking for flying talent when Richthofen came to Russia. Each of the new Jastas would consist of about 130 men, 18 of whom would be officer pilots. Boelcke was to organize them and to lead one of them himself. Impressed by the alert and enthusiastic Richthofen, Boelcke asked him if he'd like to return with him to the Western Front and 'do some real fighting on the Somme.' Richthofen could hardly believe his luck; with another pilot, he boarded a west-bound train.

As soon as his charges had arrived at Lagnicourt – their new base – Boelcke began to teach them the principles of aerial warfare. A gifted leader, Boelcke inspired his young novices, none of whom had an official kill to his credit. His remarkable eyesight made him the first to spot the tiny dots in the sky that would materialize into hostile Nieuports or Spads. Determined that his personal command – Jasta 2 – should become the most efficient in the Service, Boelcke hammered home his chief strategy: combine the twin elements of altitude and surprise and the enemy was doomed.

The Somme sector in 1916 was made to order for aggressive and daring fliers like Boelcke and his pupil; the British kept from 40 to 60 planes over the river from dawn to dusk. Every time Boelcke led Jasta 2 into the air, dogfights soon developed.

These dogfights – one pilot pitted against another – demanded that fliers practice aerobatics, especially tight turns that allowed them to swerve onto the tail of an enemy plane. The tail was the most desirable target, because single-seater fighter planes of that era did not carry a rear machine gun (as did the two-seaters); thus the enemy could shoot only forward through the propeller blade. Pilots who could make tight turns, and fast-turning planes, meant maneuverability, the key to victory. At this time Richthofen almost always flew an Albatros DII biplane, for which he devised a way to mount a machine gun above the pilot's cockpit so that he could fire upward at need.

In the early days of combat, adversaries, called 'knights of the air,' even saluted each other as they paired off for a duel to the death. Writers, especially journalists, would seize on and romanticize such gallantries. But Richthofen realized early that aerial combat was not a knightly joust but a simple mandate to kill or be killed. His life depended on his skill and his twin Spandau machine guns.

On 17 September 1916 Boelcke, ready to test his young charges in combat, led Jasta 2 out over the Somme and soon spotted 14 low-flying planes headed for them. Hand-signals told his pilots to climb slowly behind the enemy, who had not yet sighted them. The British BE2 bombers, with an escort of FE2 scout fighters, were intent on the ground below en route to bomb a railway station. On their return run, Jasta 2, having bided its time, screamed down on them from out of the morning sun. Richthofen picked out an FE2 and positioned his Albatros directly under it to rake its belly with his Spandaus. The FE2 began to spin helplessly and then spiraled down toward the earth several thousand feet below, with Richthofen in pursuit. Miraculously, the Englishman regained control and managed to land in a rough field behind the German lines.

Eager to confirm and claim his first victim,

Richthofen also landed, nearly crashing his Albatros in the process. Alighting and racing across the field, he found the stricken enemy machine with both pilot and observer riddled with rounds and the cockpit covered with blood. Aghast, Richthofen realized at last something of the true meaning of war. Assisted by some of his own infantry nearby, he lifted the Englishmen out. One died as he was placed on a stretcher and the other soon after in a field station. Later, back at the Jasta 2 mess, a proud Boelcke presented Richthofen and other victorious pilots with a commemorative beer stein, the first of many trophies that the flyer collected avidly.

With each succeeding victim, Richthofen drew closer to the coveted Blue Max, then awarded to those who had eight kills to their credit. But as the prowess of the German pilots increased, in effect devaluing the medal, the Air Service staff raised the minimum to 16.

On 28 October 1916 Richthofen was stunned by the loss of his god. He and other members of Jasta 2 watched in disbelief as Boelcke's plane went down in a freak accident with a Royal Flying Corps De Havilland scout. The German ace was killed instantly. At the funeral, Richthofen carried Boelcke's decorations, and in honor of Germany's top pilot, a British plane flew over the area and dropped a laurel wreath to be placed on Boelcke's grave with the message, 'To the memory of Captain Boelcke, our brave and chivalrous foe. From the Royal Flying Corps.'

By order of Kaiser Wilhelm himself, Jasta 2 was renamed *Jagdstaffel Boelcke* and a new (but short-lived) commander was appointed. Richthofen brought down another bomber near Lagnicourt on 9 November, and 11 days later he got two in one day – an FE2 scout and a BE2 bomber. His score now stood at 10 kills – six away from The Blue Max.

After Boelcke's death Richthofen became the scourge of the skies over the Western Front, roaring in with his Albatros, regardless of the odds, to get in the first burst from his guns. He became a confident killer, hating the English, yet also preparing himself for the day when his own turn might come. He wrote during this period: 'Nothing happens without God's will. That is the only consolation which any of us can put to our souls during this war.'

On 23 November Richthofen met in combat the famous British ace Major Lanoe G. Hawker, sometimes called the English Immelmann, after the German ace Max Immelmann. Holder of the Victoria Cross, Hawker was a formidable opponent. He was on a routine patrol over the German lines in his single-seater De Havilland 2 when he paired off against Richthofen. A chase at 9000 feet descended to about 3000 feet, where the real combat began. The Englishman's plane was more responsive than the German's, but Richthofen's could climb faster. At one point he was startled to see Hawker wave cheerily up at him.

Richthofen realized that Hawker must be low on fuel and would soon have to make a dash for his own lines. He attempted this by breaking out of a circling maneuver into a series of intricate low loops – one of the stunts for which he was famous. He would throttle back at the apex of a loop and allow his DH2 to side-slip for several seconds, thus evading the German's sights at the critical moment. Then Hawker would make a short nose dive, seizing a few precious yards of direct flight homeward. But the superior power of Richthofen's plane allowed him to catch up, and the Englishman lost valuable altitude each time he weaved his way out of range.

Some 15 minutes into the battle, the duellists were only a few hundred feet above the ground. Unable to turn or loop effectively now, Hawker dodged desperately around tall trees and over farm buildings. Richthofen held his relentless pursuit as the two ships screamed over the fields at 150 feet. Then, within 1000 yards of the British lines, Richthofen's guns jammed – he managed to clear them and squeezed off a steady stream of bullets at Hawker's tail section. The English-

Werner Voss, who had shot down 48 Allied planes before he was killed in action in September 1917, was one of the most notable of the German fighter leaders.

A cutaway drawing of the Albatros D Va fighter plane, the most numerous fighter aircraft in German service for much of 1917.

man's plane shuddered as the rounds tore through the thin fabric. Then the DH2's nose dipped abruptly and the British ace plowed into the field with sickening impact. During the duel, Richthofen had fired some 900 rounds from his Spandaus – one was found to have lodged in Hawker's brain.

Now his superiors at the High Command were watching him with special interest: this young aristocrat could help boost morale within the armed forces as a hero – someone everyone could look up to. Laudatory news articles and features soon began to appear, and before long the press was following his every move and he had become a national figure.

Richthofen was neither shy of his rising fame nor indifferent to being recognized by the enemy. To the astonishment of the other Jasta members, he decided to paint his 'packing case,' as he called it, a brilliant red, so the enemy would recognize him as a formidable adversary. Manfred's brother, Lothar, who had recently joined the Jasta, painted his machine yellow. Pilots in other squadrons followed suit. Young Hermann Goering painted his plane all black with a white tail fin. Ernst Udet – to become the leading German ace after Richthofen, with 62 victories – had his done in gold with a yellow propeller.

Some of the German pilots adorned their engine cowlings with hideous faces or painted their names in enormous letters on wing surfaces so that their Allied opponents would recognize them and quail. One flier of Jasta 12 emphasized his identity by adding under his name 'Kennst mich noch?' ('Don't you remember me?')

But it was Richthofen's own scarlet Albatros that caught and held the German public's fancy. Newspapers began calling him The Red Battle Flier and The Red Falcon. Actually, it was the foreign papers, largely English, which started calling him 'The Red Baron.' The varied colors of his planes, and their occasional disposition along the Front via special trains, accounted for the label 'Richthofen's Flying Circus.' Richthofen himself was widely quoted in the press. 'I am a hunter,' went one of his pronouncements. 'My brother, Lothar, is a butcher. When I have shot down an Englishman, my hunting passion is satisfied for a quarter of an hour.'

The young and popular ace still yearned for his Blue Max. A week after Christmas 1916, he downed his fifteenth enemy plane. On 4 January 1917 he sent a Sopwith Pup – forerunner of the famous Camel – careening earthward with a long burst from his twin Spandaus. Presumably the Blue Max was now his, and he notified the authorities. Hearing nothing for several days, Richthofen became depressed, fearing that the minimum had been raised again. Even the good news that he was to receive his own Jasta command failed to raise his spirits.

On 16 January he heard at last, It turned out

that the Kaiser himself would graciously award him the *Ordre pour le Mérite*. At 25, with his sixteenth kill, he was now Germany's leading living ace: the Fatherland had its newest colorful hero.

Richthofen, now a *Rittmeister* or Captain, looked forward to forging a new 'Circus' from his freshly awarded command, which he took over on 23 January at Douai.

His young pilots, though inexperienced, were all handpicked men and he drove them hard – just as his own mentor, Boelcke, had driven him. When he took over the new Jasta 11, it had no kills to its credit, while his old Jasta 2 had over 100. As he quickly whipped the respectful new unit into fighting shape, he added to his personal score. By the end of March 1917, he had shot down 31 planes and was well within Boelcke's all-time record of 40.

Richthofen continued to fly and fight in scarlet-painted aircraft, now usually a single-seater Halberstadt biplane. His men had seen how their commander's colorful ship made a prime target, so in a loyal effort to take some of the pressure off Richthofen, they urged him to let them paint their planes red too. This he agreed to – with one

stipulation; each aircraft was also to be marked in some way with other striking colors.

For the British pilots of the Royal Flying Corps, April 1917 came to be known as 'Bloody April': the German Circuses, as all the Jastas were now being called, destroyed 151 of their 385 planes over the Western Front. The Germans had stricter training schedules and the rigid discipline of their tightly knit formations increased their dominance of the contested air space. Furthermore, such German tactics as Richthofen's massing of planes in decisive numbers were more realistic and effective. The British, by contrast, were still tied to the requirements of ground-based Corps and Army Headquarters. The Army Staff saw the Royal Flying Corps as useful primarily as an adjunct to their own functions of picture-taking and spotting for the big guns. When bomber and reconnaissance flights failed to fulfill their objectives, their fighter escorts were blamed. Thus much British fighter strength was committed to cumbersome escort flying on slow and steady courses, while the German Circuses could roam freely and flexibly to as high as 15,000 feet. So positioned, they could

Left: The Fokker Triplane used by Leutnant von Linsingen of Jasta 11.

Below: The red-painted Triplane popularly associated with the Red Baron. Richtofen was flying Triplane Nr 425/17 when he was shot down and killed, 21st April 1918.

attack downward – ideally, out of the sun – and pick off the British escorts.

On the evening of 30 April, while eating in the officers' mess at Douai, Richthofen was summoned to the telephone. He listened with mounting incredulity as a telegram was read to him:

I have just received the message today that you have been for the fiftieth time victor in an air battle. I heartily congratulate you upon this magnificent success with my complete acknowledgement. The Fatherland looks to you with thanks for its courageous flier. May God further keep you safe.

Wilhelm II, R., Kaiser of Germany

The young ace was overwhelmed, even more so when, later that same night, he received another call informing him that the Kaiser wished to meet him personally. Forthwith he was given six weeks' leave and told to present himself at Imperial Headquarters in Berlin, where he met the Emperor and such other dignitaries as Generals Hindenburg and Ludendorff.

Although Richthofen was suffering from battle fatigue and the doctors at Douai had ordered him to rest, the propaganda machine at headquarters sent him on an exhausting morale-boosting tour. America had just entered the war, and the flagging spirits of the German people wanted bolster-

Oberleutnant Hermann Goering seen late in the war posing beside his all-white Fokker D VII. At this time Goering was commander of Jasta 1.

ing. Postcards appeared by the millions all over the Fatherland bearing his picture. He was greeted with wild cheering by adoring crowds wherever he went and received sacks full of mail, including many proposals of marriage. Richthofen was also ordered to write his autobiography and provided with a secretary to assist him.

Sick at last of fame and the sense that he was being used as a propaganda puppet, he escaped to his home at Schweidnitz to wander in the quiet woods, add to his war memorabilia (bits of fuselages and wing number plates of planes he had shot down) and work on his book. Titled *The Red Battle Flier*, it was eventually printed in huge quantities and widely read by Germans, even by soldiers in the trenches.

By mid-June of 1917 Richthofen was glad to be back at the battlefront in command of JG 1, a newly formed combination of four Jastas. He went back to flying his first love – a bright red Albatros – in which he nearly met his end leading a sortie on 6 July. In an aerial free-for-all against some RFC FE2s and Royal Navy Sopwiths, four of his eight planes were shot down. Richthofen eventually paired off with a two-seater that carried an observer/gunner who could point his Lewis machine gun in any direction, while Richthofen, with his fixed Spandaus, could only fire ahead. As Richthofen maneuvered behind the FE2's tail to come within range, the British pilot banked suddenly and the observer poured a stream of bullets into the scarlet Albatros.

The observer, Lieutenant Woodbridge of the RFC, later wrote:

We could hardly have been 20 yards apart when the Albatros pointed her nose down suddenly and passed under us. . . . We saw the red plane slip into a spin. It turned over and over and round and round. It was no maneuver. He was completely out of control. His motor was going full on, so I figured I had at least wounded him. As his head was the only part of him that wasn't protected from my fire by his motor, I thought that was where he was hit.

Lieutenant Woodbridge was correct. One of his slugs had plowed into the left side of Richthofen's head, tearing a three-inch furrow in the scalp and exposing the skull. Fighting the blood flow and intense pain, he shut off his engine, checked the spin and put the plane into a long gliding descent. Heading back to his own lines, he nearly blacked out before landing in a shell-pitted field, taking a few telephone poles with him before his machine staggered to a halt. He fainted among several of his own infantrymen after prising himself out of the cockpit. A nearby field hospital treated his ugly wound.

When he returned to duty, Richthofen seemed a changed man, increasingly introspective and moody; he spent much of his time in the company of his Great Dane, Moritz, who sometimes flew

with him. His wound continued to pain him severely and he was often forced to return to the hospital for treatment. He still commanded his JG 1 Circus with his old efficiency and iron will, but as his favorite pilots were lost one by one, he grew more morose and sometimes openly questioned the sanity of Germany's continuing the war he felt she could not now win.

As the winter of 1918 passed and the flying weather got better, Richthofen's men saw some action. But it was not until March, when the first big German offensive began along a 50-mile sector in Flanders, that JG 1 mounted a flurry of sorties. By this time Richthofen had given up the Albatros for his famous red Fokker DR1 triplane, a highly maneuverable ship increasingly favored by German fliers. At the end of the month, his score had reached an amazing 74.

Richthofen's 75th victory won him the Order of the Red Eagle (Third Class) with Crown and Swords, an unprecedented honor for a man of his rank. His tunic was now so heavy with decorations that he was unable to wear all of them at once. His 80th and last victim was 19-year-old Lieutenant David Lewis, flying a Sopwith Camel, who hit the earth northeast of Villiers-Bretonneaux at a speed of 60 miles an hour – and lived to tell about it.

When Manfred von Richthofen took off in his scarlet Fokker on the morning of 21 April 1918, it was for the last time. Before he climbed into the cockpit, a young mechanic stepped forward and asked for his autograph for his little boy. Richt-

hofen gave it, then snapped, 'What's the matter? Don't you think I'll return?'

A few minutes later, leading his flight of Circus pilots over the Somme in search of enemy English pilots, he spotted eight Camels boring through the clouds. Diving on his prospective victim, he was suddenly caught in a crossfire of bullets from Australian anti-aircraft gunners on the ground and the Vickers guns of Canadian Captain Arthur Brown in the air. Richthofen's scarlet triplane staggered, glided a few hundred yards, nosed over and crashed near the Australian gunners. So hard did the German ace's ship hit the shell-pocked earth that its propeller was never found. Thus died the Red Baron, and the controversy was never resolved as to whether Brown or the Australians fired the single bullet that drilled into his chest.

With the death of Richthofen, the magic of the Circuses – even when their new Pfalz machines arrived – seemed to decline. The roll-call of those who succeeded Richthofen as commanders of the JGs rang with memorable names: Wilhelm Reinhard, Erich Loewenhardt, Hermann Goering and others. But their life expectancy was often measured in days. The Circuses still daubed on their colorful war paint; after Richthofen's death, JG 2, in deference to Richthofen's own JG 1, switched from red to royal blue fuselages. Mere color, however, no longer mattered. The dwindling Circuses fought on until November without either mercy for their enemies or hope for themselves.

A group of Jasta 10 pilots pose for a photograph before a flight in September 1918. The aircraft in the background are Fokker D VIIs which were among the best fighter aircraft produced during World War I.

Opposite: Sergeant Fred Prince of the Lafayette Escadrille poses beside his Nieuport scout in 1916. The pipe-like fittings attached to the wing struts were designed to fire rockets at observation balloons.

Below: Lafayette Escadrille pilots, from left, Soubiran, Rockwell, Chicomski, Thenault, Campbell and Thaw at an airfield near the Somme front. They pose in front of Sergeant Campbell's Nieuport which he was able to land safely despite losing the lower left wing.

The Escadrille Lafayette

Of all the Allied flying units clashing with the Germans over the Western Front, the French Air Force's *Escadrille Americaine*, as it was first named, was unique. An all-volunteer outfit, it was composed variously of college boys, soldiers-of-fortune, professional aviators, playboys, drifters and expatriates. A strange and in some ways astonishingly romantic assortment of Americans, they all had three things in common – bravery, a taste for adventure and a US passport. At first they flew Nieuports, then Spads. They took as their insignia a feathered, screaming Indian chief copied from a corporate trademark.

While the *Escadrille* (squadron) had originated in the minds of several adventurous Americans, it was Norman Prince, a New England expatriate, who was the main driving force in forming this group. Prince himself was one of the few Americans to earn a pilot's license before the outbreak of war. In Paris in 1916 he obtained the backing of Dr. Edmund L. Gros, a wealthy physician who had organized and built up the American Ambulance Field Service.

For likely recruits, the two men began combing the various French units to which American volunteers had been drawn in the glamorous opening months of the war. At first there was opposition from the French authorities. But with the French Army bogged down embarrassingly around Verdun, they soon decided to capitalize on the value of aerial warfare.

There were also objections from Washington after the Escadrille was officially formed on 16 April 1916. At this time, of course, the United States was allegedly neutral and could not officially favor either side in the war. When it was learned that a flying unit called the *Escadrille Americaine* was being organized as a part of the French Army, the Germans were able to exert diplomatic pressure on powerful isolationist circles in the United States, which resulted in Washington's complaining to the French. However, the French then designated the Escadrille by a simple code letter and number – N 124,

the 'N' standing for Nieuport. Later an Escadrille pilot named Claude Gênet had the idea of adding the name 'Lafayette' and this appellation stayed with the unit until 18 February 1918, when it was officially incorporated into the United States Air Service.

In addition to Norman Prince, the original founding group included Kiffin Rockwell, a medical student from North Carolina; William Thaw, who had raced a hydroplane at Yale; Victor Chapman, who had been at the *École des Beaux Arts* in Paris and joined the Foreign Legion as a private; Bert Hall, a tough Texan who had been a pre-war stunt flier and who had already flown in the French Air Force; and James

Above: Dudley Hill, seen here as a sergeant pilot of the Lafayette Escadrille in 1916, later commanded a fighter squadron when America joined the war.

Opposite, top: Edmond Genet, a pilot of the Lafayette Escadrille, who had the unfortunate distinction to be the first American to be killed in action after the United States declared war. Genet was killed on 16 April 1917.

Opposite, bottom: Victor Chapman, Kiffin Rockwell and James McConnell relax with a game of billiards. All three were later killed in action.

McConnell and Elliot Cowdin, who came from the Ambulance Service.

The squadron was first posted to Luxeuil-les-Bains in the Vosges district for training. Because the French propaganda machine meant to capitalize on their achievements, the Americans were treated with kid gloves, quartered in a sumptuous villa and fed with their officers at the best hotel in town. In spite of their low ranks and small pay as non-coms, the pilots found that money flowed freely from French grants, while some had private incomes of their own. The local citizens soon began to complain about their loose living and hell-raising.

One of the original seven, James McConnell – who was later shot down over the Western Front – wrote home with foreboding: 'I thought of the luxury we were enjoying; our comfortable beds, baths and motor cars, and I recalled the ancient custom of giving the man selected for the sacrifice a royal time of it before the appointed day.'

But the Escadrille trained hard – and recklessly – often making life hell for their French officers. Their patient commander, Capitaine Georges Thénault, watched silently as the young men wrecked newly issued Nieuports in bad landings and ran them into hangars.

In May of 1916, the Escadrille was moved to Bar-le-Duc near the battle area around the vast trench system that had developed at Verdun. In this struggle of attrition, with the Germans determined to break through and advance on Paris, the long-range artillery guns reigned supreme. To supply them with 'eyes' for better accuracy,

the Germans used spotting balloons (called 'sausages' by Allied soldiers); the elite of the German air strength, led by the aces Oswald Boelcke and Max Immelmann, was engaged in protecting the balloons against Allied sorties. The Germans at Verdun were flying mostly Fokkers, against which the Nieuport was considered the best defense. Since the Escadrille was a Nieuport squadron, it was committed to the aerial duels over Verdun. Meanwhile, Dr. Gros in Paris had been recruiting more Americans for the Escadrille, among them Clyde Balsley; Dudley Hill; and future co-authors of *Mutiny on the Bounty*, Charles Nordhoff and James Norman Hall; and Raoul Lufbery, who was to become the unit's 'ace of aces.'

On 18 June Capitaine Thénault led a patrol consisting of Kiffin Rockwell, Clyde Balsley and Norman Prince toward enemy skies over Verdun, where they ran smack into 14 Fokkers. The Germans dove on the patrol with their Spandaus blazing. Thénault, the veteran, wisely signalled to the others to make a dash back to their own lines, but young Balsley was unable to give them the slip. No matter which way he banked or dove, the Germans were always on his tail. Many of the Jasta fliers at this time were using exploding dum-dum bullets – theoretically outlawed by international agreement. As Balsley was desperately trying to make his escape, one of these tore into his leg and laid it open. At last, he outran his pursuers and managed to land. His mechanics had to lift him from the cockpit. Taken to a nearby hospital, he contracted gangrene but eventually recovered. That same week Victor Chapman became the first American pilot to lose his life in the war.

As summer ended, the French decided that these Americans, whom one officer branded as 'inexperienced and brash,' should be withdrawn and sent back to Luxeuil-les-Bains. There they found some two dozen Royal Flying Corps pilots in residence. The Americans and the British quickly hit it off, bottles of wine and whiskey passed freely back and forth and there was much group singing of 'Pack Up Your Troubles'.

It became something of a ritual for the young Americans to go carousing in Paris on leave, where they acquired such colorful mascots as two lion cubs named 'Whiskey' and 'Soda.' Some pilots would pay a visit to the famous expatriate Gertrude Stein, who was then driving a Model T ambulance with her friend Alice B. Toklas as their contribution to the war effort. The Americans became well known in the French capital, where they frequently gathered at the Cafe Maxwell or another favorite, Harry's American Bar.

In their official French (and later American) uniforms, the Escadrille pilots were always snappy dressers. They were quick to renew their pink Bedford breeches, tight-fitting tunics, Sam Browne belts and high-cut Savile Row leather boots. Some even carried swagger sticks. In the air they were fond of wearing either the short 'combination' flying jackets or sturdy one-piece coveralls.

After Chapman's death, Kiffin Rockwell wrote to his brother: 'Prince and I are going to fly 10 hours tomorrow and we'll do our best to kill one or two Germans for Victor.' The next day Rockwell, as good as his word, went out of his formation in pursuit of a Fokker. As he did so, another German dove out of the sun at 100 miles an hour, staying on his tail to riddle him with bursts of illegal dum-dum bullets. When his body was found, it was fearfully mutilated and his throat had been torn open by an exploding round. Photographs were sent in protest to the Geneva Convention authorities, but they did nothing to halt the carnage.

Less than a week later, Norman Prince, returning from a flight after dark, stayed out too long over enemy lines. Unable to see clearly, he ran into a high-tension cable wire. His machine, spinning wildly, broke up in the air and Prince was thrown violently to the ground. In trying to stand, he found that both his legs were broken and that he was bleeding internally. Three days later he was dead of his injuries. As a founder of the Escadrille, Prince was given a full military funeral, complete with firing squad and bugle calls.

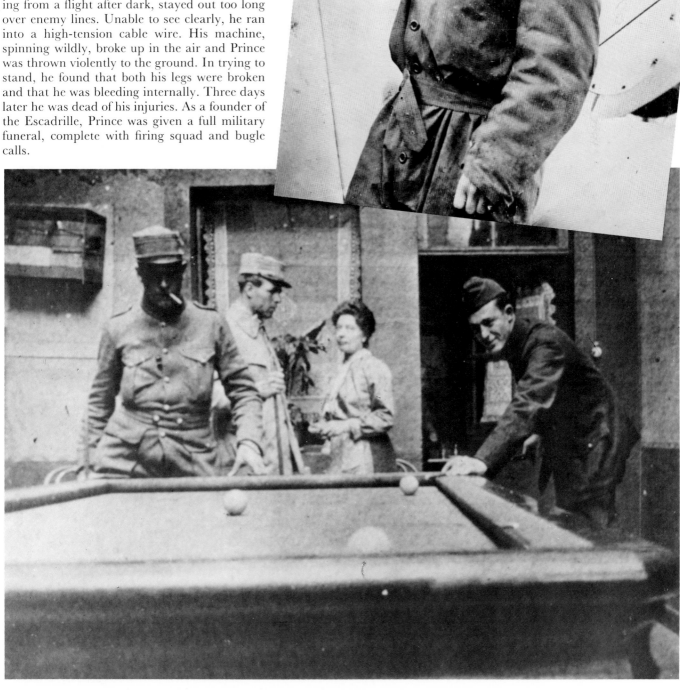

During the fall of 1916 the attitude of the French military authorities toward the Escadrille underwent a complete reversal. Instead of conserving the American fliers lest one of their deaths should cause adverse reaction, they seemed to believe that a freer expenditure of the pilots' lives might invoke a deeper commitment on the part of America to the Allied cause. The French Command now put the Americans to bomber escort work, a duty whose rigid formations made it easier for German fliers to pick them off.

In Paris, Dr. Gros called for new volunteers as replacements, and fresh faces began to show up at Luxeuil. A few of these new Americans came from French flying units like the famous Escadrille N 3, known as *Les Cigognes*, or 'The Storks.' But most of them were greenhorns who had to learn from scratch.

Of the total of 209 American nationals who volunteered for duty in the French Air Force, the majority went through the training schools at Buc, Pau and Avord, where they learned on the clipped-wing *Pingouins* before graduating to Caudrons or Nieuports (and later, to Spads). In fact, of these Americans only 38 – the original seven and 31 others – passed through the ranks of the *Escadrille Lafayette*. The rest served – until the United States entered the war – with various other French squadrons.

After its merciless mauling over Verdun and its subsequent regrouping at Luxeuil, the Escadrille was issued new Spad VII single-seaters with V8 Hispana-Suiza engines – the most reliable

and maneuverable airplane yet developed by the Allies. For nearly a year after the United States' entry into the war, on 6 April 1917, the Escadrille continued to fly under French colors and orders. Raoul Lufbery was turning into the highest-scoring ace of the squadron. As he continued to amass victories, he was built up by the French and American journalists. By late 1917 the French policy of husbanding American pilots seemed to have returned, along with renewed publicity. In Lufbery, the French press had a 'natural,' for the ace had been born in France of French parents before emigrating with his family to the United States.

In February of 1918, the Escadrille was formally absorbed into the US Air Service and redesignated the 103rd Aero Squadron of the American Expeditionary Forces. Thaw, who had been wounded but survived to become a major, remained its commander for a time. Eventually it became the Escadrille Jeanne d'Arc and was staffed by French officers and fliers.

Meanwhile, the Americans of the old *Escadrille Lafayette* had to be discharged from the French service before they could join the US Air Service. Due to US delay and red tape and a two-month wait for commissions, the former Escadrille pilots continued to fly and down German planes as civilians. But the old alumni were breaking up fast. Many were dispersed to fly with other new American units besides the 103rd. Lufbery, soon to be a major, went to command the 94th ('Hat in the Ring') Squadron, which had among its members Captain Eddie Rickenbacker, who would

Opposite: Bill Thaw parades with an American flag in May 1917 while still, as his uniform shows, serving with the Escadrille Lafayette as part of the French air force.

Below: Sergeant Soubiran poses in front of his aircraft at Cachy airfield in the Somme sector in 1916. Soubiran later commanded the 103rd Aero Squadron, which the Escadrille Lafayette became when its pilots transferred to the US Air Service.

end his AEF career with 26 kills. Captain Charles Biddle went to the 13th Aero Squadron. Captain James Norman Hall went to the 94th. Bert Hall went off to one of the 'Storks' units. Even Whiskey, the lion cub, was packed off to the Paris Zoo. When their commissions finally came through, the former Escadrille fliers put away their natty French uniforms and donned American ones.

Three months after the old Escadrille ceased to exist, the last link with the halcyon days of the proud squadron was severed with the death of Lufbery on the morning of 18 May 1918. In full view of his new command, Lufbery, in pursuit of a German photo-reconnaissance plane over Toul near Nancy, was hit by a quick burst from the gunner in the rear seat. Lufbery's Nieuport seemed to dissolve into flaming bubbles and he went into a long dive. The ace, who had always sworn that he would never burn, switched off his motor and coolly tried to put out the flames by sideslipping back and forth. But it didn't work and the flames soon made the cockpit intolerable.

His men on the ground watched what happened next in petrified horror. They saw Lufbery climb out and try to operate the joy stick from the head fairing. Then he retreated from this position and crawled back along the fuselage toward the tail. When he was about 250 feet above the earth, they watched him jump. Perhaps he had been aiming for a nearby canal. If so, he missed, and landed hard enough to be killed by the fall. Rickenbacker later wrote that when they found him, 'The charred body was entirely covered with flowers from nearby gardens.'

Eleven Lafayette Escadrille fliers became aces. Among the dead were Lufbery with 17, David Putnam with 12 and Frank Baylies with 12. Paul Baer got 8 enemy planes; T. G. Cassady, 8; Edwin Parsons, 8; Charles Biddle, 8; Gorman Larner, 8; W. T. Ponder, 6; F. Connerley, 6; and William Thaw, of the original seven, 6.

Many who denigrated the importance of the American contribution to the air war and pointed to the low scores of its aces tended to forget the heroism and devotion of the early pilots of the Escadrille. As they battled over the trenches of Verdun, two years were to pass before other American airmen came close to matching the deeds of this early gallant unit. Even the latter-day aces like Rickenbacker and Frank Luke had to be trained in tactical matters by the French. And before the advent of the German Circuses, before the onset of 'Bloody April,' this small band of volunteers had gone willingly into combat with an enemy far better trained and several times their number.

The members of the Escadrille as a whole personified those special characteristics of the flying volunteer elite of World War I. They flew and fought without parachutes. They saw their comrades come and go and measured their own existences by the hour, knowing that death from wounds would come to four out of five. They were true expatriates who fought without formal allegiance to any country, surrounded by commanders who spoke a different language and whose values and their cultural attachments were alien to them.

Opposite: The much-decorated Raoul Lufbery poses in front of his aircraft in 1917.

Below: The Lafayette Escadrille's base at Ham in 1917.

The Commandos

The British commando organization was created in adversity to strike back at the German domination of Europe. The commandos' fighting qualities were evident from the first but were never better displayed than in the culminating D-Day triumph.

The term 'Commando,' employed in the Boer War to denote certain raiding units in service against the British in South Africa, was used again in World War II for specialized British amphibious troops which raided Axis-held territory. Until the actual invasion of the Continent in 1944, when they were used as first-assault shock troops, the commandos were generally employed in harassing German forces occupying the European and North African coastlines. They were volunteers from the British Army, organized in units called Commandos, and rigorously trained at Achnacarry and other bases in Scotland and England for such operations as raids on St. Nazaire, Spitzbergen and Vaasgö, Norway. In 1942 and 1943, Commandos of Royal Marine volunteers were also formed.

As the war moved toward larger amphibious operations, the number of Commandos increased. The strength of a full Commando was apt to vary with periodic reorganizations, but in late 1942 a typical Commando consisted of 24 officers and 435 enlisted men. In combat there could be up to 630 men. Each Commando had a headquarters and several Troops, which were the equivalent of platoons in regular infantry companies. The usual arrangement was to have six Troops to a Commando, one of which was a Heavy Weapons Troop armed with medium machine guns and heavy mortars. Thus a Commando was not unlike an infantry battalion; however, instead of a battalion's four companies, the Commando had only five small rifle or combat Troops, each with an overall complement of 120 men of all ranks. All Commandos were, of course, organized under the British Special Forces in a Special Service Brigade until spring 1943, and thereafter in a Special Service Group.

In early 1940 the Commandos were really a handful of what were called Independent Companies. That year, ten Independent Companies were organized, each with 20 officers and 270 men drawn from Territorial Army volunteers plus regulars and reservists. Four of these companies were the first British Special Service Forces in combat in World War II. They went ashore from their parent ship, HMS *Royal Ulsterman*, on 15 May at small fishing ports south of

Opposite: Commandos train in overcoming enemy sentries, a picture taken in 1942.

Narvik, Norway to try – unsuccessfully – to delay the German advance.

Meanwhile, Prime Minister Churchill was pressing for stronger assault units. 'If,' he wrote early in June, at the end of the Dunkirk evacuation, 'it is so easy for the Germans to invade us . . . why should it be impossible . . . for us to do anything of the same kind to them?' An imaginative British Army officer, Lieutenant Colonel Dudley Clarke, devised a plan for larger raiding parties to be drawn from a special force and carried to France by ship to harass the enemy. From his boyhood in South Africa, he remembered the tales of daring Boer farmers' raiding parties called Commandos (from Afrikaans 'commands') in the war of 1899-1902. This he thought would be an appropriate name for these new units. Clarke interested his superior, Sir John Dill, Chief of the Imperial General Staff, who presented the idea to the Prime Minister. A few days later the enthusiastic Churchill approved it, and Clarke was ordered to mount a raid across the Channel 'at the earliest possible moment.' That same afternoon, the War Office Section MO (Military Operations) 9 came into being and took steps to organize the special force of Commandos. Liaison with the Royal Navy procured some air-sea rescue boats for Clarke's raid, launched on 23 June, the night that France surrendered. The 115 participants were selected from the Independent Companies and, faces blackened with theatrical grease paint (later mud and burnt cork would be used), they made a series of four landings along a twenty-mile stretch of French coastline around Boulogne. The four

parties remained ashore for about an hour and did only minor damage; the lone casualty was Dudley Clarke himself, who was hit in the ear. Although it was only a token raid, it showed the necessity for some means of distinguishing friend from foe on a hostile shore and for pin-point navigation in assault landings. And it proved that landings on enemy-held shores were possible.

In that first year of the commandos' existence, the only other raid was in mid-June on the German-occupied Channel island of Guernsey. It was carried out by some 100 men drawn from No. 3 Commando (one of ten newly organized units) and No. 11 Independent Company. Under one of the first Commando leaders, Colonel John Durnford-Slater, the raiders boarded two destroyers and then transferred to crash motorboats for the landing. This raid, described later by Durnford-Slater himself as a 'very amateurish affair,' accomplished little, and some men had to be left ashore where they were taken prisoner. Throughout that summer and fall of 1940, Churchill's desire for big raids involving from 5000 to 10,000 men was simply not feasible. First, there were not as yet that many trained commandos and, second, there were few adequate invasion-type small craft to take them ashore.

In the desperate year of 1940 many future commanders – Durnford-Slater, Clarke, Peter Young and others – were preparing their men for a new kind of hit-and-run soldiering, although an abstruse command set-up made raids from England hard to conduct. High-level red tape decreed that each Army Command was responsible

Prime Minister Churchill on a visit to a commando training center in Scotland during World War II. Churchill was instrumental in establishing the commandos, hoping that their raids would encourage the formation of resistance movements in Occupied Europe.

for attacking coastlines opposite their district in England. Moreover, only the Royal Navy could give the OK for any seaborne operation. Only Norway was exempt from this web of red tape. Hence the only important raid during this period was an assault in the early spring of 1941 on the Lofoten Islands by about 500 men of 3 and 4 Commandos with some Royal Engineers and Free Norwegian units.

The Lofotens were picked for this first big raid because they offered a chance not only to strike back at the Germans, but also to destroy economic objectives, including large fish oil supplies needed for Nazi manufacture of nitroglycerine and vitamin tablets. Sailing for Norway aboard two transport ships with Landing Craft Assaults (LCAs) launchable from davits, the force met the submarine HMS *Sunfish* off Stamsund as a navigation check and were piloted to their landing points by sailors of the Free Norwegian Navy. In the pre-dawn hours of 4 March, the commandos landed unopposed at three harbors besides Stamsund – each on a different island. By noon they had set fire to several oil factories and smashed electrical installations. They also sank a handful of small ships and set fire to many thousands of gallons of oil and gasoline. The commandos took back with them over 300 volunteers for the Free Norwegian forces and some 200 German prisoners. Before wrecking the telephone exchange at Stamsund, one lieutenant used the mainland cable to send a telegram to Berlin addressed to A. Hitler. It read: 'You said in your last speech German troops would meet the English wherever they landed STOP Where are your troops?'

As spring turned to summer, there were several proposals for fresh commando targets. It was decided that a raid on Spitzbergen, a strategic coal-mining island in the Svalbard group belonging to Norway, would be a good bet. This landing was made chiefly by Canadian troops trained as commandos and was unopposed, since the Germans had not garrisoned the island. With the help of some Norwegians, the Canadians destroyed several mines in late August and then returned to England.

By October 1941 Lord Louis Mountbatten had replaced the aging Admiral Sir Roger Keyes as Chief of Combined Operations, and all Special Forces, including the Commandos, came under his imaginative direction. Lord Louis had been pressed by Churchill to 'conduct a program of raids in ever-increasing intensity' on the European coast. Mountbatten, who had great charm and a flair for organization, quickly established the necessary liaison with the Chiefs-of-Staff, ministries and others upon whom the Commandos relied for badly needed weapons and supplies. In a few short weeks, headquarters was humming with a vigor unknown under Sir Roger.

In December 1941 Combined Operations planned a diversionary raid, again in the Lofotens. Since the raiding had now become more organized, greater use could be made of feints to distract the enemy from principal assault targets. Moreover, in overall strategy, it was hoped that these northerly missions would cause the enemy to think that the Allies intended to invade not France, but Norway. On this feint, 300 men of 12 Commando landed in the Lofotens at six o'clock in the evening of the day after Christmas. They were unopposed by a sleepy German garrison who, stuffed with their holiday dinners, were off their guard. Specially trained for snow warfare, and wearing white hooded coveralls, the commandos swiftly occupied the two harbors on the island of Mostenesöy. While they did some damage ashore and took prisoners, they remained only two days on the island because their supporting ships were attracting enemy bombings.

While these commandos were making their feint, Troops from 2 and 3 Commando were hitting the principal target – Vaagsö Island, in a rugged fjord off central Norway. Fish factories, oil tanks and radio stations were again the objectives. This raid was unique because it was the first against a defended port, conducted by five assault groups. Group 1 was to land at Hollevik on Vaagsö's south shore to take defense points and villages about a mile from the town of South Vaagsö. Then it was to join and support Group 2, which was to go ashore just south of that town and capture it. Group 3 was to take the small nearby island of Maaloy while Group 4 was to lie offshore in reserve, ready to assist any of the other groups. Group 5 was to go by destroyer up the Ulvesund Channel and land near Kapelnoes

King George VI, left, and Admiral Roger Keyes, right, watch commandos assemble an assault boat during an inspection of commando training in October 1941.

THE COMMANDOS

Right: Commandos in training in Scotland. The first man falls on the barbed wire flattening it down so that the rest of his squad can advance.

Left: A commando sergeant instructs men of the American 1st Ranger Battalion in unarmed combat during training in 1942.

Commandos charge through a smoke screen during an exercise. The soldier in the center carries a Thompson submachine gun, a weapon the commandos favored.

Commandos help a wounded comrade back to their landing craft during the Vaagsö raid in December 1941.

Point north of the town; it would cut the road there so that German reinforcements from North Vaagsö could not reach South Vaagsö. The latter was thought to be defended by 150 Germans of the 181st Division. There was also known to be a battery of four coastal guns on Maaloy to protect Ulvesund Harbor. No enemy warships were thought to be in the vicinity, and only about 40 planes were believed to be based at cities some distance away.

Sailing on December 26, the Vaagsö force rendezvoused with a submarine off the Vaagsfjord as their navigation check and then steamed up the fjord between snowy hills just visible in the predawn. The landing would take place at 8:50 AM. Until then, the LSIs (Landing Ship Infantry) anchored in a bay protected from the Maaloy batteries, a short run up the coast from the beaches. When the attack began, the cruiser with the Vaagsö force opened up on Maaloy and the destroyers fired at other targets. All 50 men of Group 1 landed without opposition at Hollevik, cleared the villages there and took prisoners. The leader of this group was then ordered by radio to move up the coast and form a reserve for the Troops attacking South Vaagsö.

Group 2, led by Durnford-Slater, signalled the Navy with Very shells to stop its bombardment as they went ashore. But before they did so one of the RAF bombers assisting in the landing was hit by a German trawler, went out of control and dropped a bomb among the landing craft, causing several casualties in one of the boats. This landing was purposely made at the base of some sheer snow-covered rocks, because it was thought unlikely that enemy machine guns would be covering such an apparently inaccessible point. These Troops got ashore and began working their way north toward South Vaagsö. Meanwhile, Group 3 was only some 60 yards from Maaloy Island when the cruiser Kenya's bombardment lifted. This naval fire had kept the German batteries' crews in their trenches; before they could get their guns into action, the commandos had overrun and taken Maaloy.

Up around South Vaagsö, attacking Troops were meeting fiercer opposition than expected. The town lay on a narrow strip of shoreline beneath a sheer rock wall several hundred feet high. The main road went through the town, and down this road No. 3 Troops worked its way, taking house after house and killing several Germans. No. 4 Troop had killed several more Germans early in the fight, but others tenaciously defended the town's strongpoints, including the Ulvesund Hotel around which savage combat raged. Here the attacking Troops took heavy casualties. Reinforcements from the Maaloy group were called over, and Captain Peter Young, with men of his No. 6 Troop, joined in the hotel fight. With the help of mortar fire, running attacks with grenades and submachine-gun fire, the hotel, now ablaze, was taken and resistance stamped out.

During the fight for the town, antiaircraft fire from the Navy ships was directed against attacking Messerschmitts. Durnford-Slater told his demolition squads to start destroying fish oil factories and other objectives. Other squads were blowing up guns and exploding stores of unlaid mines at the waterfront. Meanwhile, Groups 4 and 5 were landing north of the town to cut off the defenders from that direction. At last the fighting in South Vaagsö centered around a few German defenders holed up in a red warehouse. Grenade-throwing sorties by Peter Young and other leaders helped wear them down, as did bren-gun and mortar fire. Gasoline had been splashed about in part of the warehouse, so a mortar shell hit on the roof sent the whole structure up in flames. As air combat by the RAF protected the force's ships from Nazi bombers, the warehouse action ended the hardest fighting of the raid.

The short Arctic day was now waning and No. 2 Troop led the rest back down toward the beaches. Durnford-Slater urged his men through the flames of several burning buildings by leading the way himself. Many wounded had to be lowered from the high rock faces on stretchers, while the walking wounded made the boats with a hand from their mates. Despite continuous sniper fire, the withdrawal went well and Slater, who had been the first commando ashore, was the last to leave. The unqualified success of the **Vaagsö** raid, when reported in the press, gave Allied spirits a considerable boost. In addition, it caused the Germans to deploy thousands of extra troops northward from their Atlantic Wall defenses. And among the captured German documents, the commandos discovered some German Navy code information that aided in deciphering many secret papers.

All through the years 1942-44 the Norwegian raids continued, with others mounted in various theaters as more commandos were trained. One of the most successful raids on the French coast was carried out on 28-29 February 1942 at Bruneval, using both parachutists and seaborne commandos to capture valuable German radar equipment. This apparatus helped British scientists to develop 'Window,' an effective counter-measure against enemy radar.

In what has been called the most profitable amphibious raid of modern times, the men of 2 Commando carried out the brilliantly planned and executed assault on St. Nazaire on 27-28 March. With demolition parties drawn from several Commandos, 2 Commando, led by Colonel A. C. Newman, had the objective of destroying the big dry dock that housed German submarine pens. St. Nazaire, situated at the mouth of the Loire on an estuary, had only one deep-water channel, well covered by enemy batteries. The river's wide mud flats were thought impassable, but the planners believed that lightly loaded ships and assault craft could scrape over the flats on the high water of the spring tide. And

A Corporal armed with a Thompson submachine gun leads two commando riflemen in a cautious advance during the Vaagsö raid.

aerial photos showed that there was no boom protecting the huge dry dock. The final plan was to make an explosive blockship of HMS *Campbeltown*, one of the 50 over-age destroyers given to Britain by President Roosevelt. Formerly an old four-stacker, the *Campbeltown* (the late USS *Buchanan*) was fitted out with two raked-back stacks so she would resemble an enemy *Möwe*-class destroyer. She was stripped of all extra weight, manned by a skeleton crew and fitted with a warhead with a delayed 8-hour fuse to ram solidly up against the dock gate.

The commandos were to go ashore at three points; some would go over the side of the *Campbeltown*, while others would land by boat on the Old Entrance quays and the Old Mole, or breakwater. Formed into small assault parties, demolition squads and protection parties, they would first knock out gun batteries around these positions. Then they would proceed to destroy

British prisoners pay their last respects to fallen comrades after the raid on St Nazaire.

the lock gates at the Old Entrance and, if they could, those at the New South Lock. This would make the U-boat basin tidal, preventing the submarines from passing freely in and out of their pens. They would also destroy the pumps used to empty the dry dock and the gate winching gear that hauled the gates aside to allow ships to enter. After two weeks of intensive training at Cardiff and Southampton, where there were similar docks, the raiding force assembled at Falmouth and set sail on the afternoon of 26 March. That night, the force, consisting of a motor gunboat in the lead, the *Campbeltown*, 17 Fairmile motor launches with wooden hulls and two escort destroyers, hoisted German colors and headed in toward the mouth of the Loire. There was also to be a diversionary air raid. An hour before midnight, the fuses on the *Campbeltown* were set to go

off at about 5 o'clock the next morning. With ten miles still to go, the force in two columns stole into the St. Nazaire estuary.

Soon after midnight they were spotted by the Germans and bracketed in the powerful beam of a searchlight from the Old Mole. But the German-type silhouette of the *Campbeltown* enabled the raiding force to bluff its way along for several more minutes. When the old destroyer was about 1700 yards short of ramming, her German colors were hauled down and her own ensign hoisted. The enemy guns ashore opened fire mercilessly. Several crew members were killed, and at the last moment a stray bomb from an RAF plane hit the destroyer's foredeck. But she plowed on in spite of it and, surging over the anti-torpedo nets, smashed solidly into the dry dock gate. Now under very heavy fire, the left column of motor launches veered off toward the Old Mole to land their commandos; the opposite column bored on, intending to slip under the stern of the *Campbeltown* in toward the Old Entrance. Even though these assault craft were returning excellent fire of their own, many were so badly mauled that they sank or were forced to withdraw. Around the Mole, whose searchlight had never been shot out, a few commandos struggled ashore, but many were drowned in their heavy equipment, killed by gunfire or badly burned in sheets of flaming gasoline. Despite the deadly fire and German soldiers tossing grenades down on them, three squads got ashore and started clearing the Mole, then hastened on toward their objectives through the old part of town toward the New South Lock. Other commandos also made it to shore and started on their objectives around the Old Entrance. Aboard the *Campbeltown*, the assault parties dropped their scaling ladders over the bow and proceeded to knock out gun positions on the docks.

Under cover of their protection parties, the demolition squads – those who had made it ashore – got to work on their missions. One team reached the pumping station and blew in its steel door, then ran below and set charges on the pumps themselves. Dashing clear of the building, they heard the pumphouse windows blow out with a terrific roar – and a rain of concrete blocks. Other commandos sledgehammered oil pipes and electrical gear. Three squads making for the northern dock gate and its winch house in the dark took heavy casualties, but managed to blow up their objectives. They could now hear the gurgle of water flowing into the breached dry dock. All feasible demolitions north and south of the dry dock had now been achieved. However, all efforts to destroy the New South Lock and the steel bridge leading to it were frustrated. Some commandos had fought their way through the Old Town and even beyond around the rear of the submarine pens, but many of these were soon forced to surrender to German *Stosstruppen* (Shock Troops) who were now arriving on the scene. Ninety minutes after the landing, Colonel Newman decided to regroup and withdraw his force of about 100 men.

Those who could make it to the *Campbeltown* came aboard the gunboat alongside it, whose decks were already littered with wounded and dead. Others headed back into the Old Town, got scattered and were taken prisoner. At length, the gunboat started back down the estuary, to run a fire-gauntlet of six miles before reaching the open sea. Some commando boats had never been able to land their launches at all; these followed her. Raiders still ashore clambered aboard whatever launches they could. Some escaped but others were sunk and their occupants picked up by enemy vessels. The motor gunboat finally reached the destroyer escorts waiting at sea. Six of the launches also managed to reach England.

At about 10:30 AM – after a delay caused by faulty fuzes – the warhead on the *Campbeltown* blew up with a terrific roar; the dock gate burst apart and the waters of the Loire surged into the dry dock. Two delayed-action torpedoes fired at the outer lock at the Old Entrance also went up a couple of days later, adding to the ruin of the huge dry dock, the only one in western France capable of accommodating the German battleship *Tirpitz*. So badly damaged was this facility that it was not repaired until well after the war. But the price had been high. The British had lost 160 raiders killed and some 200 taken prisoner.

Small and large commando raids continued throughout the spring and early summer of 1942. Indeed, they were so frequent that Lord Mountbatten's desire for 'a raid every fortnight' was fast becoming a reality. The next major target was the town of Dieppe, with its narrow streets and harbor set between chalk cliffs 150 feet high.

Above: Commando landing craft pass a supporting motor launch on their way ashore during the Dieppe raid.

Left: Men of No 4 Commando come ashore in England on their return from the attack on Dieppe.

Below: Knocked-out Churchill tanks and a burning landing craft on the beach at Dieppe.

Main picture: Men of the 4th Special Service Brigade land on Juno Beach on D-Day.

Below: Men of a commando headquarters unit land on D-Day. Among the equipment they carry are bicycles and small motor cycles, designed to speed the first stages of the advance.

Covering the sea approaches to Dieppe were two powerful coastal batteries on either side of the town; these had a range of over ten miles and could traverse through 360 degrees. They would have to be knocked out before the main force carrier ships could come in and land the Canadian 2nd Division plus a company of American Rangers and some Free French. Number 40 Royal Marine (RM) Commando would be in floating reserve. Chosen to land against the eastern battery at Berneval was 3 Commando, led by Durnford-Slater, with Major Peter Young second in command. The battery on the west would be taken care of by 4 Commando under Lieutenant-Colonel Lord Lovat; it would be split into Group 1 under Major Derek Mills-Roberts and Group 2 led by Lovat himself.

The force sailed from England on August 18 in four columns of various types of landing craft, with destroyer escorts. On the way, several of the frail wooden assault boats were damaged and scattered by fire from German ships. This resulted in only four of the landing craft of 3 Commando reaching their target beaches of Yellow 1 and 2. One of these was Major Young's boat with 18 men, which got ashore at Yellow 2 west of the Berneval battery. Later, under covering fire, five other boats approached Yellow 1, but only three

got their commandos ashore. German fire had been heavy at the outset and many aboard the boats were either dead or wounded. On Yellow 1, Captain Richard Wills with some 50 men fought his way through wire beach defenses to take several machine-gun posts. When the Germans counterattacked in strength, Wills' small party was forced back down to the beach, only to discover that the outgoing tide had left their boats stranded on the rocks. These commandos were then taken prisoner.

Wills' action, however, had served to draw off an estimated 350 of the Berneval batteries' defenders, which left Peter Young and his men free for the moment to scale the cliff where the guns were situated. Skirting a minefield, obligingly posted *Achtung Minen!*, Young fought his way into the village, looking for suitable positions where his

Royal Navy motor launches of the type often used to support commando raids. Motor launches played an especially important role at St Nazaire.

men could snipe at the Germans manning the battery. Finding none, they worked their way through a wheat field to about 200 yards from the guns. There they proceeded to pepper away and irritate the gunners – so much so that one of the guns swung around toward them and began to fire, but to little effect. Meanwhile, the main force was moving in toward Dieppe. Wisely, Young with his handful of men did not attempt to rush the battery manned by some 200 Germans. In any case, their ammunition soon ran low, and enemy reinforcements were sure to make an appearance. But they did shoot up a German observation post before withdrawing and making their way safely back down to the beach.

The battery to the west near Varengeville mounted six 150-mm guns set some 1000 yards inland behind high cliffs about 400 feet above sea level. The best approach from the beach was up two gullies at a point designated Orange 1 beach; Mills-Roberts' Group 1 of 88 men would land here, move up one of the gullies and engage the battery with mortars and small arms fire from a wood about 300 yards away. A mile and a half farther west, the cliff line was broken where the Saane River emptied into the sea; here at Orange 2, Lord Lovat's Group 2 would land and double around back of the battery to positions where they could launch a fire-and-movement charge.

Coming into Dieppe waters on HMS *Prince Albert*, this western force launched its assault craft from their davits in calm seas and landed within minutes of their scheduled five o'clock. Mills-Roberts' men blew a gap in one of the gully's barbed-wire defenses with a bangalore torpedo and proceeded upward in single file. When they reached the top it was daylight, but

the Germans manning the battery had not yet discovered their presence. A patrol was sent out to the right to cut telephone lines in a nearby lighthouse that served as the battery's observation post. Mills-Roberts moved his men through the shuttered houses of Vesterival toward the wood and the battery, which had begun to fire at the incoming carrier force. Setting up his headquarters near an old barn, the major sent out snipers and bren-gun teams, and soon had mortar fire zeroed in on the battery. One of these shells hit a stack of cordite charges near one of the guns, and the resulting explosion put the battery out of action. But the German small-arms fire was intensifying and the group was taking more and more casualties. Then Group 2 reported by radio that they were forming up for their assault.

Lord Lovat's Group 2 had landed at Orange 2 at 4:30 AM and speed-marched half a mile along the banks of the Saave River before cutting east over open country toward the German battery. Using fire-and-movement – for German patrols had now discovered their presence – they continued to advance. Ninety minutes after landing, they were in position for their final assault. It was kicked off when Lord Lovat fired the signal – a series of white Very shells. What followed was savage fighting, much of it hand-to-hand, with heavy casualties on both sides. One commando officer later described it as 'Screams, smoke, the smell of burning cordite – mad moments soon over . . .' But finally the emplacements were cleared of Germans and demolition charges were set to blow the guns' breech blocks and underground magazines. Fallen commandos were then laid at the foot of the battery's flagstaff and the Union Jack was hoisted over them. German corpses lay everywhere – behind breastworks, around guns, outside bunkers, and in slit-trenches, many badly burned from the cordite. Then 4 Commando's withdrawal was effected as rapidly as possible, with Lord Lovat leading them on back down to Orange beach 1 under heavy mortar fire. Carrying their wounded, they managed to reach their Goatley boats with the aid of smoke generators, and made their way out to the destroyers and safety.

As these commando flank operations were performing their jobs so gallantly, the principal assault by some 5000 Canadians directly off Dieppe itself was being met by fierce opposition. Their extremely heavy losses were due to a number of telling factors. For one thing, the German commander was in the habit of drilling his gun-crews each week – and this particular morning happened to be that time. Also, an offshore southerly wind wafted the British smoke screen off the beaches in several vulnerable places, giving the Germans a clear field of fire at the approaching landing craft. The first wave of Canadians was to have been supported by nine tanks – but these were late in landing. After the initial bombardment by naval gunfire and a low-level attack by RAF Hurricanes, the German gunners overlooking the beaches had a chance to recover and man their weapons. In those few minutes, they had a field day and the result was slaughter. Without covering fire or effective smoke-screen concealment, the struggling Canadian infantrymen and engineers were sitting ducks. The second wave surged in under the same heavy fire and compounded the confusion. The few tanks that landed were largely knocked out and, while some Canadian infantry actually reached the town, they were quickly killed, wounded or taken prisoner. The few Marines who made it ashore from No. 40 (RM) Commando kept up a steady fire from behind a beached LCT, but inside an hour all were slain.

For the Canadians, the price of Dieppe was high indeed. They took a total of 3369 casualties, of whom 907 were killed outright or died later as prisoners of war. Yet the big raid was not entirely the disaster some military historians make it out to be. The Canadians' sacrifice taught the Allies lessons that would save thousands of lives two years hence in Normandy. These lessons, though bitter, proved that the cost of taking a defended port was too high, that preliminary naval and air bombardments must be more intense and that

landing timetables must be more elastic. As the war progressed through the rest of 1942 and the two years following, commando units carried out dozens of smaller raids along the French coast, as well as larger actions in the Mediterranean.

When the big invasion day – D-Day, 6 June 1944 – finally arrived, the commandos were ready. From east to west along the Bay of Seine in Normandy, the landing beaches were code-named Sword, Juno and Gold for British sectors, and Omaha and Utah for American. Initially the British landed at five points, each about a mile wide across a 24-mile front. Their westernmost flank was some ten miles from the Americans' Omaha Beach. Most of the points thought open to counterattack on the flanks or between landing points were assigned to the Special Forces. The principal divisions making the first wave landings were the British 50th at Gold, the Canadian 3rd at Juno and the British 3rd at Sword.

The Special Service Group to take part in the landings was headed by Major General Robert Sturges, with Brigadier John Durnford-Slater as his second in command. They were to land in two brigades, the 1st and 4th, with 47 (RM) Commando playing an independent role by pushing

Men of 40 (Royal Marine) Commando take cover at a roadside on the outskirts of St Aubin-sur-Mer shortly after their landing on Juno Beach on D-Day.

Lieutenant Colonel Peter Young briefs two commando snipers near Breville, Normandy on 17 June 1944.

Opposite: Men of 47 Royal Marine Commando wait for orders in the streets of Arromanches, Normandy, on D-Day.

west on the extreme western flank and capturing the town of Port-en-Bessin between the British and American sectors. The 3, 4, 6 and 45 (RM) Commandos formed the 1st Brigade. These Commandos would take the town of Ouistreham at the mouth of the Orne River and then push rapidly inland. Advancing to the bridges at Blouville and Ranville, they would link up with elements of the British 6th Airborne. These combined forces would then comprise the eastern flank guard of the whole beachhead along the line east of the Orne and on the high ground in that area among orchards, woods and fields with their hedgerows. The Commandos of the 4th Brigade – 41, 47 and 48 (RM) – were to form two sides of the hinge between Juno and Sword. No. 41 (RM)

would land west of Lion-sur-Mer and move west while 48 (RM) would land at St. Aubin-sur-Mer and push east. These forces would form a pincers, clearing the fortified points assigned to them, and then move inland to take the heavily defended radar station at Douvres.

The 1st Brigade's 4 Commando's LCAs came ashore from the HMS *Queen Astrid* at 8:20 AM, which was H plus 55. They found a British infantry brigade pinned to the shore by mortar and pillbox fire. The leading Troop took the pillbox ahead of them, forced their way through the German line of beach defenses and reached their assembly area in the dunes beyond. The column of 4 Commando then pushed on toward Ouistreham to take the Casino, a fortified point overlook-

ing the left flank of Sword Beach. After savage fighting against an enemy battery and several machine gun emplacements, Ouistreham was taken, and the Commando re-formed and advanced toward their main objective – the Orne bridges. Coming ashore right behind No. 4, the men of 6 Commando encountered a ghastly sight on the beaches. 'Bodies,' wrote one survivor, 'were sprawled all over . . . some with heads, arms, and legs missing, the blood clotting the wet sand.' They then infiltrated through the Germans' second line of defense, slogged through a swamp and attacked four strongpoints and an enemy battery. Speed-marching some seven miles to the Orne bridges, they arrived only minutes behind schedule.

These Troops were followed by 3 Commando and 45 (RM) Commando. A bicycle Troop of No. 6 had already crossed the bridges, and the commandos had joined a battalion of the 6th Airborne in taking the town of Le Plein. At dusk the 1st Brigade, joined by the rest of the 6th Airborne who had just flown in, dug in on high ground above a flat coastal plain east of the Sword beachhead. Even though they had landed in the third wave after H-hour, all these Commandos had taken casualties on the beaches.

The commandos of the 4th Brigade had a more rugged landing on Sword Beach. No. 41 (RM) Commando was put ashore several hundred yards from their intended point near Lion-sur-Mer, which one Section reached to find its main defenses deserted. The rest attacked a fortified chateau farther west, and lost their colonel and two officers in the attempt. Having lost contact with their tanks, they had to be satisfied with neutralizing the strongpoint, which was taken the next day. The Marines of 48 Commando had a very rough time trying to land in wooden LCIs off St. Aubin. H-hour at this part of Sword Beach had been delayed three-quarters of an hour, and the tide covered much of what was called 'Rommel's asparagus' – anti-landing boat obstacles in the water. Some of the boats were hung up on these and others were held offshore under fire. Three did manage to get ashore, but not squarely on the beach; their ramps plunged and rose in the swells, causing the Marines to flounder in waist-deep water and take grim casualties. Forcing their way up the beach past the assault's human debris – some dead, many wounded, others dazed – they managed to reassemble and made for the village of Langrune. Here they met only one strongpoint and by dusk had taken up positions to defend it against a counterattack.

The next day, D plus 1, 46 (RM) Commando, which had been in floating reserve, landed and swung around the Commando holding Langrune, then cleared the narrow forested Mue Valley and the town of Douves, beyond which lay the heavily fortified radar station. By D plus 5 these commandos had advanced inland as far as the villages of Rots and Le Hamel. Meanwhile, far to the west on Gold Beach, the independently

acting 47 (RM) Commando had come ashore on D-Day, losing four of their 14 LCAs on the way in. They fought their way inland and at dusk reached a knoll behind their objective – the harbor town of Port-en-Bessin. The next afternoon, supported by naval gunfire from HMS *Emerald,* the Marines attacked the town to stiff resistance by the Germans. Finally, after a night attack by 50 commandos, the last strongpoint fell and the German commander surrendered.

Over on the eastward flank of the Canadian and British sector on D plus 1, the 1st Brigade was holding its line around Merville beyond the Orne. But later that day, many commandos of No. 3 were killed trying to take back a battery reoccupied by the Germans. The high ground around Le Plein was the key to the Brigade's positions, and in the next few days the enemy made desperate efforts to dislodge it. By D plus 3, the commandos were dog-tired, fighting off German night probes like zombies from their pits and trenches. The combat was often close and heavy from trench to trench, with Germans outnumbering commandos two to one. One Troop had taken so many losses that it was down to only 15 men. Next morning, D plus 4, they were so exhausted that they dropped off to sleep while talking to one another, oblivious of the mortar shells exploding around them. No. 4 Commando was very hard hit, but the Brigade held on and at last the German attacks faltered and ceased. As for the 4th Brigade, its 48 (RM) Commando, down to some 220 men after D-Day, reconned the strongly held radar station at Douves but could do little more than harass it; six days later it was taken by 41 (RM) with the aid of tanks, with 225 Germans taken prisoner.

A week after D-Day, Lord Lovat was badly wounded in an attack on Bréville by 6 Commando. This village, at the base of the only salient projecting into 1st Brigade's lines, was finally taken on 12 June, with very heavy losses on both sides. Mills-Roberts then took over the brigade, although he too had suffered wounds at Bréville. On 12 June No. 4 Brigade moved into the Orne line, and for the next two months both brigades held these ridges before the city of Caen, which was the ultimate objective of the British sector. That city finally fell on 9 July, D plus 33. On 16 August, the Americans took Orléans, and that same week two German armies were caught in the Falaise pocket by British, Canadian and American armies. By 1 September, the Allies had crossed the Seine and liberated Paris, while a few days later the British took the city of Antwerp.

In the final push across Europe and into the German heartland itself, Commando units played a noteworthy part, particularly in the German river crossings. Sometimes they fought side by side with their American counterparts, the Ranger battalions. Other commando units, performing with equal valor, were invaluable assets to the Allied war effort in such theaters of operations as the Balkans and Burma.

Opposite: A soldier of a Free French commando unit greets some newly-liberated civilians on D-Day.

The Waffen SS

The SS uniform has come to symbolize the worst of Nazi brutality but the Nazi's enemies also learned to respect the fighting qualities shown by the fanatical young volunteers even when Germany was going down to defeat.

The *Schutzstaffel*, or SS, was a body of German troops which grew out of the Adolf Hitler headquarters guard, the *Sturmbateilung*, or SA – largely a group of professional hoodlums and bouncers organized in 1923. The SS, which means literally 'protective echelon,' was more familiarly known in World War II as the Elite Guard. In 1929 Heinrich Himmler, its leader, defined its purpose as 'to find out, to fight and to destroy all open and secret enemies of the Führer, the National Socialist movement and our racial resurrection.' – in short, political terrorism. In 1933 the SS was divided into three groups, one of which the Verfügungstruppe (SS-VT), was to develop into the notorious Waffen-SS – the fully militarized arm of the SS which ultimately provided nearly 40 divisions in World War II.

Another unit consisted of 120 men selected from Hitler's former Munich bodyguard and was to evolve into the most famous force in Nazi history – the Leibstandarte Adolf Hitler, or Adolf Hitler Bodyguard Regiment. Under the tough and quick-witted Bavarian major general Josef (Sepp) Dietrich, it grew to true regiment size and

was assigned for training to the 9th Infantry Regiment at Potsdam. Actually, the new unit was not intended to be a regular military fighting force, but the Third Reich's household troops and ceremonial unit. It assumed the responsibility for the protection of Hitler's person at the new Reich Chancellery. The double sentries in their black uniform with white belts, gloves and shirts posted at the door to Hitler's study symbolized the opening of a new era – the creation of a second armed force parallel with the Wehrmacht.

Unlike the Wehrmacht, with its rigid Prussian traditions, no preference was given to an SS officer candidate's background or education. Future officers had to serve two years in the ranks before going to one of the cadet academies. All of this, wrote one historian, 'fostered among officers, NCOs and enlisted men a sense of fellowship generally unknown in the army.'

An innovative SS-Sturmbannführer (Major), Felix Steiner, wished to organize his regiment into small battle groups that were mobile enough to deal effectively with the enemy but still able to retain their regimental structure. Steiner aban-

Opposite: An SS recruiting poster calls on Dutchmen to join in the fight against Bolshevism. Increasingly as the war went on the SS tried to recruit throughout the occupied territories beginning with the 'racially acceptable' Dutch and Norwegians.

officers with the gift of command and the social standing born of generations of military service. Where the Army could boast that 50 percent of its officers came of traditional military families, only a scant five percent of VT officers were of that background. And while a bare two percent of Wehrmacht officers came of peasant stock, as many as 90 percent of VT officers had been raised on the land. The VT remained largely an army of peasants, yokels and artisans. In Lower Saxony, Schleswig-Holstein, Franconia and the Saar, one in three farmers' sons joined the VT or, later, the Waffen-SS.

For this lack of tradition, the VT substituted enthusiasm and devotion to the cult of Hitler. They came to believe that in contrast to the 'old fogyism' of the Wehrmacht, the Verfügungstruppe was the only trustworthy armed force in the Nazi regime. Steiner's reforms had imbued these farm lads and mechanics with the idea that they were a military elite of far finer stripe than the Wehrmacht. Similarly, their new commanders, raised in the Hitler Youth and indoctrinated in the SS cadet schools, suffused their soldiers with a Nazi ideological fervor that brought them into ill-concealed opposition to all that the Army represented. Indeed, this hostility toward the Wehrmacht became a heady elixir to the VT troops. The Army generals, although they had never recognized the VT as a fully-fledged arm of the service, feared that this growing armed force under Himmler, who was also in charge of the police machinery, might suddenly multiply into a fatal threat to the very existence of the Wehrmacht.

This feeling of elitism was also enhanced by various ingenious trappings and flummery dreamed up by Himmler for the SS as a whole. Shunning the Army grey and brown of the old SA, the SS man was now clad from head to foot in black – black cap with chinstrap and silver death's head, black tunic over a brown shirt with black leather buttons and black tie, black Sam Browne belt, breeches, and jackboots. All kinds of mysterious badges and markings contributed to the mystique. An 'old fighter' (alter Kämpfer, or veteran) wore an aluminum chevron on his right forearm. A member of the notorious Sicherheitsdienst (SD) – the Security Service – wore a diamond insignia enclosing the letters 'SD.' The SS symbol itself, in the form of twin lightning bolts, was copied from an ancient Teutonic rune with supposedly occult connotations. Upon acceptance into the SS, this same runic symbol was tattooed on the inside upper forearm of the recruit.

All of this gimmickry was designed to show that in the SS an elite corps was forming – an Imperial Guard of strict puritans and guardians of the Reich. Its purpose was to symbolize the SS man's spirit of obedience, which in Himmler's words 'hesitates not for a single instant, but executes unquestioningly any order coming from the Führer.'

Top: SS Reichsfuhrer Himmler and SS general Sepp Dietrich take the salute at a parade in 1940. Dietrich had begun his career as bodyguard and chaffeur to Hitler; in 1940 he commanded the Liebstandarte Regiment and by the end of the war was an army commander.

Above: Himmler inspects an SS unit on the Eastern Front early in 1945 during his brief period in command of Army Group Vistula, opposing the main Soviet advance into Germany.

doned the standard Wehrmacht rifle and gave his men more mobile weapons, chiefly submachine guns, grenades and explosives. He also furnished them with a new battle dress, a camouflage blouse and suit in place of the army's field grey. In time, Steiner created a force of military athletes that made even the Wehrmacht's eyebrows rise. Here were troops who could march nearly two miles in twenty minutes – a feat unheard of before. In Steiner's words, here was 'a supple, adaptable type of soldier, athletic in bearing, capable of more than average endurance on the march and in combat.'

So complete was Steiner's success that the VT came to look on him as its real commander and Himmler himself, always impressed by innovation, made him, in the words of a jealous rival, 'his favorite baby.' Steiner retained his star status for years, because he was one of the precious few professional soldiers in the SS. But it was painfully clear that the VT still lacked experienced

Himmler devised similar inducements to attract Foerderne Mitglieder (sponsoring members) – sympathizers who gave the SS monthly financial support. These included a silver badge consisting of an oval enclosing the Hackenkreuz (Swastika), the runic double S and the letters 'FM.' His FM periodical reached a circulation of 365,000 by the outbreak of war. And to every sponsoring member he dispatched the motto:

It is an honor to be an SS man
It is an honor to be an honorary member
Let each continue to do his duty
We SS men and their honorary members
Each in his appointed place
And Germany will be great once more.

So unexpectedly successful was this propaganda that soon Himmler's shadowy army of sponsoring members actually outnumbered the SS itself and a flood of money came pouring into the welcoming SS coffers.

In mid-1933 Himmler, suspecting that bad elements had entered the SS to the detriment of its Praetorian Guard image, called a temporary halt to all SS recruiting. In a massive purge that lasted through 1935, he combed out of the officer corps and enlisted ranks the alcoholics, unemployed, opportunists, homosexuals and men of doubtfully Aryan background. Even some of the old thugs of the Sepp Dietrich type were ousted, having served their purpose during what Himmler described as the 'struggle period'. They no longer fitted into the new Nazi elite picture. During this period Himmler expunged from the SS no fewer than 60,000 men. From 1935 on every SS officer was required to present proof that neither he nor his wife had Jewish ancestors; this was soon extended to all SS men of every rank.

What was still lacking was a more cohesive corps spirit, stricter entry requirements and a binding code of honor. Himmler now decreed that the SS was to become an Order rather than a mere organization. An avid and romantic student of history, the Reichsführer-SS had discovered the group upon which he proposed to model his Order – the Jesuits! And indeed, the parallels between these two groups were to be astonishing. Each was subject to no temporal authority, conferred many privileges upon its initiates, was protected by strict conditions of admission and cohered through an oath of absolute obedience to its overlord, whether Pope or Führer.

Late in the 1930s, the SS developed a set of criteria to which all applicants had to measure up before their final acceptance. These criteria fell into three groups: racial appearance, physical condition and general bearing (intellectual attainments were not mentioned). As to race, there were supposedly five groupings: pure Nordic, predominantly Nordic or Phallic, harmonious bastard with slight Alpine, Dinaric or Mediterranean characteristics, bastards of pre-

Right: An extract from an SS manual.

Below: SS Sturmbannfuhrer Otto Skorzeny led the commando unit which rescued Mussolini from captivity in 1943 and in 1944 infiltrated German troops in American uniforms behind the Allied lines during the Battle of the Bulge.

Die Schutzstaffeln
Meine Ehre heißt Treue
der NSDAP.

Führung:

Die Schutzstaffel — SS. —, eine selbständige Gliederung der Partei. wird vom Reichsführer SS. geführt.

Aufgaben:

Die ursprüngliche und vornehmste Aufgabe der SS. ist es, für den Schutz des Führers zu sorgen.

Durch den Auftrag des Führers ist das Aufgabengebiet der SS. dahin erweitert worden, das Reich im Innern zu sichern.

Mitgliedsauslese:

Zur Erfüllung dieser Aufgaben ist eine gleichartige, festgefügte und weltanschaulich zusammen verschworene Kampftruppe geschaffen, deren Kämpfer aus bestem arischen Menschentum ausgesucht werden.

Die Erkenntnis vom Werte des Blutes und Bodens ist richtungweisend für die Auslese in der Schutzstaffel. Jeder Staffelmann muß vom Sinn und Wesen der nationalsozialistischen Bewegung tief durchdrungen sein. Er wird weltanschaulich und körperlich vorbildlich ausgebildet, damit er einzeln und im Verband im entschlossenen Kampf um die nationalsozialistische Weltanschauung erfolgreich eingesetzt werden kann.

Nur die blutsmäßig besten Deutschen sind für diesen Kampfeinsatz tauglich. Deshalb ist es notwendig, daß in den Reihen der Schutzstaffel unaufhörlich Auslese gehalten wird, erst grob, dann immer feiner.

Diese beschränkt sich aber nicht nur auf die Männer, denn ihr Zweck ist die Erhaltung einer artreinen Sippe. Darum wird von jedem Schutzstaffelmann gefordert, daß er nur die ihm arteigene Frau heiratet. Von Jahr zu Jahr werden die Ansprüche gesteigert, die an die Reinerhaltung der Schutzstaffel gestellt werden.

Treue, Ehre, Gehorsam und Tapferkeit bestimmen das Handeln des Staffelmannes. Seine Waffe trägt die vom Führer verliehene Inschrift: „Meine Ehre heißt Treue!" Beide Tugenden sind unlöslich miteinander verbunden. Wer hiergegen verstößt, ist unwürdig geworden, der Schutzstaffel anzugehören.

27 Die Organisation der NSDAP.   417

WAFFEN SS

Eintritt mit vollendetem 17. Lebensjahr
Kürzere oder längere Dienstzeitverpflichtung
Auskunft erteilt: Ergänzungsamt der Waffen-SS, Ergänzungsstelle V
(Süd), München 27, Pienzenauer Str. 15

Left: A German recruiting poster for the SS. As the war went on the SS ranks were increasingly filled with fanatical former members of the Hitler Youth who, as the poster points out, could join when 17 years old.

Right: A poster designed for use in Holland featuring Paul Kruger, leader of the Afrikaners in the Boer War against the British, who the Nazis believed would appeal to the Dutch population.

Above: Senior SS officers including Sepp Dietrich and Fritz Witt observe the training of the Hitler Jugend (Hitler Youth) Division in Belgium in the summer of 1943.

Opposite: Standard bearers of the Liebstandarte Adolf Hitler Regiment on parade at Nuremberg at a Nazi Party rally before the war.

dominantly East Baltic or Alpine origin and bastards of extra-European origin. Only applicants falling into the first three groups were considered worthy of acceptance into the SS.

Himmler was also fanatical on the subject of an applicant's physical proportions. He had an aversion to 'people who might be tall but were in some way disproportioned.' With the selectivity of a professional breeder, he insisted that the SS man be 'of well proportioned build; for instance, there must be no disproportion between the lower leg and the thigh or between the legs and the body; otherwise, an exceptional bodily effort is required to carry out long marches.'

The applicant then began a prolonged testing period, for which Himmler again took his cue from the Jesuits. Just as a Jesuit novice had to undergo two years of examinations before taking his vows of poverty, chastity and obedience, so that SS recruit had to be tested before he was allowed to swear the sacred *Sippeneid*, or oath of 'kith and kin'. The several phases of the SS novitiate were keyed to the Nazi calendar. On 9 November, the anniversary of the Munich Beer Hall Putsch, the candidate was permitted to wear his SS uniform – but without collar patches. On 30 January, the date of the Nazi seizure of power, the applicant became a cadet and was given a provisional SS ID card. The high point came on 20 April, Hitler's birthday, when the new cadet received his collar patches and permanent SS card. Then he swore his oath to his Führer:

I swear to thee, Adolf Hitler
As Führer and Chancellor of the German

Reich, Loyalty and Bravery.
I vow to thee and to the superiors
Whom thou shalt appoint
Obedience unto death
So help me God.

Between 20 April and entry into the service on 1 October, the new cadet had to earn the Reich Sport Badge and learn the SS catechism, another reinforcement of the Hitler cult. For example: 'Why do we believe in Germany and the Führer?' Answer: 'Because we believe in God, we believe in Germany which He created in His world, and in the Führer, Adolf Hitler, whom He has sent us.' Next, the cadet completed a few months service in the Arbeitsdienst (Labor Service) and the Wehrmacht. If his Wehrmacht report were good, he might finally be accepted into the Order soon thereafter. He then underwent another ceremony in which he pledged himself and his future family to obey Himmler's marriage law prescribing that SS members might marry 'solely if the necessary conditions of race and healthy stock were fulfilled' and only after approval by SS headquarters.

Now the new member of the Order was awarded his coveted SS dagger and was at last admitted into the black-clad brotherhood in which the fanaticism of the religious sect, the rites and customs of a feudal age and the romantic cult of Germanism merged strangely with contemporary power politics as dispensed by National Socialism. The SS man was no longer answerable to the normal court system; he had his own code, which he defended jealously and of which his

Left: A typical SS appeal for recruits referring to the supposed Nordic, Viking ancestry of the Norwegians.

Right:
Despite their
often
impressive
graphics,
recruiting
appeals met
little response
in Norway.

Til vakt ved Nordens grense mot øst!
SS-SKIJEGERBATALJON NORGE

dagger was the symbol. Another of Himmler's elite touches was to resurrect that hallmark of aristocratic arrogance, the duel. Subject to the permission of the Reichsführer-SS himself, every SS man was entitled to challenge another.

Meanwhile, in 1936, the Army generals were still pressing Hitler to limit the expansion of the SS-Verfügungstruppe. Alarmed at alienating the Wehrmacht, the Führer temporarily forbade any further expansion. The VT was not allowed to form a division, was refused artillery and was forbidden to publish recruiting notices. The last straw – a bitter one for the VT – was that the Wehrmacht now had the right to inspect SS units at will. But in February 1938 an unexpected crisis developed within the Wehrmacht itself. Both the commanding general and the Reich Minister of War fell from power, and Hitler seized command of the Army himself.

Six months later the VT's uneasiness was over.

turism, especially in the East, soon forced the SS onto the field of combat in the invasion of Poland. Steiner's Deutschland Regiment, Sepp Dietrich's Leibstandarte and the Germania Regiment were incorporated into General Werner Kempf's regular Wehrmacht division, itself a part of the German 3rd Army.

While Steiner's SS unit distinguished itself in the advance on Mlava and Modlin, the Leibstandarte fought in the battle of Bzura in central Poland and the Germania advanced on Lwow with the 14th Army. But military critics denounced the SS soldiers' showing as less than satisfactory; compared with regular Army units, they suffered astonishing casualties. It soon became clear – even to SS commanders – that the SS men simply had not been trained to fight as part of a division, nor were VT officers able to command their troops in complicated infantry maneuvers. To the VT high command, there

Below: Men destined for the ranks of the Liebstandarte Regiment during training in Berlin in 1933.

Above right: A machine gun team of the Liebstandarte during maneuvers in 1935.

On 17 August 1938 Hitler signed a decree which in effect announced the future Waffen-SS, because it recognized the VT as a permanent security force in both peace and war. It was to be available for 'certain special internal political tasks' at Hitler's own discretion, but the Führer made it clear that the VT would remain primarily a force for the protection of his regime. Ideological instruction drummed into Himmler's soldiers the notion that they had to protect the Hitler State even against their own countrymen, if necessary.

A wave of anti-Christian propaganda was unleashed on SS men to compel them to renounce all 'bourgeois' Christian morality. The VT became a bastion of atheism, and young officers were required to prove their opposition to the Christian message of reconciliation and tolerance, which the SS regarded as un-German, effeminate and destructive to the race.

Actually, Himmler had never thought of the VT as anything but an internal regulatory force for political power and a counterweight to a possible putsch by the Wehrmacht, which he never really trusted. But Hitler's military adven-

seemed only one logical solution: the Verfügungstruppe must form a self-contained division with its own artillery and supply units. Needless to say, the Wehrmacht generals vigorously opposed this, in their resolve to keep Himmler's army as tiny as possible. Since the Army generals could regulate any such combat numerical strengths, they could set a ceiling low enough to prevent the VT from expanding – a privilege of which the generals made full use.

Fortunately for the VT, in the meantime, a new champion had appeared on the scene who would liberate the Verfügungstruppe from the shackles of the Army. The real founder of the Waffen-SS, he was SS-Brigadeführer (Brigadier General) Gottlob Berger, a loquacious and energetic Swabian and one of Himmler's closest confidants. Sharing Himmler's ambition to build up the VT into a full-scale army, he was made head of the recruiting office in the SS-Haupamt (Central Office). When the Army threatened to block the VT's expansion program, Berger obtained carte blanche from Hitler to build up the VT with men who were exempt from Wehrmacht service for SS purposes; over this the Army had no control. Thus Berger got the go-ahead to start forming an entirely new army with a new overall name – the Waffen-SS.

In fact, however, Berger's subterfuge automatically linked the VT with the most despised unit in the whole SS – the thugs, yokels and embittered concentration camp guards of the Totenkopfverbände. Many VT commanders regarded this as an insult to any soldier. Where the VT was trying to become a military force, the Totenkopfverbände affected an anti-military outlook. Many a Gasthaus brawl occurred between them. Their leader, Theodore Eicke, was

the inventor of systematized concentration camps and the murderer of the maverick SA chief Ernst Röhm. He had been dismissed from the Army and had failed in the police as well. Thus he instilled in his men all his own pent-up resentments and, in his tirades against professional soldiers, Jews and Marxists, he found willing pupils among his motley crew.

But Berger and his SS organizers brushed aside these differences and raided the new sources of manpower to form division after division. Eicke, somewhat mollified, was allowed to form his own Totenkopf Division. Ex-Wehrmacht General Paul Hausser was given the Deutschland, Germania and Der Führer Regiments to mold into a motorized VT division called Das Reich. Later Sepp Dietrich's Leibstandarte also became a division. Thus at a single stroke, Berger had succeeded in creating a sizable Waffen-SS. At the onset of the Polish campaign, the VT had been barely 17,000 strong; now Himmler had no fewer than 100,000 SS soldiers.

But as the continued fighting in Poland and elsewhere began thinning out the ranks of the Waffen-SS, Berger met a check in finding replacements. The Wehrmacht, which had first choice of new conscripts, reserved the right to decide whether its recruits should be released to serve in the SS. In March 1940 the Army High Command stipulated those units which it would recognize as part of the Waffen-SS, thus effectively limiting its expansion. Hitler, always unwilling to alarm his professional soldiers with the bogey of a second Wehrmacht, sided with his generals. He forbade the formation of an SS army corps and decreed that the strength of the Waffen-SS was never to exceed five to ten percent of that of the Wehrmacht.

Left: A heavily-armed stormtrooper prepares for an attack.

Below: Hitler inspects an SS unit at the cadet school at Lichterfelde.

Rebuffed but not deterred, Berger cast his eye beyond the borders of Germany itself toward the thousands of 'racial Germans' in neighboring states, especially in the Balkans. Here lived many young men who were awed by Hitler's lightning campaigns of conquest and intoxicated by the propaganda of a 'Greater Germany.' Soon young Roumanians, converts to the Hitler cult, were being smuggled out of their country under the very noses of Roumanian officials anxious that no man of military age should desert to some foreign army. Racial German volunteers were variously hidden in German hospital trains, disguised as laborers and often simply picked up by the supply columns of SS divisions sweeping cross southeastern Europe.

When the siren song of Nazi propaganda failed to entice recruits, strong-arm squads aided in the process. In the later years of World War II, pure press-gang methods were used in the Balkans, where men of German blood who refused to 'volunteer' were threatened with the destruction of their homes. When even these sources began to dry up, Berger turned to the nations known as 'Germanic.' Many impressionable young men of northern and western Europe had come to believe in the new era as the conquerors marched through their cities of Oslo, the Hague and Brussels. Motivated by the prospect of rich spoils and adventure, many also succumbed to the propaganda about becoming 'warrior peasants' who would eventually come to rule millions of European 'sub-humans.'

By the spring of 1941, the first major non-German force had been put together – the SS

Viking Division, composed of Danish, Dutch, Flemish and Norwegian volunteers with German officers and cadres. But it was the racial German influx that really swelled the ranks of the Waffen-SS. By the end of 1943 these men comprised 25 percent of its manpower. When the war ended, 310,000 of them, drawn from all parts of Europe, were serving in SS units. By 1944 Himmler and Berger's army had almost a million soldiers.

In actual combat, the Waffen-SS entered upon a career that had few parallels in World War II. In the 1940 blitzkrieg, the SS proved it could hold its own with any Wehrmacht division. Its men stormed through France, Belgium and the Low Countries in a kind of ecstasy. Disdainful of losses, they seemed impelled by a fury in the assault that soon distinguished Himmler's soldiers from all other German units. Sepp Dietrich's Leibstandarte, in particular, displayed a fearless nonchalance – toward both the enemy and its superior officers – that was unknown in the regular Army.

In its pursuit of the British forces toward Dunkirk, the Leibstandarte was ordered to cross the heavily defended Aa Canal and seize the village of Watten. When the Führer's headquarters countermanded the order on 24 May, Dietrich simply disregarded the dispatch. He and his troops were across the canal only hours later. As the advance point of General von Kleist's Panzer Group, they prevented the French from forming a line of resistance along the Loire. Then, in a wide southward sweep, Dietrich's soldiers reached St. Etienne, leaving the main body of the Wehrmacht far behind. Other SS forces boasted equal successes. The Der Führer Regiment forced the Grebbe Line in Holland; Eicke's Totenkopf Division seized a crossing over the Seine and bridgeheads over the Loire; and the Verfügungstruppe Division chased the enemy right down to the Spanish frontier.

The Wehrmacht generals and officers observed the SS thirst for combat with mingled admiration and dismay. To the professionals, these soldiers seemed to herald a new form of warfare which made a mockery of all reasonable tactics. They were appalled by the fact that the

Opposite, top: Josef 'Sepp' Dietrich led the Sixth SS Panzer Army in the Battle of the Bulge in December 1944 and was convicted of war crimes after the war because of the murders committed by his men at Malmedy during the battle.

Opposite, bottom: A Sturmgeschutze (assault gun) of an SS unit in the streets of Athens in April 1941.

Below: A column of SS vehicles outside Milan in the summer of 1943. The SS were given priority in the supply of equipment even when their units were inexperienced and veteran army units were going short.

Waffen-SS commanders had apparently never learned to use any form of caution in the employment of their men. Indeed, some of the more audacious SS units had been known to attack singing such songs as the *Horst Wessel Lied*. Yet many SS leaders were merely putting into practice the relentless lesson of the cadet schools: that a soldier's duty was to deal out and accept death. As a result, of course, the SS units suffered casualties on a scale unknown to the Army. As early as the onset of the Battle of France, officer losses alone were such that replacements had to be drafted in directly from the cadet schools. Inevitably, this reckless esprit de corps began to impress the Führer himself; in a speech to the Reichstag he referred to 'the brave Divisions and Standarten of the Waffen-SS.' Praise from their leader was heady medicine and reinforced their spirit – an arrogant spirit that looked down on the ordinary soldiery around them with the guardsman's traditional contempt.

By spring of 1941, when the war turned eastward, the Waffen-SS had expanded to four divisions and one brigade. SS forces were summoned to the Balkans and again they spearheaded the

Right: SS leader Kurt Meyer confers with subordinates during the early stages of the invasion of Russia in the summer of 1941.

Above: Kurt Meyer, Fritz Witt and Max Wünsche were among the leaders of the SS forces in Normandy in the summer of 1944. They are seen here in July after a staff conference.

invading German armies. In central Serbia, Das Reich took Belgrade in a sudden and slashing attack and overran the Bacska. Dietrich's Leibstandarte broke into Albania, stormed through Thessaly, and forced a passage into Greece. These units had scarcely caught their breath, however, before new orders came from Berlin. Hitler had decided to invade Russia. Now numbering over 160,000 men, Himmler's army moved into assembly areas on the eastern frontier for the jump-off toward Moscow. The Leibstandarte and the Viking Division were allotted to Army Group South, Das Reich to Army Group Center, and the Totenkopf and other divisions to Army Group North.

As the invasion progressed, Himmler was dismayed by the demand for more and more SS formations. And the more deeply they penetrated into the expanses of Russia, the more his commanders divorced themselves from his orders

and wishes. His SS soldiers were living in another world, driven through the steppes and marshes by belief in their Führer and in the ultimate victory of the Reich. Both heroes and victims of a fearful chapter of human error and hallucination, they fought as under a spell. Yet in their delusion they won a place of their own in the annals of war. Whether in the north, center or south, wherever the shocked enemy had recovered enough to stand and fight, wherever he mounted a counterattack and tore gaps in the German advance, orders would go out for the SS units to hold.

In January 1942, after the Soviet breakthrough west of Moscow, strong Russian forces moved forward in the rear of Army Group Center. General Model then moved the SS regiment Der Führer, under Obersturmbahnführer Otto Kumm, into the bend of the Volga near Rzhev. Here it was to form a thin screen linking the front with the army forces farther west – and it held until Model had enough troops in the south to deal a death blow to the enemy.

In a temperature of minus 25 degrees Centigrade, the SS soldiers held on, driving the Russians back hour after hour, day after day. By 18 February Model had his victory. When Der Führer was finally relieved, Kumm met Model, who said: 'I know what your regiment must have been through, Kumm. But I need it still. How strong is it now?' Waving his hand toward the window, Kumm replied: 'My regiment is on parade outside.' Model looked out and counted 35 men – all that remained of 2000.

One captured Russian general commented that the SS Viking Division had shown greater fortitude than any other unit on either side and that his own men had breathed a sigh of relief when it was relieved by Wehrmacht units. Even a few German Army generals voiced praise for the SS divisions. In a letter to Himmler, General von Mackensen, commanding the 3rd Panzer Corps, extolled the Leibstandarte for its 'discipline, and refreshing, cheerful energy and unshakable steadfastness in crisis.' Yet not all Army officers were of the same mind. Jealousy and rivalry ruled many professional soldiers as they saw the Waffen-SS pushing itself to the fore and getting favored treatment. The Wehrmacht's aversion to the Waffen-SS was an open secret. In fact, many SS commanders already suspected the Army of deliberately giving them the dangerous hotspots so as to burn out their rival.

But many Army officers had another aversion to the Waffen-SS. They detected in this new force a fanaticism foreign to military tradition, and directed not only toward the enemy in combat but also against helpless prisoners of war and civilians. Stories of barbaric shootings of both by SS units were as numerous as the tales of their courage. Apologists for the Waffen-SS later protested that the soldiers were merely reacting to the inhuman Soviet methods of warfare. And in fact, German commanders had found in captured files orders by Soviet headquarters proving that German prisoners had been murdered by the Russians. But the bestial reprisals made by some SS soldiers were repugnant to many Germans. Some senior SS leaders, including Sepp Dietrich, tried to prevent such reprisals. 'We owe it,' said Dietrich, 'to the insignia on our sleeve.' But they were often unheeded.

In parts of the Ukraine, for example, the Waffen-SS behaved with such savagery that the people deserted their villages and took refuge with the Soviet Army. In Galicia, the Viking Division shot 600 Jews as a reprisal for Soviet crimes. In June 1944 a company of Das Reich soldiers, searching for one of their officers captured by the *maquis*, destroyed the village of Oradour and killed its entire population. The fact remains that such crimes were very seldom committed by the Wehrmacht.

Because of its successes, Hitler allowed the SS to grow ever larger and eventually lifted all restrictions on it, permitting the service to do as it wished. As the war advanced, the Waffen-SS became the Dictator's best hope, and finally he clung to the conviction that only they could save him. In time, too, the SS managed to break the Army's stranglehold on equipment and Hitler gave it the latest assault guns, armored troop carriers and at last Panzer armor itself.

Thus slowly, in the face of continual Army resistance, the three original Waffen-SS divisions were re-equiped as Panzer divisions, and the 1st SS Panzer Corps was formed under the generalship of Paul Hausser. In March 1943 Obergruppenführer Hausser and his armored forces rolled through the Ukraine. This corps repulsed a major Soviet attack in the Kharkov sector and in the summer of 1943 spearheaded the last powerful thrust in Russia. By the summer of

1944, according to one historian, these Waffen-SS divisions 'had on two separate occasions prevented another Stalingrad' by breaking up menacing Soviet moves. 'Wherever they were committed, they attacked; sometimes with great success and sometimes with none. But whatever the outcome . . . the end result was to delay the enemy advances.'

Despite its military triumphs, however, the Waffen-SS could not long conceal the fact that it had, in Steiner's own words, 'been burnt to a cinder.' Its Panzer armor had come too late. In one period between mid-June and mid-November of 1941, the SS lost 1239 officers and 35,377 men, of whom 13,037 had been killed. By 1943 one-third of the original divisions had fallen in Russia. In the breakout from the Cherkassy pocket, the Viking Division lost all its tanks, all its equipment and half its men. In February 1943 Eicke was killed near Kharkov, and similar high-ranking casualties in other divisions began to curb their efficiency. Totenkopf sent back a report to Berlin that 'Losses in NCOs are catastrophic . . . a company which has lost it old experienced non-coms and section commanders cannot attack . . . its backbone is not there.'

As SS casualties zoomed, their cries for replacements grew increasingly strident. But the quality of the now scarcely trained recruits was so low that the fighting ability of the whole Waffen-SS was curtailed. The new men – many of them pressed into service – were reluctant soldiers at best. Poorly trained, they soon became sullen skeptics. A typical report to SS headquarters from the Munich recruiting office advised: 'Readiness to enlist not good. Young men do not wish to volunteer, but wait until they are conscripted.' Shocked by the reports of ruthless

General Paul Hausser, one of the most successful of the fighting leaders of the Waffen SS.

Men of the Liebstandarte Division pause at an improvised burial ground on the Russian Front. Note the camouflaged smocks they wear, a characteristic of SS units.

Opposite: An archetypal SS soldier at the controls of an antiaircraft gun. Note the camouflaged jacket, and the goggles to protect against dust from the Russian steppe.

methods and towering casualties, many Germans were now openly anti-Waffen-SS. And the SS anti-Christian campaign began to boomerang as well, with parents and churches actively opposing SS recruiting efforts. The old appeal to the glory of Greater Germany now fell on indifferent or hostile ears. Berger was reduced to raiding the Hitler Youth and Labor Service camps for replacements.

As the war reached its mid-point and ground on to the inevitable Allied victory, the world in which the Waffen-SS leaders had believed was slowly collapsing. The ideological cord linking the army of Hausser, Steiner and Dietrich to the Reich and the Führer began to fray. While they still paid lip-service to the stereotyped ideals, the SS units were withdrawing into themselves, owning allegiance to no one. For the soldiers of the Waffen-SS, their outfits became their true homes. The hard-fought battles, the divisional insignia, the memory of fallen comrades – these elements forged a bond that held the units together in the face of lost illusions.

After D-Day the bitter fighting in Normandy saw regiment after regiment destroyed, under orders from Berlin to fight to the last man and give up no ground. They were simply sacrificed by a Führer walled up in his self-deluded world at Wolfsschanze, impervious to pleas for withdraw-

al on the grounds of enemy superiority and the exhaustion of German troops. As Paris fell and the Allies swarmed toward the Rhine, the Waffen-SS was now in danger of total annihilation, for the greater part of it was fighting in the West. There were six divisions in all, including the Leibstandarte, forming the 1st SS Panzer Corps under Sepp Dietrich and the 2nd under Paul Hausser.

By April 1945, with Germany's enemies on German soil in both east and west, it was clear even to Hitler that he was beaten. Small groups of SS men fought grimly on, many with a fury born of fear, for the rumor had spread that the double lightning runes tattoed on their arms would identify them to the Allies as war criminals and they would be given no quarter.

The remnant of the Waffen-SS, however, was not to commit suicide, as officially ordered. Instead, they surrendered before they were totally surrounded. Afterward, languishing in the huts and compounds of Allied prisoner-of-war camps, many were tormented by a sense of guilt. They were unable to quell the nagging question: How had it happened that with all their devotion and enthusiasm, they had turned into blind instruments of force, into slaves of a perverted honor that had made them mindless tools of the Führer's will?

Rangers, Marines and Marauders

Amphibious operations and developing techniques of air supply gave the US forces in World War II many opportunities to exploit the particular qualities of elite troops in terrain as diverse as North Africa, the Pacific islands and the Burmese jungle.

Inspired chiefly by the exploits of the British Commandos, and partly by the successes of Himmler's Waffen-SS early in the war, some American military men began to turn over the feasibility of forming small, elite hit-and-run assault units. These would be all-volunteer units and would take special training in attack and quick withdrawal tactics. Using their own resourcefulness wherever possible, their mission would be to confuse, terrorize and demoralize the enemy by throwing him off-balance – and to survive to do the same another day. While several of these American forces came into being during World War II, three emerged as the most famous, due not only to the courage of the men serving in them but also to the drive, imagination and personalities of their commanders. These units were popularly known as Darby's Rangers, Carlson's Raiders and Merrill's Marauders.

Darby's Rangers

From December 1941 to late 1943, the United States found herself in the same position as the British. Attacked and humiliated, she had not yet succeeded in coming to grips with the enemy on a large scale. The Commando model, symbolic of aggressiveness, was a naturally attractive one to emulate. Thus in June 1942, the first Ranger companies, based on the Commando idea, were formed in Northern Ireland from among the US troops stationed there. Many of their members were volunteers from the 1st Armored and 34th Infantry Divisions, which were the first American fighting units to have landed in Great Britain. Earlier in the year, at the suggestion of Brigadier General Lucian Truscott, head of the US Mission to Combined Operations, General George C. Marshall, the Army Chief of Staff, had approved their formation.

Prospective volunteers for the Rangers were told that all men of excellent physical condition might apply for service in a new type of combat unit to be formed along the lines of the British Commandos. They were also told that the Rangers required a superior type of soldier of excellent character who was not averse to seeing dangerous action. Further, all volunteers had to be athletically inclined, possess good wind and

Opposite: Men of the 2nd Ranger Battalion, US First Army, get ready to lead the Army's advance farther into Germany in March 1945.

stamina, be good swimmers and be able to make decisions on the spot. They were also warned that the Commando training they would receive could be even more dangerous in some cases than actual combat.

Those volunteers who were accepted – about 2000 men – spent their first weeks at Carrickfergus in Northern Ireland, where the 1st Ranger Battalion was organized. Unlike a regular infantry battalion, the Ranger battalion had small companies, consisting of three officers and 64 enlisted men. The six line companies – A through F – had only two (instead of four) platoons. Each platoon consisted of two assault sections composed of twelve men and a mortar section with

Below: Major Darby points out a detail of equipment to General Truscott during an inspection of one of the first Ranger units shortly before the Dieppe raid, in which a very small Ranger contingent participated.

individual's progress. Men have come and men have gone – until now the chosen few remain. You few are now known as the 1st American Ranger Battalion, a name honored in American military-history annals, since it was first used by Rogers' Rangers of Indian war fame. . . .'

From Ireland, the Rangers crossed to Scotland and their new training ground, the Commando camp at Achnacarry, a few miles outside Inverness. Their instructor, a fiery Scot named Cowerson, harangued them at length on the rigors of the coming program and assured them that 'Only the half dead will be accepted for sick-call.' Nodding toward two husky, mustachioed Scots, he added, 'Assisting me will be Sarn't Blimt and Sarn't Brown.' Immediately afterward, the 'Sarn'ts' informed the Rangers that all ammunition used in their training would be live.

For the next four weeks, the Commando instructors lived ruthlessly up to their promises. Daily the Rangers made grueling seven-mile 'speed marches' with rifles and full packs in an hour or less. When exhausted GIs straggled, they were grabbed by the seats of their pants and rushed back into line. If they fell out again, they were jeered and called weaklings and cowards. When men could not take the pace and keeled over, they were ordered to make the same speed march after duty hours. Ranger officers, as well as their men, had to take everything the Commando instructors handed out.

The regimen was soon to harden them into true shock troops. All companies worked on a rigid schedule that included unarmed combat, physical training, bayonet drill, scouting and patrolling, small-unit tactics, assault landings, cliff climbing, river crossing with ropes, weapons training, map and compass reading, street

Right: Darby, seen later in the war when serving as a regimental commander with a Fifth Army unit in Italy.

five men. The Commandos had found that for short decisive encounters, such as night raids or establishing beachheads, smaller units were more effective.

In late May, General Truscott consulted Major General Russell Hartle, commander of the 34th Division, about a leader for the Ranger battalion. Without thinking twice, Hartle pointed to his aide, Major William Orlando Darby. 'You're looking at him right now,' said Hartle. To the delighted Darby the offer was just the challenge he had been looking for, and he accepted on the spot. A West Pointer and a stickler for discipline, Darby was of medium height with wide shoulders, a slender waist and a broad chest. As his men got to know him, they found he had a magnetic quality that was difficult to describe and a dynamic energy that infected others. A tough leader but a fair one, Darby was a man born to command.

'For three weeks,' he said in his first address to his men, 'I have watched you train, observed your spirit, and noted your appearance as soldiers. . . . I have received daily reports on each

fighting and combat problems with live rounds. The whole set-up resembled a well-coordinated assembly line. When a man blundered, a 'Sarn't' was always there to explain patiently: 'Now, look here, Laddie, what would the bloody Hun be doing if you did it that way in battle?'

Not the least of the Rangers' training was cliff climbing. Many who were not in the least fazed by exploding grenades and whizzing bullets grew terrified at the cliffs of Achnacarry. The Commandos, however, insisted that it was crucial, because much of the enemy-occupied coastline, especially France's, was rimmed by steep, nearly perpendicular cliffs. Because the enemy least expected attacks along the heights, they seldom kept large garrisons there and were vulnerable to surprise raids. So the Rangers climbed the Scottish cliffs – and sometimes casualties resulted.

The Rangers stay in Scotland ended at Corker Hill on the Firth of Forth, where they waited eagerly for the ships to take them on their first combat venture. Early in October 1942 they boarded the HMS *Royal Ulsterman*, which sailed westward to join a large convoy – actually part of the gigantic invasion force of Operation Torch. With the Rangers were General Terry Allen's 1st Infantry Division – 'Big Red One.' Speculation was keen among the men as to what their destination would be, until they were given the word: Go ashore and take a town called Arzew, thirty miles east of Oran in French Algeria. Already aboard was an elaborate sand table mock-up of the town with its harbor defenses. Dominating the town above the harbor was a huge French Foreign Legion fortress; adjacent to that was their main objective – a powerful 4-inch gun battery.

On D-Day, 9 November, the Ranger companies shoved off for the Arzew beaches in their assault boats. The inky outline of the Atlas Mountains loomed ahead. The Americans ·charged ashore, poured a mortar barrage on the Fort and battery and achieved their missions in a matter of hours when the French conceded. In fact, the French forces – including the normally fierce-fighting Legionnaires – put up only token resistance, since they were titularly under the Vichy government. Soon they were to be incorporated with the Americans and British against the real enemy: Rommel's Afrika Korps and their Italian Allies. After Darby's men had secured Arzew, General Terry Allen asked the Ranger leader for two companies to assist in taking the nearby towns of St. Cloud and La Macta – and got them.

The press now discovered 'Darby's Rangers,' and they appeared on the front page of *Stars and Stripes* with the banner headline 'CRACK NIGHTFIGHTERS TAKE ARZEW ... THEN SMASH WAY TO ORAN.' *The New York Times* carried pictures of Rangers training in Scotland.

Yet Darby and his men knew that the easy landing at Arzew had not really proved them. That was to come with the raid on Sened Pass, in

Among the skills learned by the Rangers were a range of street fighting techniques, some of which were practiced in bomb-damaged areas of London.

Tunisia, where Field Marshal Rommel and General von Arnim were boring through the thinly held American line. The enemy was well entrenched on the heights of El Geuttar, a few miles from the Rangers' bivouac at Gafsa.

Sened had been won and lost twice by Allied forces; it was the key to the Maknassy Plain. The goal of their raid was to knock the enemy – Italian Bersaglieri and massing German armored forces – off balance. 'We've got to leave our mark on these people,' one Ranger commander told his men. 'They've got to know they've been worked over by Rangers.' When it was all over, some 100 Italians had fallen on the slopes of Sened, with only one Ranger fatality.

Two days later Rommel's Afrika Korps hurled several Panzer divisions against the American positions at Faid and Kasserine Passes, and all American forces in the south were ordered to bolster strength. The 1st Ranger Battalion was assigned to rearguard the entire 2nd Corps withdrawal to Derna Pass. Colonel Darby gathered his Rangers around him and gave them the facts: 'Rangers, we are the last unit to pull out of this mess. Behind us and on our flanks are enemy armored columns looking for straggling units to cut up. We have no tanks, we have no trucks. We have only a few rocket guns and grenades to fight against armor. . . . But I know you won't let them get us cheap.'

In fact, the tanks did soon come. But thanks to mist and tireless Ranger legs, the two armored columns paralleling their route of march failed to destroy Darby's men. In the most urgent speed march of their history, without water or sleep for 48 hours, the Rangers made the protective foothills of Derna Pass just as the German cannon went to work on the tail-end of their columns. For several weeks the 1st Rangers were stretched out on a seven-mile front on the flanks of the Pass astride the Féiana-Tebéssa highway. Darby's men went out on patrol every night to reconnoiter, harass and report new targets for Allied artillery and aircraft. Off-balance, the Germans and Italians were unable to mount an all-out attack. Meanwhile, General Terry Allen's Big Red One Division, part of the 34th, and the 1st Armored were holding at Kasserine. When General Patton assumed command of the 2nd Corps, American forces prepared to assume the offensive again and the Rangers rested, true veterans now and waiting for their next job.

Combat orders were swift in coming. Patton attached Darby's force to Allen's 1st Division again and sent them back to Gafsa with the command: 'Find 'em . . . attack 'em . . . destroy 'em.' They found that the Axis forces had strategically retreated to the high mountains near El Guettar with two Panzer and four infantry divisions. Their orders were, supported by the 1st Armored, to mount the first main American push of the war in Tunisia to be spearheaded by the Rangers. The key was a funnel-like pass that overlooked the two main roads leading to the east – where the Americans were to make their thrust. But from positions blasted out of solid rock, the enemy had all approaches covered with anti-tank and machine guns. The mouth of the pass was also blocked with rocks and barbed wire. A frontal attack would be pure suicide into crisscrossing artillery and other fire. There seemed only one

Above right: Rangers demonstrate typical combat equipment.

Below: Men of a Ranger unit during training in the north of Scotland in February 1943.

Opposite, top left: A commando sergeant supervises bayonet training of the 1st Ranger Battalion in August 1942.

Opposite, top right: An instructor demonstrates how to disarm an enemy.

RANGERS, MARINES AND MARAUDERS

Above: American troops advance inland on the first day of the landings in Tunisia.

Above right: General Terry Allen, seen here after the war, under whose command the Ranger units fought many of their actions of the Tunisian campaign.

way to clear the pass – stun the enemy with a surprise attack from his rear. It was a made-to-order mission for Darby's men.

To the rear and flanks of the enemy were steep cliff-faceted mountains, in which Ranger scouts found a series of fissures and saddles that could form a route. On the night of 21 March Darby led his men nearly twelve miles up the slanting cliff walls to a plateau overlooking the Italian positions. At dawn an ear-splitting Ranger bugle call rent the air and Darby's troops, shouting Indian battle cries, swooped down on the sleepy Italians, tossing grenades, spraying slugs and thrusting with their bayonets. Three hours later most of the strategic pass was in Ranger hands. Darby radioed Allen: 'You can send in your troops . . . The pass is clear.' By keeping up relentless pressure, the Rangers kept the enemy from recovering at El Guettar, took the entire pass and bagged 1400 prisoners. This operation unquestionably saved hundreds of American lives.

Back at Gafsa, Darby told his men that they were going back to Algeria to form and train two more Ranger Battalions. General Eisenhower, he said, was 'sold' on the Rangers. Some returned to the States to help train the 2nd and 5th Rangers, while the original battalions split into three groups to form the new 1st, 3rd and 4th Battalions. Volunteers were found by raiding other outfits – and even by recruiting suitably bellicose prospects in local bars. The old-timers poured it on relentlessly, and six weeks later three new battalions packed their gear to join the 1st Division in what was to be the invasion of Sicily.

This huge Sicilian invasion armada started off from North Africa in calm seas, but during the 24 hours before landing a heavy storm blew up. Most of the Rangers were seasick by the time they hit the beaches. Weighted down by their heavy

equipment, several drowned when deadly mortar fire struck their landing boats. As the Rangers tumbled out over the lowered ramps into the seething surf, the darkness ahead was sporadically broken by powerful sweeping searchlights. Cannon and tracer ammunition stitched the night with lethal lines of red and blue as they sprinted up the beach.

One platoon blundered into a field of land mines, where the dreaded Bouncing Bettys ripsawed their way through their fatal advance. One sergeant, seeing his lieutenant literally disintegrate ahead of him, was lifted up bodily and thrown back onto his companions. He picked himself up and yelled to those behind him to stop where they were. Moving quickly among others still in the mine field, he found a path back to the beach and guided the others to momentary safety. Feeling a pain in his abdomen, he probed with his fingers and found a gaping hole several inches long through which his viscera were protruding. He staunched the wound with his hand and took command of his leaderless platoon. A few minutes later this courageous non-com, Randall Harris, aided by another sergeant, silenced a series of seven pillboxes that were decimating his company by flinging grenades through their apertures. Afterward, weak from loss of blood, Harris gave himself first aid, tightened his rifle belt and led his company toward their objective: the heavily fortified citadel of Gela

The action soon concentrated on the main enemy strongpoint – the cathedral square of Gela. In twos and threes the Rangers darted into doorways, spraying rifle and submachine-gun fire into house after house until all resistance was squelched except in the sanctuary itself. The Rangers then invaded the cathedral and flushed out the last enemy snipers.

108

Throughout the beachhead, the news of Sergeant Harris's amazing feats spread quickly. Leading his company, he had knocked out four more pillboxes and cleaned out several city blocks of gunners and snipers. Fortunately a young medical officer, seeing Harris clutch his abdomen in pain, treated his wound just in time to save his life, after which he was evacuated to a hospital ship. Meanwhile, the Rangers and GIs of the 1st Division, who were advancing on the Ponte Olivo Airport, were under constant attack by Luftwaffe planes. The Italians had scuttled the Gela landing pier, and large sandbars prevented the Navy from unloading what the troops ashore needed so badly – tanks and artillery.

Then what the Americans had dreaded most became a reality: sixteen Italian tanks came roaring toward Gela on the Neciema road. Clanking into the town, they headed for Cathedral Square, blasting buildings with their 47mm guns. The Rangers, who had neither tanks nor antitank guns, rained down grenades, dynamite, bazooka and mortar shells from upper stories to little effect. But just then, a near miracle happened. A

miles of the town, the Navy began to come through with devastating effect. Blistering gunfire from the cruisers *Savannah* and *Boise* and the destroyers *Glennon* and *Butler*, joined by heavy mortar and divisional artillery ashore, splintered the Panzers into smoking, twisted junk. Meanwhile, the Navy had also rammed a pontoon causeway across the sandbars, and several tanks had finally come ashore. Before the day ended, the German attempt to wipe out the beachhead had been smashed.

By mid-August the 1st and 4th Battalions were camped at the town of Corleone, where new Ranger replacements were trained for the approaching invasion of Italy itself. The fall of Messina on 17 August 1943 ended the campaign in Sicily, and men of the 3rd Battalion were among the first Americans to enter the city. Medals were passed out to heroes like Harris and Shundstrom, but everyone knew that fresh action was not far off.

Then bad luck struck the Rangers. First, several of them were killed in training maneuvers. Next came virulent epidemics of malaria, dysen-

Below left: A 105mm howitzer fires in support of the defending forces during the Germans' Kasserine attack.

Below: Even before the fighting in North Africa was over the Rangers were training for their next landing operation. Here a Ranger battalion comes ashore on an Algerian beach in December 1942.

solitary soldier in a jeep arrived towing the most coveted object on the beachhead – a 37mm anti-tank gun. Darby bellowed: 'Hey there, soldier – swing that damned thing around here!' He and Captain Chuck Shundstrom, his second in command, got the 37 working and blasted away at the lead tank until it burst into flames. This heroic action galvanized the Rangers, who prevented the rest of the tanks from passing. Soon the enemy was streaking back across the burning wheatfields from whence they had come.

Next day, D plus 1, the weary Americans saw an even more ominous sight: a three-mile-long line of Mark VI Tiger tanks of the Hermann Goering Panzer Division surging toward Gela, followed by tough Panzer Grenadier infantrymen. But, when they were within a couple of

tery and jaundice. Half the Rangers shivered with fever while the other half spent the day racing for latrine boxes and slit trenches. But most regained their strength in time and found their old Ranger spirit returning – perhaps aided by a bevy of attractive nurses working at the field hospitals. When news came that the Ranger force was boarding ship at Palermo for the invasion with General Mark Clark's 5th Army, scores of Rangers went AWOL from the hospitals and made it back to their companies in time.

A daring landing on a narrow mountain-rimmed beach at Maiori, just west of Salerno, enabled them to surprise and wipe out a German armored company. Then they marched seven miles inland over mountainous country to take the high hills overlooking the plain of Naples.

The Germans, discovering they had lost this key high ground, counterattacked with wave after wave of paratroops and SS. The thinly manned Ranger line sometimes wavered but never broke. For 18 days, every surge was beaten back with heavy losses, with the help of the 82nd Airborne. The enemy was forced to syphon off as replacements troops that might have turned the tide on the American beachhead at Salerno.

After the bitterest fighting in Ranger history, Darby's men led the way down the winding road on 22 September for the big push to Naples. This time the Rangers were committed to dislodge the Germans from their famous Winter (Gustav) Line in the mountains of the Venafro area north of Naples. They secured peak after peak until the American lines advanced to San Pietro, as heavy German mortar and artillery fire took almost 40 percent Ranger casualties. After nearly four weeks of continuous battle, the three battalions were withdrawn to Lucrino to prepare for the Anzio beach landing.

On the chill night of 22 January 1944, the Rangers made a silent and unopposed landing in Anzio Harbor. Inside three hours the port was secured, as the Rangers fanned out to enlarge the beachhead, netting 40 German victims and a battery of coastal guns. Next day the aroused Germans pounded the port with shells and Stuka dive bombers, circling the seven-by-ten-mile

beachhead with ten divisions. For the next four days Darby's men held the furthermost tip, with savage fighting raging day and night until the battered Rangers were relieved by British troops.

Their next task was to spearhead the 3rd Division attack against Cisterna di Latina and there to cut the two main highways from Rome to Cassino. The 1st and 3rd Battalions advanced by night behind the German lines, while the 4th moved out surreptitiously along the enemy-held road until they ran into a wall of steel. The Germans had set up a perfect cross-fire system that covered all avenues of approach. Whenever a team of Rangers tried to leave their ditches, they were cut down like cordwood.

By now the Germans were alerted to the presence of the 1st and 3rd, who found themselves squarely in the middle of a German paratroop division. Thus began the costliest fight in Ranger history – the battle of the Ranger pocket. As the Germans poured all types of fire into them, they could do little except dig in on the banks of their ditches and return what fire they could.

Back with the 4th, Darby tried frantically to direct the attack to break through to the two beleaguered battalions. The Germans were much stronger than expected – outnumbering the Rangers ten to one – and, in fact, the entire American attack had now bogged down. The only units that had reached their objectives – the

Below: A German bombardment rains down on the beaches at Salerno, a bitterly contested battle for the Rangers and all the other Allied units.

Left: A landing craft
approaches Omaha
beach, most fiercely
contested of the D-Day
landing beaches.

1st and 3rd – were now battling for their lives. German tanks now joined the battle, and the trapped Rangers leaped aboard them in an attempt to lift the turrets and spray the interiors with fire. Beset from all sides, their ammo completely gone, the Rangers could fight with little but knives and bayonets. The pocket became smaller and smaller.

A desperate Darby now received this message from the 1st's sergeant-major: 'They're closing in on us, Colonel; we're out of ammo – but they won't get us cheap!' The iron-willed Darby, his once-proud force now shattered, fought in vain to hold back his tears. Asking his staff to leave him, he went inside a farmhouse and wept. Next day, the 4th launched another attack, this time pushing forward a mile and destroying hundreds of paratroopers, but they were too late to save their sister battalions.

In these two bitter days, the Ranger lost more men than in all of their previous campaigns put together. A bare 18 men managed to infiltrate back from the corpse-strewn Ranger pocket. But the two battalions had not been wiped out in vain.` German prisoners later revealed that the Germans had been marshaling heavy forces in the Cisterna area for an all-out push to drive the Americans back into the sea. But the Rangers' sudden attack had disorganized it and helped save the Anzio beachhead at its critical moment.

For sixty more days the lone 4th Ranger Battalion continued to fight alongside the 504th Parachute Regiment at Hell's Corner, the most hotly contested real estate at Anzio. In the end, Anzio held firm and from it the 5th Army launched its attack on Rome. But the men of the 4th were not to see Rome, and Darby was no longer with them, having been given a new command. What was left of the war-weary Rangers (about 200 men), were ordered back to the States to train new troops. Among these would be the new 5th Ranger Battalion which would land at Omaha Beach on D-Day. Other Rangers – some 250 who joined Darby after Tunisia – were transferred to the crack Canadian-American Special Service Brigade. Thus the fighting history of Darby's Rangers drew to a close.

On 16 April 1945 Colonel William Orlando Darby, now assistant division commander of the 10th Mountain Division, was killed leading an assault team in the Po Valley when a shell fragment penetrated his heart. He was not yet thirty-five. Forty-eight hours later, all German forces in Italy surrendered.

Abandoned German trenches in the aftermath of the D-Day landings. Ranger units spearheaded the landings, being assigned to attack strongpoints and gun batteries.

Carlson's Raiders
(2nd Marine Raider Battalion)

The US Marine Corps, itself an elite military organization during World War II, spawned four noteworthy Raider Battalions during that conflict. The second of these battalions became known unofficially as 'Carlson's Raiders' and performed admirably at Makin Island in August 1942 and later on Guadalcanal.

The 2nd Raider Battalion was the brainchild of Lieutenant Colonel Evans Fordyce Carlson. A former Army captain, he had enlisted in the Army when he was sixteen and served on General Pershing's staff in World War I. In 1922, detesting his peacetime job as a salesman, he enlisted as a private in the Marine Corps. Commissioned a second lieutenant some months later, he spent several tours of duty at various stations in China. In 1935 he was assigned to the military guard at Warm Springs, Georgia, President Roosevelt's private retreat. There Carlson, a tall, lean, hawknosed man, formed a friendship with the President that led to a private correspondence when he returned to China in 1937 as an observer with Chinese guerrilla armies fighting the Japanese.

Evans Carlson became fascinated with the 8th Route Army, the principal Communist force in northern China, and made two long marches with it through the interior. His outspoken praise of the Communists' discipline, determination to oust the Japanese, guerrilla tactics and democracy (which was in sharp contrast to the Nationalist regime of Chaing Kai Shek) led to a dispute with his superiors and Carlson resigned from the Corps in April 1939. For the next two years he traveled in China, lecturing and writing prolifically on China, the Red Army and Japan. After Pearl Harbor Carlson was recommissioned as a major in the Marine Corps at his own request. Early in 1942 he was promoted to lieutenant colonel and placed in command of the 2nd Raider Battalion.

Utilizing some of the principles he so admired in the Chinese guerrilla forces, Evans Carlson started organizing his special Marine unit. The Raiders would be strictly hit-and-run Marines who specialized in private wars of their own against the enemy. All would be volunteers, willing to answer yes to Carlson's demand: 'Could you cut a Jap's throat without flinching?'

Carlson chose as the Raiders' motto and battle cry the Chinese guerrillas' shout 'Gung-Ho!' This slogan was actually derived from the name of a Chinese industrial corporation, but Carlson misconstrued it as meaning 'Work together!' and, under his eagle eye, this is what Gung-Ho came to mean. Organizing his unit on radically democratic principles, Carlson abolished the officers' mess and other privileges of rank. Officers and enlisted men were issued identical equipment and battle dress; to confuse the enemy, Carlson decreed that Raiders would wear no badges of rank such as bars or chevrons in the field. He also insisted that there be equality among ranks at all times and encouraged free discussions of missions. His Raiders must be able to march and fight on an unchanging ration of rice, tea and bacon. All Carlson's men were handpicked, and he had for his executive officer the President's son, Major James Roosevelt.

The 2nd Raider Battalion first saw action on the night of 24 August 1942, when they slipped

Marine Raiders get set to paddle ashore from their assault transports at the start of the Guadalcanal operations.

113

Above: Marines jump
ashore from their landing
craft to join the fighting
on Guadalcanal.

Left: A pause during the
advance inland for a
raider unit on
Guadalcanal.

ashore from two submarines, USS *Nautilus* and *Argonaut,* on tiny Makin Island, the approaches to the atoll being patrolled by enemy sea and air forces. The Makin raid was to divert Japanese reinforcements from reaching Guadalcanal. The landing was made with great difficulty in a squally, pounding surf on the southern beach of Butaritari Island, which formed the base of the atoll's triangle of islands around its lagoon. In a spectacular 40 hours of running fire-fights, sniper attacks by Japanese and enemy strafing, the Raiders destroyed aviation gasoline and took a heavy toll of the enemy. That night they carried their rubber boats across the island and launched them on the smoother waters of another part of the lagoon. Then they lashed them to a native outrigger, and minutes later the outboards of this makeshift raft brought them alongside the *Nautilus.* Of 221 men landed, the Raiders lost 30 – 14 killed in action, seven drowned, and nine whose fate was unknown until after the war. Behind them they had left about 100 Japanese dead. The

alarmed Japanese High Command set about beefing up their defenses on Tarawa and other islands in the Gilberts and Marshalls.

Carlson's success in the Makin raid was wildly acclaimed back in the States, but, the 'ordinary' Marine – if such there was – in the South Pacific was not impressed by the 'Gung-Ho boys' of Evans Carlson. This was especially true of the dogged Marine defenders of Guadalcanal in the Solomon Islands. In fact, Carlson's Gung-Ho motto, far from commanding their awe, more often than not called forth their sarcasm. When the 2nd Raider Battalion landed at Aola Bay on Guadalcanal on 3 November 1942, they knew they would have to prove themselves to their brother Marines.

General Vandegrift, attempting to close the trap on a few hundred Japanese around Kukumbona in the Point Cruz area of the huge island, assigned Evans Carlson's Raiders to a position to the south. Their orders were to cut off and annihilate the feared 230th Japanese Infantry Regiment

Below: Carlson and his men come ashore on Guadalcanal in November 1942. Fortunately their landing was unopposed and they were able to form up properly before advancing inland.

should they burst out of the trap. On 5 November, the Raiders started moving west from Aola Bay toward the 230th Regiment, which had been giving the 7th Marines plenty of trouble. By 10 November, Vandegrift's Marines to the north had killed some 350 Japanese soldiers and captured much of their artillery. But most of the 230th managed to wriggle out of the snare, and they poured through a gap blasted in the inland line held by the US Army's 164th Infantry Regiment. As they fled westward, Carlson's Raiders followed them like a scourge.

Here was the hit-and-run private war Evans Carlson's men had been trained for. Disdainful of outside help, receiving only an occasional airdrop of rice and ammunition, the Raiders began to whittle down the fleeing 230th Infantry. Twelve times they struck the Japanese column, falling savagely on its rear and flanks, then vanishing as suddenly as they had appeared. This was the same guerrilla tactic that Carlson had learned so well from the Chinese 8th Route Army some five years before.

The main body of the 2nd Raider Battalion marched in a line parallel to the retreat of the Japanese, its snipers picking off enemy officers and non-coms. Right behind the 230th came Raider patrols which opened fire each time they ran into large numbers of the enemy. Japanese commanders would then rush reinforcements to the rear of the column, whereupon the main body of the Raider Battalion would pour concentrated fire into them from its flank position.

Using these guerrilla tactics, Carlson's men killed over 500 soldiers of the 230th Regiment with a loss of only 17 of their own men. When they returned to the Marine lines 30 days after they had set out from Aola Bay, the Raiders found that Gung-Ho was no longer a derisive catcall among their fellow Marines.

After their actions on Guadalcanal, both the 1st – under Colonel Merrill (Red) Edson – and the 2nd Battalions were regrouped with the other Raider Battalions into the 1st Raider Regiment in March 1943. From their bases in American Samoa and French New Caledonia, they were used to spearhead a number of landings in the south Pacific. One of these was a daring assault landing on Bougainville at Empress Augusta Bay on 1 November 1943. Coming ashore on Green 2 beach, they moved east to a mission station and on the 9th fought a stubborn action for a trail junction. For the rest of the month and into December, they fought in support of the 3rd Marines before being withdrawn to Guadalcanal in January of 1944.

Evans Carlson continued to lead his Raiders personally until they were merged into the Raider Regiment, of which he became second in command. As an observer at the assault on Saipan in June 1944, he was badly wounded. He returned to the United States, was awarded the Legion of Merit and then retired on account of his wounds with the rank of brigadier general.

Right: Admiral Mountbatten addresses men of an American air supply unit supporting Merrill's Marauders. Mountbatten had been Chief of Combined Operations in Britain before being sent to Southeast Asia so he was thoroughly familiar with the operations of irregular units like commandos or marauders.

Merrill's Marauders (Galahad Force)

Early in 1944, when the war between Japan and the Allies was three years old, some 20,000 specially trained troops invaded enemy-held Burma. Roughly 17,000 of these were known as 'Chindits,' mainly British soldiers with some battalions of Gurkhas, Nigerians, Chinese and Burmese. Chindit was a corruption of 'Chinthe,' the Burmese temple gargoyle which General Orde Wingate of the British Long Range Penetration Force had chosen as a symbol of allied air-ground cooperation. The remaining 3000 were Americans who came to be known as 'Merrill's Marauders.' Trained in guerrilla warfare, these 20,000 men penetrated Burma by secret routes or landed on remote airfields hacked out of the jungle. Their mission: to liberate the land route, blocked by the troops of the wily and brilliant General Tanaka, along which aid could reach China.

The Southeast Asia Command had been recently organized under Vice-Admiral Louis Mountbatten, with Lieutenant General Joseph Stilwell as his Deputy Supreme Allied Commander. 'Vinegar Joe,' as he was known, had an old score to settle with Tanaka. As Chief of Staff to Chiang Kai Shek, Stilwell had campaigned in Burma with the Chinese 5th and 6th Armies, but he had not been able to hold the Burma Road against the Japanese. He withdrew into India and prepared his Chinese and Allied forces to

retake Burma, with the goal of smashing the enemy at the important rail and air center at Myitkyina on the Ledo Road.

The 3000 Americans in Stilwell's invasion army were officially designated the Galahad Force, from the knight of Arthurian legend. Galahad was an offspring of the Quebec Conference and represented the US Army's first venture into long-range penetration. Since the British had an edge in experience and comprised the bulk of the forces in Burma, Chief of Staff Marshall sent Galahad to them for training.

Galahad was a maverick outfit from the first. A call for volunteers produced few with combat experience. The force was raised chiefly from volunteers among US servicemen stationed at such tropical bases as Panama and the West Indies. One of its veterans later commented that 'It contained far more than its share of drunkards, derelicts and guardhouse graduates.' These 3000 unscreened volunteers were lumped together under the unimpressive label of Casual Detachment 1688 and shipped out for training with Lieutenant Colonel Charles N. Hunter.

In Gwalior, British India, far from home and even from the neon lights of garrison towns, the members of the 1688th grumbled and griped. They felt cheated at not being sent out immediately on the 'hazardous mission' for which they had volunteered. A wild lot, they kept the MPs busy, their guardhouses full and the local Indians in a state of terror. At Christmastime

they celebrated by firing their weapons into the air despite their officers' every effort to stop them. One large group, bent on hellraising, flagged down the Bombay Express as it passed near their camp and took off for a spot of leave – AWOL.

What the group needed was a leader who could take their individual talents and turn them to good use. To this point they had had only makeshift leaders on temporary assignment over Hunter. It was not until New Year's Day of 1944 that Vinegar Joe named as their CO one of his favorites, Brigadier General Frank D. Merrill. Then a *Time* correspondent dubbed the unit 'Merrill's Marauders,' and Galahad's image began to form through journalism, military folklore and their status as the only American ground troops in combat in Burma.

Unpromising as these men might have seemed – indeed, many British officers regarded them as little more than hooligans – the fact was that there were many highly adaptable individuals among them. One of their best platoon leaders was a man waiting only for the end of the war to be ordained a minister. Another was a dedicated career Army officer. The best shot among them was a Sioux Indian. Some men in the radio sections had taught themselves whatever electronics they needed to know. The reconnaissance platoons so essential in jungle fighting included several alert Nisei, American-born Japanese. And when the pack mules arrived, dozens of GIs learned how to be mule-skinners on the spot.

Above: Lieutenant Colonel Hunter makes a speech to his men on 1 January 1944 when the Marauder force was officially activated as the 5307th Composite Regiment (Provisional).

Above left: General Stilwell enjoys his Christmas dinner (1943) at a forward base in Burma.

They had the material for a top fighting outfit, and the leader they needed turned out to be their own Colonel Chuck Hunter rather than the genial Frank Merrill, who commanded them for only a short time. Even as a subordinate commander, it was Hunter who had trained them in India. And it would be Hunter, a West Pointer and a strict 'by the book' disciplinarian, who would turn this motley bunch of GIs into a part of American military history.

Ordered at last to Burma, Hunter elected to march his troops down the Ledo Road instead of going by truck; this would help harden the battalions and give the mule-skinners a chance to get used to their animals. It was a grueling hundred-mile hike, with each man carrying a full field pack, but it gave the Marauders a sense of unity and achievement. After a three-day rest, they jumped-off into the jungle to join forces with Stilwell's Chinese troops in pursuit of Tanaka.

bly area. These recon platoons were the elite of both the Chindit and Galahad forces. They had the nervewracking job of approaching a concealed enemy without betraying their own position. This took the bravest of men for, in the silent jungle, a careless step might snap a dry branch like a pistol shot and a burst of enemy fire could be expected at any bend in the trail.

In charge of the leading recon platoon was Lieutenant Sam Wilson, who had been a protégé of Hunter's at the Infantry School at Fort Benning, Georgia. After a thirty-mile march, he found an abandoned enemy camp which was well behind Tanaka's 18th Division and which would make a good forward assembly area for Galahad. Judging the information too important to send back with a dispatch rider, Wilson, an expert horseman, took it back himself on a pony which had been among his mule herd. Merrill wasted little time in moving out Galahad's main body.

Below left; The Marauders begin their advance in Burma. Fording jungle streams was often more difficult than in the location shown here.

Below: A Marauder platoon leader shows his field glasses to two Burmese boys early in 1944.

If Galahad (as Stilwell still called the Marauders) could effect a flanking march through the jungles to the village of Walawbum, crossing twelve sizable rivers on the way, it would be in an ideal position to block and perhaps trap Tanaka's men. Meanwhile, the Chinese 1st Army would attack directly southward on the road that eventually led to Kamaing, where Tanaka had his forward supply depots. If Kamaing fell, Stilwell was sure the way to Myitkyina would be open. If it did not, he would be content for the moment with positions taken in the Mogaung Valley some twenty miles west of Myitkyina. But putting Galahad in the right position to storm Walawbum was critical.

Merrill chose a route swinging wide around Tanaka's right flank and started down it with his main body. Reconnaissance platoons from each of the three battalions scouted ahead, locating the Japanese so as to establish a forward assem-

In five days the battalions crossed two big rivers, received an essential supply drop, blooded their men in a brush with the enemy and finally arrived at the small rise on the east bank of the Nyumpyek River where stood their objective – Walawbum village.

Merrill deployed his forces widely so as to block the entire area with his four battalions under Lieutenant Colonels McGee, Beach and Osborne. A regiment of the Chinese 1st Army was supposed to move southeast and eventually link up with Galahad. The astute Tanaka, however, seeing how slowly the Chinese were moving, decided to throw his main force at Galahad. What followed was a confused close-range battle, largely of isolated platoons and companies. In reconnoitering a position, Beach ran smack into a Japanese soldier whom his alert orderly shot dead. Hunter went out with a patrol to locate a Colonel Brown, who was leading an

Opposite, main picture: Brigadier General Frank D. Merrill commander of the Marauders.

Inset: General Merrill looks out from a C-47 cargo plane on a supply dropping flight over North Burma on 16 April 1944, during the advance to Myitkyina. Air supply played a vital part in all jungle operations.

A group of reinforcements moves forward to join the Marauders in the final attacks on Myitkyina.

advance of Chinese tanks, and clashed almost immediately with the enemy.

The chief thrust of the enemy attack fell first on McGee's men in their forward position, but they held on for 36 hours and took a heavy toll of Tanaka's soldiers. Running short of ammo and unable to get more, they had to fall back to the main position. An outstanding action was fought by one of Beach's platoon leaders, Lieutenant Logan Weston, whose men were pinned against the river bank by an enemy company. In order to hold out, Weston formed a tight perimeter. One of his Nisei, Private Henry Gosho, translated the shouted Japanese orders for Weston, who could then deploy men left or right to meet each new enemy rush. Under cover of 81-mm mortar fire delivered by a Pacific veteran, Lieutenant Woomer (known as 'Woomer the Boomer'), Weston was able at last to cross to the safety of the other bank.

Finally, it was Beach's battalion that halted the enemy advance. The Marauders had performed well, firing fast and straight, as the Japanese rushed forward with suicidal courage screaming 'Banzai!' Soon Tanaka wisely withdrew his tattered men and escaped south toward Kamaing. Before the village of Walawbum, the victorious Galahads counted some 400 Japanese bodies of the 56th Regiment. While Walawbum was a stunning success for Merrill, he was still unable to close the jaws of his trap and bag Tanaka's main force. This was due in part to footdragging by the Chinese troops and slipshod staff communications work in keeping in touch with Galahad. As a result, Tanaka could not be

ensnared on the Kamaing Road and he was able to slip away to the Mogaung Valley.

The Galahad Force was unwisely split up, with Osborne's 1st Battalion joining the 113th Chinese Regiment to try to seize the Jambu Bum (mountain range) Pass for the best chance of meeting the main 1st Chinese Army. Hunter, commanding the 2nd and 3rd Battalions, was to follow the Tanai River, aiming to cut the Kamaing Road around Shaduzup. Eventually Osborne's forces would join up with Hunter in that area. At this point the Marauders were in top form, having slain some 800 Japanese in all with the loss of very few men. Battalion commanders had proved their mettle and natural leaders were beginning to emerge from the ranks. Even so, with malaria and other sicknesses and their casualties, the unit was now 2300 strong.

Osborne's operation went well enough. After a few bitter skirmishes, he cut his way through the jungles to make the Jambu Bum undetected. There, with a quick dawn bayonet charge, he overwhelmed a complete enemy supply depot. Thus the line of the Jambu Pass was secured. As usual, however, the Chinese forces lagged behind, and the resourceful Tanaka was able to elude them. By this time the 1st Battalion had fought through some dozen actions on the march; relieved by the Chinese, the men were given a rest – after which Osborne marched them off at a leisurely pace to rejoin Hunter. Little did they know, until they received a frantic message from Merrill, that the rest of Galahad was even then engaged in its worst ordeal: the Battle of Nphum Ga (pronounced 'Noom Ga').

On 24 March, after a hectic march, Hunter had arrived according to plan in the Mogaung Valley. McGee's men had successfully crossed the Moguang River to block the Kamaing Road, and they were engaged in rooting out an enemy outpost from a small village. Hunter was carrying out his objectives, undeterred by the news that Osborne would be delayed in reaching the Shaduzup area, when information reached Merrill that a strong Japanese force had arrived from the south. From a captured enemy map, Merrill correctly deduced that the enemy was making a wide enveloping movement up the Tanai Valley, which would threaten and perhaps evict the Chinese forces at Shaduzup. When Stilwell heard of this, he ordered Merrill to block this thrust. A good trail which ran through Nphum Ga to Shaduzup seemed the logical route for the enemy to follow on such a mission. General Merrill, himself then at Nphum Ga, ordered Hunter and McGee, then around the Auche vicinity, to join him for a stand there.

The Japanese force, which was thought to be three first-rate battalions, was in fact only part of Tanaka's 114th reserve regiment under Colonel Fusayama Maruyama, based on Myitkyina. All of Tanaka's units were now at half-strength or less. Maruyama had with him only about 700

infantry and as many clerks and supply men as he could scrape up and form into two weak battalions, with four light guns. Moreover, he had been shaken by an attack of P-51s which had caught him fairly in the open on the trail to Auche. Still, he and his ragged men had plodded up through the jungle toward Nphum Ga, fighting the Galahad rearguard units as they went.

And those rearguard units, platoons under Lieutenants Weston and Smith, were giving Maruyama a very hard time. With only some 70 soldiers between them, these two Galahad leaders arranged several ambushes, spraying Maruyama's advance columns with bullets and then slipping away to do the same again. When they finally broke away toward their own lines, Weston and Smith's Marauders had inflicted some 60 casualties on Maruyama's force and reduced his advance to a turtle-like creep up the bamboo trail.

This brave rearguard action was extremely fortunate because it bought a little time for McGee's battalion which, after hard action and some wild rumors, momentarily panicked. At the point where McGee's men were, the trail was perfectly straight and an excellent enfilade target for Maruyama's 75-mm guns, which raked the

A Marauder unit rests on the trail near Nphum Ga on 28 April 1944. Note the pack mules carrying ammunition and other supplies.

trail mercilessly. Part of the battalion bolted, many throwing away packs and weapons, and there was nothing McGee could do to stop them. The leaders of the rout ran on to Galahad headquarters, where Merrill, Hunter and other officers tried to restore. some kind of order until McGee, with the harder core of the battalion, caught up with the fugitives. Merrill wanted McGee to go back to Auche, but this was now no longer possible. Indeed, the entire Galahad Force was quickly being cut off from any escape from the Nphum Ga heights. Setting up a tiny perimeter, McGee ordered everyone to dig in as fast as he could, adding that if a man felt he couldn't fight, he was to go away and hide. Under this reproach, many of the panicked men recovered their composure and rejoined their fellows. Finally, on 27 March, Maruyama caught up with McGee and all but surrounded him, and the siege of Nphum Ga was on in earnest.

Merrill finally consolidated his forces on the heights, which offered many good defensive positions in the form of ridges, while the bowl below it, where the village was situated, provided cover for the mules, signal and headquarters sections. There was also an invaluable spring of water here. As a part of Galahad's defense perimeter, the 3rd Battalion took up a position at the hamlet of Hsamshingyang to protect a small airstrip for the dropping of supplies. In their effort to reach the mountaintop, the Marauders were in a state of near exhaustion. Men in both battalions had marched over 70 miles, crossed dozens of streams and made the last dash up the slopes through mud and exploding shells. Even so, they began whipping the hilltop into a tenable position.

What the panicked men of the 2nd Battalion might have lost in dignity, they quickly regained in their heroic defense of this obscure Burmese village. Despite the ferocity of the Japanese attacks, McGee's tiny perimeter held fast. At first Maruyama made an attempt to advance past McGee down to the Hsamshingyang airstrip and Merrill's heaquarters, where victory would have been his. Unable to do this, he settled for keeping the pressure on McGee's ever-contracting perimeter. In spite of their courage in the attack, the morale of Maruyama's men – and indeed all of Tanaka's forces – had reached a very low ebb. Their uniforms were so tattered that many were nearly naked; great numbers had no shoes and nearly all suffered from beri-beri, malaria and skin diseases. Their daily ration consisted of a handful of rice. Most of the sick and wounded could not be treated due to lack of medical suplies, and evacuation was impossible.

Tanaka's ammunition was also pitifully scarce, with forward troops allowed only 150 rounds per weapon of every kind. Any supplies reaching him had to go over the rough road to Bhamo or be shipped up the Irrawaddy, and from thence over even poorer roads to Kamaing. Along this route they were always subject to the Chindit raiders. Also, Maruyama's troops were constantly battered by bombs and strafing from P-51s of the American 10th Air Force, sometimes to within 100 yards of McGee's perimeter. Thus the Japanese were only comparatively 'safe' when they were engaged in close fighting with the Marauders. The upshot of this was close-in combat of the dirtiest and bloodiest kind. A few Galahads whose nerve had broken were bayoneted as they huddled paralyzed in their fox holes. But this occurred on the other side as well. Logan Weston, leading a small force attempting to take the pressure off McGee, kicked aside a piece of cloth and found beneath it two terrified young Japanese soldiers, whom he shot dead.

On the 28th meanwhile, as McGee was being cut off by Maruyama, General Merrill was incapacitated by a heart attack. The Galahad surgeon insisted he be evacuated along with other casualties, but Merrill refused. Hunter privately apprised Stilwell of the situation and the latter ordered Merrill to leave. But he refused to go until the last wounded man was flown out, which did not happen until 31 March. Hunter then took over command of Galahad.

On the 31st, after savage fighting, the enemy took the water hole and McGee did not have sufficient men to recapture it. Every available man was in a foxhole in the perimeter. As the hours dragged by, the water shortage grew serious and the Galahads had to drink the brackish rainwater in a hollow where several dead mules lay. On 1 April, the enemy launched a simultaneous attack on McGee from the east and northeast. It failed. Shrouding the mountain top now like a fog was the miasma of scores of Japanese corpses and decaying animals. So acute became the water situation that McGee requested by radio a drop of 500 gallons of water in plastic bags, which saved the 2nd Battalion from certain annihilation.

Hunter, meanwhile, had not been able to relieve McGee. On 3 April he announced to his staff that no help could be expected from Osborne's 1st Battalion for at least four days. He added, 'Gentlemen, in the morning we start an attack that will drive through to the 2nd Battalion. It may take two or three days, but we *will* get through.' Up at Nphum Ga, however, McGee's situation had not improved. Some of the wounded had died and were buried in the perimeter. The 2nd's success in beating back enemy rushes was due largely to a Nisei sergeant, Roy Matsumoto, who relayed attack plans from a point near the enemy line where he could overhear the Japanese commands. On one occasion, he decoyed the enemy into a trap by shouting 'Charge!' in Japanese.

Hunter's attack was successful in gaining – for jungle warfare – considerable ground. The enemy force blocking the Nphum Ga trail was pushed back until it merged with the enemy line surrounding McGee's perimeter. Meanwhile, the Japanese made a heavy assault on McGee and succeeded in gaining a slight penetration.

Opposite: Men of a Marauder unit practice an attack on a Japanese pillbox. The soldier on the left is armed with a flame thrower, a very effective weapon in close range fighting.

MYITKYINA
NORTH AIRFIELD
CONS. BY 1888 INGR.AVN.BN
10TH U.S. ARMY AIR FORCE

The control tower at Mytkyina airfield constructed soon after the airfield was captured by the Marauders.

But the Marauders counterattacked with grenades and beat them back. For the next two days McGee continued to hold.

On 6 April the 3rd Battalion gained another 200 yards, most of it due to the extraordinary mortar-fire direction of Lieutenant Woomer. 'The Boomer' had worked his way to within 25 yards of a position where two enemy machine guns had been holding up progress for hours – so close that they were inside the zone of error of his own mortars. Then over his radio he gave the now-classic order: 'Deflection correct. Bring it in 25 yards and if you don't hear from me you'll know you came this way too far.' With the next rounds, the enemy guns were silenced and 'The Boomer' came through unscathed.

At last, on 7 April, Osborne's 1st Battalion appeared on the scene after a forced march of nearly four days. His men were exhausted and riddled with malaria and dysentery, but Hunter picked 250 of them fit enough to fight the next day, half to work around east to create a diversion while the rest crept around to the west to cut the enemy supply line. With the trails blocked, the Japanese took heavy fire in several directions. By the 9th, Easter Sunday, Beach linked up with McGee's weary men and the ring around Nphum Ga simply dissolved. Maruyama had had his fill

and, leaving nearly 400 dead soldiers behind, he melted away. The Marauders found his camp-fires with rice still cooking over them.

After this action, Stilwell committed Galahad to a major push to break the stalemate at Myitkyina. This was to become known as his 'end-run' – a secret march across the Kumon Bum range to seize the town. Stilwell's task force was organized in three columns, two of a Galahad battalion and a Chinese regiment, and the third of a Galahad battalion and 300 Kachin (warlike Burmese) tribesmen. The Myitkyina Task Force was given to General Merrill who, after his heart attack, had been retained at Shaduzup as the nominal commander of Galahad. Hunter – never a Stilwell favorite – was relegated to the command of the 1st Battalion and the 150th Chinese Regiment. Merrill's first objective was the town's south airfield, to be approached over a secret route through the thick jungles of the Kumon Bum – as tough an obstacle as any in Burma. It took the Marauders some 20 days to cover the grueling 50 miles to the airfield. Two of the 'end-run' columns got bogged down in clashes with Japanese outposts. But the redoubtable Hunter wormed his way around them and on 17 May radioed an exultant Stilwell that the airfield was in his hands.

What Merrill did not understand, however, was that the capture of the field was only the first step toward the goal of taking the town itself. All he had gained was a jumping-off place for an attack. It was then believed that Myitkyina was held by some 350 Japanese, but the real figure was ten times that. Moreover, the pathetic physical condition of Galahad at this time was completely ignored. Nearly the entire force now had malaria or dysentery or both. One of the battalions was so afflicted with dysentery that the men had cut the seats out of their fatigue pants to avoid fouling themselves on the march.

The day after the fall of the airfield, Stilwell arrived at Myitkyina in a state of euphoria with a dozen American war correspondents in tow. He gave no specific instructions to Hunter and left by plane almost immediately. Hunter, left with the entire responsibility, twice sent the Chinese 150th to probe the town's defenses, but enemy resistance was very stiff and they were badly beaten back. Stilwell then placed various commanders in charge of the Myitkyina Task Force, but the Japanese still held firm. Vinegar Joe, who disliked the British, refused the offer of the crack British 36th Infantry Division; he was determined that the town must be taken only by his American-Chinese forces. Yet by June the 'old' Galahad, wracked with sickness and exhaustion, had virtually ceased to exist as a fighting force. Stilwell tried filling its ranks with untrained engineer troops from road construction detachments, but these more than once broke and ran before enemy counterattacks. Thus the siege of Myitkyina dragged on through June and July, with the enemy holding off attacks by the Task

Force, which had grown to two Chinese divisions, the wreck of the original Galahad and a 'new' Galahad made up of raw replacements from the States.

By late summer the terrain around Myitkyina had become Verdun-like. The condition of the hollow-eyed veteran Marauders, the unending combat, the stench of unburied bodies – all were horrendous. As a measure to compensate for the failure of his Chinese troops, who were incapable of coordinated attack, Stilwell and his staff ordered the hospitals combed for marginal effectives. Of the 200 Marauders ordered back to duty at Myitkyina, 50 were immediately sent back to the hospital by Galahad's own officers. This attempt to hustle half-healed and half-cured soldiers back into action became a scandal. Moreover, conditions at the convalescent camp had become so bad that men rioted, giving rise to false rumors that the Galahads had mutinied. Just

prior to his return to the States, Stilwell visited the camp of the aggrieved Marauders – where even the MPs refused to patrol – to talk to their spokesmen. But his temerity in doing so did not impress the men. As for the indomitable Hunter, he hammered the 'new' Galahad into shape, and it was making good inroads on the defenses of Myitkyina when the town finally fell in August.

The scandal of the Marauders' shabby treatment was eventually hushed up, conditions got better and medals were handed out. The ill-used regiment was redesignated the 475th Infantry – complete with its own colors emblazoned with 'Myitkyina.' But few of the old Marauders remained to taste these belated fruits of their accomplishments. Before Stilwell boarded his plane for the States, he offered Hunter official command of the regiment. But Hunter refused. He had had enough of Vinegar Joe and was ordered home.

A fortified hilltop position typical of many in Burma defended by the Marauders.

Flying Tigers and Kamikazes

Both the Flying Tigers and the Kamikazes began their operations from a position of inferiority. However, Chennault's men scored increasing successes to the end of the war while the Kamikazes' sacrifice proved futile.

By the outbreak of World War II, aviation had progressed to the point where those nations who could command the skies were very likely to win the war. With fleets of large, high-flying bombers able to demolish whole cities and squadrons of well-armed fighters and interceptors capable of strafing and killing whole battalions of ground troops, air power had become – as General Billy Mitchell had predicted many years before – the supreme and decisive weapon of modern warfare.

Many brave men of all sides fought in the air during this war in all theaters of operation. Yet the war produced two flying units that by all criteria can be said to have attained elite status. One flew for the Allies; the other for the Axis powers. On the Allied side, the war against the Japanese in the air began with a ragtag group of barely six dozen American reservist pilots commanded by a craggy-faced tactical genius named Chennault. On the Axis side, the air war ended with several thousand young and fanatical Japanese pilots hurling both their planes and their bodies into the aircraft carriers and other ships of the US Pacific Fleet.

Chennault's 'Flying Tigers'

At the age of 51, General Claire Lee Chennault began in the summer of 1941 to train what would become his famous American Volunteer Group (AVG) of fliers. It was composed of three squadrons under the supreme command of China's Generalissimo Chiang Kai-Shek, and it soon began to challenge the air superiority of the powerful Japanese Air Force over Burma and China.

The AVG became known as the 'Flying Tigers' because of the carnivores painted on the sides of their Curtis P-40 fighters. However, it was the leering shark's mouth painted on their cowlings that caught everyone's imagination – and in time struck fear into many a Japanese pilot's heart. Without doubt the AVG was the most colorful and publicized air unit of World War II.

Chennault had been a career Army pilot for most of his life. From 1932 to 1936 he led the Air Corps Exhibition Group, known popularly as 'Three Men on a Flying Trapeze,' with which he worked out many intricate details of formation flying. Deeply interested in air power, he wrote a

Opposite: General Chennault chats to a group of Flying Tiger pilots in front of a P-40 fighter painted with the unit's famous shark's mouth insignia.

book called *The Role of Defensive Pursuit,* in which he set forth flying principles that he hoped would help American pilots in aerial combat. By 1937, however, his career as a military aviator seemed to be over. As an old-line pilot, he had flown for many years in single-seater planes, and the continuous noise of open cockpits had left him comparatively deaf. He had also been disfigured by engine-burn marks, and his men often called him 'Old Leatherface.' His poor hearing forced him to retire as a lieutenant colonel in 1937.

Realizing that war with the Japanese was highly probable, Chennault went to China immediately after his retirement. There he succeeded in persuading the Generalissimo that he was the man to take over and train the Chinese Air Force, which had been badly crippled by the might of the Japanese Air Force. Actually, he was offered this job by Madame Chiang who was sponsoring the establishment of a new aviation school. Chennault also talked Chiang into letting him set up an air-warning net within China to alert Chinese pilots to approaching Japanese sorties. This same net was also to be used by the Flying Tigers.

Claire Chennault had long cherished a dream of organizing a volunteer force of American airmen, flying American equipment in China against the Japanese. In proposing this idea to Chiang, Chennault told him the purpose of the volunteer unit would be fourfold: to test American equipment, to furnish air support for Chinese land forces, to train a nucleus of American pilots in real combat and to fight a delaying action against the Japanese until the Chinese armies could be better equipped to mount offensives against the enemy who had all but encircled them on their own soil.

Given the go-ahead by the Generalissimo, Chennault returned to the United States in 1940 to recruit pilots and mechanics to fight for China. He set out to attract such men from the US armed services, promising high pay and plenty of adventure. In the summer of 1941, the Army, Navy and Marine Corps permitted a few reserve officer pilots to resign their commissions and accept jobs as 'instructors' with a 'front' organization known as the Central Aircraft Manufacturing Company, or Camco, as it was nicknamed.

These 70-odd pilots and some 300 ground-crewmen proceeded in small groups on ships of various nations – Indian, British, American and some not even registered – westward from San Francisco to Java, then Singapore and thence to Rangoon, Burma. The Camco 'instructors' were carried on the passenger lists as lawyers, doctors, accountants and even acrobats. When they finally arrived in Kunming, Chennault began whipping them into shape, concentrating on pilot training, tactical drill and a thorough understanding of Japanese methods and capabilities. By November of 1941 he had two fully trained squadrons and one partially trained. On 23 December the AVG flew its first mission over Burma, intercepting bombers over Rangoon.

With the invading Japanese overrunning southern Burma and pushing the British and Chinese armies northward, Chennault's AVG units had to change bases often. In March 1942, with Rangoon being threatened, the Flying Tigers moved up to Magwe. In April – truly the darkest days of the Burma invasion – they rebased themselves as far north as Lashio. Later they would move to Loiwing, Pooshan and finally to Chennault's main headquarters at Kunming in south central China. The Imperial Japanese Air Force was now all over central Burma, and the only thing that stood between its armies and the capture of all Burma were the few pilots and planes of the First AVG. Yet the Flying Tigers would not have been able to operate without the small ABC (Assam-Burma-China) Ferrying Service flying daily supplies of bombs, food, aviation gasoline and ammunition from Assam, India,

Opposite, top: General Chennault looks on while ground controllers plot the positions of incoming Japanese aircraft. Despite the rough and ready conditions in which it operated, the ground control system was very effective.

Main picture: Chennault's personal transport plane lands at a Chinese airfield. The air bases for the Flying Tigers in China were wholly dependent on air supply for fuel, planes and ammunition. In the background can be seen the wing of a parked B-29 bomber.

over 'the Hump' of the Naga Hills into Burma.

As the early months of 1942 dragged on, however, the tide in the air began to turn. Under Chennault's clever leadership, the pilots of the AVG – often against odds of 20 to one – slowly started driving the Imperial Air Force from the skies of Burma and held the Burma Road itself, running from Lashio to Kunming, for months after it should have fallen. Considering that the AVG fought in what many experts called obsolete aircraft – P-40Bs and P-40Cs – their deeds and scores became truly legendary. They became even more so when new P-40E 'Kittyhawks' with their powerful Allison engines began to arrive from the States.

Although the First (or original) AVG – before it became a part of the US Army Air Corps – flew only for some seven months and never had more than 55 airplanes available to the unit, it became the terror of the air over Burma and southern China. Official figures vary, but during this brief period AVG pilots shot down between 286 and 299 Japanese planes of various types. The AVG lost only some 30 aircraft, with 10 pilots killed in combat and nine more dying in accidents.

Day after day – sometimes making two and three sorties per day – the American pilots would go out to bomb and strafe enemy targets and troops – and to do battle with the Japanese Zero fighters. Chennault had taught his fliers never to

turn with the Zeros, because they could outmaneuver any other airplane of the time and could outclimb the P-40s four to one. However, the P-40, which was very heavy, was one of the strongest planes then built and it could out-dive the Zeros two to one. The earlier P-40s were armed with two 50-caliber and four 30-caliber machine guns mounted in the wings. When the new Kittyhawks arrived, they carried six devastating 50s and with them AVG fliers could outgun anything in the sky. Veteran Flying Tigers like Tex Hill and Ed Rector often witnessed the lighter, flimsier Zeros completely disintegrate in the face of their six 50s. The trick was never to try to beat the Japanese pilots at their own game – climbing and quick maneuvering – but to dive on the Zeros, preferably out of the sun, get them in their sights and pulverize them with their 50-caliber guns.

In April 1942 Chennault, then a brigadier general in the Chinese Army, was recalled to active duty in the Army Air Forces as a colonel and promoted soon after to brigadier general. On 4 July the work of the AVG was absorbed by the 23rd Fighter Group and Chennault became chief of the Army Air Forces in China, organizing the China Air Task Force to carry on the war. A year later he would be promoted to major general and become commanding officer of the 14th US (Volunteer) Army Air Force.

Bottom: Armorers work on 0.30 inch machine guns from a Flying Tiger aircraft early in 1943.

Bottom right: Three pilots from the 51st Fighter Group hurry through their Christmas Dinner while on alert at an airfield in China, December 1942.

When the old AVG Flying Tigers officially became the 23rd Fighter Group, their contracts were terminated by Camco and they were offered the option of being inducted into the US military with commissions. Most of them probably would have accepted induction, for they admired General Chennault tremendously and would have gone on fighting for him in the air. However, unfortunate pressure was brought to bear on them to accept induction, which angered many of the pilots. Adding to their ire was publicity to the effect that they fought only for high salaries paid them by Camco of between $600 and $750 per month, with a bonus of $500 for each enemy plane shot down. Other stories, both in print and by word of mouth, intimated that they were unruly and undisciplined men who were little more than 'flying bums.'

Little wonder then that many of these veterans, bone-tired as they were, elected to return to the States. They had been abroad for almost a year under the most trying conditions. All were showing combat fatigue, and some were also in poor health. In the end, only five of the original Flying Tigers – Tex Hill, Ed Rector, Gil Bright, Charles Sawyer and Frank Schiel – remained to lead the 23rd's squadrons. New American Army pilots – most of them green – began to show up at Kunming – a fact that did not escape the Japanese publicists.

On the night of 3 July Radio Tokyo – the only program the Americans could ever get in China – warned the 23rd Group that Japanese fliers would quickly annihilate them, for it was common knowledge that the experienced AVG pilots were leaving. But the Japanese had not reckoned on one great ace-in-the-hole arranged by Chennault and the loyal homeward-bound veterans of the First AVG. Half a month before, two squadrons of these Flying Tigers had agreed to stay behind for a two-week period to help train the newly formed group. This gesture by such aces as Bob Neal, Charles Bond, Frank Lawlor, John Petack, Jim Howard and others, who were suffering from combat fatigue and various illnesses, was one of the most self-sacrificing instances of the war. In the two weeks that they remained, two of them gave their lives. One was Johnny Petack, killed while dive-bombing targets over Nanchang by a lucky anti-aircraft hit.

In fact, the canny Chennault had been expecting an attack on 4 July anyway, for the enemy had always shown an affinity for raids on American holidays. When they arrived over Kweilin, expecting to find inexperienced fighter pilots, they found instead many American boys who had been flying for weeks with the AVG and who now knew the ropes. They were led by Major Tex Hill and the four other veteran Tigers who had stayed with the 23rd.

Main picture: A line of the Flying Tigers' distinctive P-40s ready for take off at a base in China in October 1942.

Bottom left: Flying Tiger pilots examine the wreckage of a Mitsubishi 'Dinah' Aircraft they shot down near their Chinese base.

Above: Major John R. Alison.

Right: David 'Tex' Hill, one of the original Flying Tigers seen climbing into his aircraft before a mission in 1945 by which time he had been promoted to Colonel.

third was under Major Frank Schiel, who had charge of training the new fliers as they arrived from America. Scott himself ran Group Headquarters at Kunming and stood by for orders from 'The General,' as everyone called Chennault, to coordinate attack missions eastward. Late in July 1942 Scott, who yearned for aerial combat and who later became an ace with 12 kills and many 'probables,' was ordered to Kweilin to take charge of fighter operations there.

In Kweilin, Scott and the other Army men soon learned the value of the air-raid warning net developed by Chennault. It saved the American fighter force in China many times; without it, the Flying Tigers' chances of success against the Japanese Air Force would have been greatly reduced. To understand how it worked, one must imagine two concentric circles – one with a radius of 200 kilometers and the other with a radius of 100 – around each of most of the airfields and large cities of Free China. Inside these circles were thousands of reporting stations – some within the Japanese lines and a few right on the enemy fields themselves. One 'station' could be a coolie sitting on a city wall watching for enemy planes or listening for engine noises and reporting what he saw by visual signals to others. Another could be a mandarin in a watch tower. Still another could be a Chinese soldier in a field with a radio.

That Independence Day, as the overconfident Japanese came in over Kweilin, they brought with them, besides Zeros, some new twin-engine I-45 fighters that were supposed to able to knock any American plane out of the sky. The Japanese came in performing arrogant acrobatics, expecting to strafe the Chinese civilians in the city without opposition.

Watching them with field glasses from outside the cave he used as headquarters at Kweilin was General Chennault. Over the radio he barked directions to Bob Neal, Ed Rector and Tex Hill who were holding their P-40s up 'in the sun' at 21,000 feet. At Chennault's crisp and familiar order, 'Take 'em!' the new 23rd with the attached AVG squadrons screamed down on the enemy and massacred them. In less than half an hour, there were 13 wrecked Zeros and new I-45s smoking on the field for the Chinese to exult over.

In this way, the 23rd Fighter Group was activated, initiated and organized into combat readiness. The Group also had a new commanding officer, a career Army pilot and West Pointer named Colonel Robert L. Scott Jr. who, some months later, was to begin writing his best-selling book *God Is My Co-pilot*. When Scott took over at Kunming there were three Flying Tiger fighter squadrons and one headquarters squadron. Major Tex Hill commanded one at Hengyang; with him were his deputy leaders, Majors Gil Bright and Johnny Alison (later shot down over Hengyang) and Captain Ajax Baumler. Major Ed Rector had another squadron at Kweilin, with Captain Charlie Sawyer as his assistant. The

All of these reports finally got in to the outer circle where the information was screened. Then it went by telephone to the inner circle where it was rescreened; finally, the information wound up on the plotting board at the cave or operations shack at Kweilin – or whatever field Chennault was operating from. There Chinese interpreters got the various reports and moved pin flags along the map of China. Thus Chennault and his pilots could see at a glance where every enemy ship was in that particular attack zone and also where their own planes were. The net worked so efficiently in some areas that the Flying Tigers did not take off until the Japanese were within the 100-kilometer circle, thus conserving more fuel with which to fight.

Moreover, the Tigers knew at what altitude the Japanese were approaching and from exactly which direction. Their speed and numbers were also known. In several places, the Americans even knew when the Japanese rolled their planes out of hangars and revetments, when they started their engines and when they took off. Not only did the net system work for the obvious purposes of defense, but it also helped the Flying Tigers to locate their own lost pilots. On one occasion Colonel Scott, nearly out of gas after a bombing and strafing mission, made it back to his base just as his tanks read 'Empty,' thanks to directions given him by the net system.

In the event that Flying Tiger pilots had to bail out or land in unfamiliar Chinese territory, they all wore a Chinese identification flag on their flying jackets. Below this flag of Free China was

the seal, or 'chop' as the Chinese called it, of the Generalissimo. Chinese characters printed across the chop read: 'Chinese: Aid and protect this foreigner who has come to help China fight.'

Into the spring of 1943, Chennault and his Flying Tigers carried the air war to the enemy, including heavy bombing and strafing attacks on enemy shipping at Hong Kong and the Kowloon Peninsula. Flying now in the newer of the P-40 series – Kittyhawks, Tomahawks and Warhawks – they were clearing the air over China of enemy Zeros and bombers. As the Japanese planes approached, leaders would rally their attacks with cries of 'Tally-Ho!' or simply 'Here come the bastards!' The Tigers would maneuver for their enemies' tails, flip their gun switches on FIRE and with their three 50s in each wing – so mounted as to converge their tracers at about 200 yards – they would pour their deadly fire into the Zeros. Often those on the ground listening to radios tuned to the pilots' frequency could hear one of the Tigers mutter to an unlucky enemy 'Your mother was a turtle – your father was a snake,' – and then came the rattle of the 50s. Back on the ground, the Tigers were always greeted by the coolie workers with the thumbs-up call of 'Ding-hao,' meaning 'You are number one.'

In May 1943 General Chennault attended a Far Eastern strategy conference in Washington and there came into conflict with General Joseph Stilwell, Chiang's Chief of Staff, over the distribution of resources and future strategy. Chennault wanted to build up the Air Force even more and, having secured a larger share of material

Colonel Robert L. Scott, commander of the 23rd Fighter Group, ready to take off for an attack on a Japanese base on 4 January 1943.

133

and supplies than Stilwell, he launched on his return to China an attempt to drive the Japanese back toward the sea. Having achieved near mastery over the skies, he now tried to cut off enemy supply lines by attacking shipping. So successful was this that the alarmed Japanese were provoked in July into mounting a powerful counter-offensive called *Ichi-Go* to reconquer lost territory. Within six months, Chennault's forward base at Kweilin had fallen.

Undaunted, the Flying Tigers regrouped their squadrons at Kunming and continued their war of attrition and tactical support of American and Chinese ground forces in both Burma and China. Chennault remained in command of the 14th Air Force until July 1945, when he resigned in protest against the decision to disband the Chinese-American joint wing of the Chinese Air Force.

The Kamikaze

In October 1944, just as Claire Chennault of the Flying Tigers was serving out his last months as commander of the 14th Air Force, a new elite Japanese scourge of the air was coming into being.

As the Battle of Leyte Gulf grew more intense, many high commanders in the Imperial Japanese Navy were coming to realize that their war for conquest was a lost cause. Could there, perhaps, be some kind of an eleventh-hour miracle that could turn their faltering naval effort into a complete and lasting triumph over the American Navy? One high-ranking naval officer, Vice-Admiral Takigiro Ohnishi, was convinced that there could. Impulsive, daring, romantic and sometimes almost maniacal, Ohnishi was also a poet who had once composed the lines:

> In blossom today, then scattered
> Life is so like a delicate flower.
> How can one expect the fragrance
> To last forever?

Ohnishi, who commanded officers and men who were entirely devoted to him, had noticed isolated cases of Japanese pilots crashing their planes into enemy ships when their bombs had missed or when their planes had become badly damaged. Other Japanese military men had also noted such instances, but it was apparently Ohnishi who first came up with the idea of deliberate crashing as a formal tactic. At any rate, it was he who proposed the use of suicide planes as an answer to Japan's mortal challenge. His loyal lieutenants were in enthusiastic accord. Thus, some weeks before the Leyte landing, Ohnishi had been training a small corps known as the Special Attack Force of the Japanese Naval Air Forces. It consisted of 24 young pilots stationed at Mabalacat Airfield near Manila.

Admiral Ohnishi and other officers regarded the sacrifice of these fliers – soon to be followed by hundreds of others – as a modern counterpart to winds which had historically rescued the Japanese home islands from conquest. Such a typhoon wind blowing at great strength in 1281 was supposed to have wrecked a Mongol invasion off Japan. Again, in 1570, the Emperor of China had organized a huge amphibious force for the invasion of Japan which its defenders were ill-prepared to beat off. Then suddenly the Shinto gods had sent a Divine or Heavenly Wind – in Japanese, a *Kamikaze* – in the shape of a typhoon which scattered the Chinese fleet and blew back to China all the ships that had not been sunk.

On the morning of 20 October 1944, the day of the invasion landing on Leyte by American

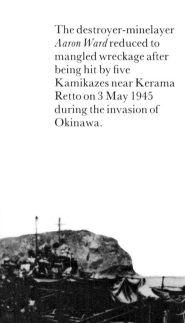

The destroyer-minelayer *Aaron Ward* reduced to mangled wreckage after being hit by five Kamikazes near Kerama Retto on 3 May 1945 during the invasion of Okinawa.

forces, Admiral Ohnishi stood before his small group of suicide pilots and issued final instructions:

'Gentlemen,' he announced, 'Japan is in mortal danger. Our country's salvation is now beyond the powers of the ministers of state, the General Staff and insignificant commanders such as I. That salvation can only come from brave young men such as yourselves. Therefore, on behalf of your hundred million countrymen, I ask of you the supreme sacrifice. And I pray for your success!'

At this point, visibly moved and his voice breaking, Ohnishi delivered his final words: 'You are at this moment gods without earthly desires. But one thing you must remember: your crash dive will not be in vain. Unfortunately, we will not be able to tell you the outcome. However, I shall be observing your performances to the end and shall report your brave deeds to the Emperor. On this point you may rest assured. I ask all of you to do your utmost.'

Actually, little experience was required of a pilot on such missions, and hundreds of obsolete Japanese aircraft could be used for them, a fact which did not escape Admiral Ohnishi and other commanders. When word of the impending heroic suicide raid spread from Mabalacat Airfield to other Japanese naval bases, squadron and group leaders were deluged by eager volunteers clamoring to make the supreme sacrifice for country and Emperor themselves. One of these Kamikaze leaders, Captain Rikihei Inoguchi (who was to survive the war and co-write a book about the *Divine Wind*) became so annoyed with some arm-waving young pilot volunteers that he shouted at them impatiently: 'Everyone wants to go! Don't be so selfish!'

During the next few days, the suicide pilots scheduled to make the first kamikaze attack made their personal farewells, professed their fidelity to their Shinto gods and on the eve of their take-off, clad in crisp dress blues, quaffed a ceremonial libation of the rice wine called *sake*. So doing, they reaffirmed their loyalty to Emperor Hirohito, whom they regarded as a god come to earth, and pledged their eagerness to die for him.

At dawn on 25 October, Lieutenant Yukio Saki led the first flight of old fighter-bombers toward Leyte. (A flight consisted of three Kamikazes and two escort planes.) Other suicide planes were also taking off from Davao on Mindinao. All were headed for the great naval battle then in progress off Samar: their main targets were the escort aircraft carriers of Admiral Thomas L. Sprague's 'Taffy 1' Group and Admiral Clifton Sprague's 'Taffy 3' Group. That morning the Kamikaze force scored hits on the small carriers *Sangamon*, *Santee*, *Suwanee*, *Kalinin Bay*, *White Plains*, *St. Lô* and some smaller craft.

While the Kamikazes from Davao hit the *Sangamon* and put the *Suwanee* and *Santee* out of action, the five who had taken off from Mabalacat Airfield jumped Taffy 3 just as Clifton Sprague's

carriers were trying to recover their own Avengers and Hellcats. They were never seen on American radar screens. Approaching from very low altitudes, they climbed rapidly and started their long dives from 5000 to 6000 feet. So sharp and sudden was their onslaught that they could not be intercepted by American planes in the vicinity.

Kitkun Bay caught the first attack, with one of the Japanese missing her bridge and island but crashing into the port catwalk. It bounced into the sea but the bomb it carried exploded and caused much damage. Two Kamikazes zoomed toward *Fanshaw Bay*, Admiral Sprague's flagship, but were shot down. The remaining two plum-

meted toward *White Plains*. At an altitude of 500 feet they pulled out of their dive, both under fire by 40mm guns. One of these planes, already smoking, turned and dived onto the *St. Lô*, crashed through her flight deck and burst into flames below. Several explosions of torpedoes and bombs on the hangar deck followed. Huge sections of the flight deck, the elevator and entire planes were hurled hundreds of feet into the air. Blazing from stem to stern, *St. Lô* foundered in a haze of dense smoke.

The second Kamikaze of this pair then started a run on *White Plains*, which tried to maneuver evasively with a hard left rudder. The plane kept on weaving in under intense fire as tracers ripped at its wings. Misssing the carrier's catwalk by inches, it exploded before it hit the water, showering the flight deck with fragments of both plane and pilot. Lieutenant Yukio Saki's first Kamikaze flight was over.

Meanwhile, three fresh Kamikazes had arrived on the scene, one of which dropped on the crippled *Kitkun Bay*. Its wings were shot off as it approached the small carrier – none too soon, for its bomb struck the water a few yards off the starboard bow and parts of the plane hit the forecastle. Another crashed through the flight deck, badly damaging the *Kitkun Bay*. Still another suicide plane crashed into her afterstack

A Japanese 'Judy' aircraft dives on the carrier *Essex*, operating off the Philippines on 25 November 1944. The photograph was in fact taken from the *Essex*, moments before the Kamikaze struck home near the forward flight deck elevator.

and two others dived but missed. Of the escort carriers making up Admiral Sprague's Taffy 3 Group, only his flagship *Fanshaw Bay* (called by her sailors 'the lucky Fanny B.') sustained no damage in this first Kamikaze attack. Less than a week later, other Kamikazes put the small carriers *Intrepid* and *Belleau Wood* out of action and permanently crippled the carrier *Franklin*, destroying 33 of her planes and killing or injuring 70 of her crew.

Thus the American Navy was confronted with a new problem in air defense: Kamikaze warfare. As a steward's mate of the *Witchita* put it, when that light cruiser sustained a suicide onslaught a few days later, 'We don't mind them planes which drops things but we don't like them what *lights* on you.'

In November the Kamikaze attacks were stepped up, particularly in the Leyte Gulf area. Many of these were successful, with the Japanese pilots crash-diving and hitting the battleships *Maryland* and *Colorado*, the cruisers *St. Louis* and *Montpelier*, seven destroyers and two attack transports. In

Below: Even before the formal establishment of the Kamikaze units wounded Japanese pilots or those with damaged planes commonly made crash dives on to their targets. Shown here is a Val dive bomber making for the carrier *Hornet* during the Battle of Santa Cruz in October 1942. *Hornet* was sunk in this battle.

December the destroyer *Ward* received a death-blow from the Kamikazes, with one plane striking her just above the waterline and entering the boiler room. Moments after a blinding explosion, the order was given to abandon ship. Some Kamikaze attacks were not so successful. One US destroyer, the *Laffey*, was attacked by 22 suicide planes. Five made direct hits, four bombed her and three grazed her, but the *Laffey* remained afloat. Oddly, however, much heavier ships were completely destroyed by a single hit.

In mapping out the strategy of the Kamikaze attacks, Admiral Ohnishi had educated his fliers with certain (so he thought) sure-fire techniques. In diving on carriers, the pilots were told to aim themselves at the elevator area amidships. With battleships and cruisers, they were advised to point their planes at the base of the bridge. Against destroyers, transports and smaller ships, they should aim themselves at any point between the bridge and the ships' center. As human torpedoes, in effect, they were expected by their superiors to achieve the goal 'One plane for one ship.'

Right: The escort carrier *St. Lô* explodes after a Kamikaze attack. With their stores of aviation fuel and bombs, the lightly-built escort carriers were very vulnerable if hit.

Above right: A Judy dive-bomber burns furiously after being hit by fire from the carrier *Wasp*. Antiaircraft gunners often had literally to shoot Kamikaze attackers apart since a damaged plane or wounded pilot could finish an attack run.

In fact, however, had the Japanese pilots pointed themselves instead near the waterlines of all warships, particularly the thinly plated carriers, destroyers and transports, their number of sinkings would surely have been greater.

In reality, the Kamikaze units – aside from the first few pilots trained by Admiral Ohnishi – followed no set pattern of organization or training. They varied from groups of thoroughly trained men, equipped with specially designed *Baka* bombs, to any Imperial Navy flier who decided to smash his bomb-laden plane into an American ship. The units were formed in several ways. Some commanding officers volunteered their entire squadrons, while others were designated by orders from higher headquarters – without regard for the wishes of the affected group. Still others consisted of small bands of fanatical pilots who offered themselves at the last minute.

Whether land-based or aboard ship, members of the more permanent suicide units – which of course were whittled down with each attack – were treated with vast respect by other personnel. They were accorded special privileges and special food was often prepared for them. Many pilots wore on their final missions a waistband called a *sen-nin-bari*, a sort of talisman woven by their wives, mothers or sweethearts which was supposed to ward off enemy bullets. Before their departure, the doomed Kamikaze pilots also sewed two 5-sen coins into their belts. This was an old Japanese superstition based on a pun: in Japanese, 'death' is *shi-sens*, which can also mean 'four sens.' Since five is superior to four, 'five sens' symbolized overcoming death. However, this was never construed to mean that a Kamikaze flier should avoid death and return with his plane; rather, it meant that he should not flinch or lose heart on his way to his destiny or karma. Only humiliation awaited the pilot who flew back to his base or ship, his mission a failure. Needless to say, no Kamikaze pilot ever wanted to wear a parachute.

One Kamikaze pilot, who miraculously survived the war, wrote of his 'last flight':

My plane seems to grow larger and larger. It is about to take me to my death, a death that is inevitable and predetermined. I begin to run. Why? To reach my death faster? I feel lighter than usual. . . . I settle into the cockpit, get out again and touch the ground; it has supported me for 21 years, I murmur my thanks to it. Never again will I be able to put my feet upon the earth. Each gesture is my last. . . . Fear plagues me. I ask myself: 'Will I suffer at the moment of the explosion?' I answer at once: 'It's not worth thinking about. The pain will last only a flash, perhaps a tenth of a second . . .' We continue to fly in tight formation.

At first the Kamikaze suicide missions were a temporary expedient only, but their early successes caused the Japanese to continue such attacks, not only in the Philippines but elsewhere. Well into the spring of 1945, Kamikazes went on hurling themselves into American ships, adding the carriers *Bunker Hill* and *Bataan* to their hit-list. The suicides also hit the *Enterprise*, and the *Franklin*, favorite target of the Kamikazes, was battered so badly in a low-level attack that 832 of her crew were killed.

In April 1945 the American assault on Okinawa gave the Japanese a final chance to defer, if not avoid, eventual defeat. Kamikazes were the principal weapons. On that island, over 1800 planes carried out well-organized suicide raids. In the first few days of April, the toll of damaged and sunk American shipping rose at an alarming rate, while naval casualties quickly mounted in proportion.

By 6 April Admiral Toyoda, commander of the Combined Japanese Fleet, completed plans to launch from Kyushu the first of ten general air attacks, called Kiki-Sui, which would continue until 22 June. Before these attacks ended, a total of 1465 Kamikaze planes from Kyushu sank 26 American ships and damaged dozens of others. However, so powerful had the US Pacific Fleet become that the Kamikaze units – very short of planes at war's end – were insufficient to stave off the American victory.

Even so, in the Japanese High Command's plan for a final defense of the home islands, the role of the Kamikazes was to be paramount. Fortunately for both sides, the war ended before these plans could be carried out.

Opposite, top: A comrade tightens the 'hachimaki' of a Kamikaze pilot. The 'hachimaki' was a scarf bearing a Samurai symbol of courage and was worn by most Kamikaze pilots.

Opposite, bottom: A group of Navy Kamikaze pilots are given their final orders before setting out on a mission.

Below: The crew of a Mitsubishi G4M 'Betty' bomber relax at an airfield in Japan before taking off to attack the American forces near Okinawa. Their aircraft behind carries an Ohka piloted bomb slung underneath. The Betty would fly to within about 15 miles of the target before releasing the rocket-powered bomb whose pilot would guide it until the 2640-pound warhead exploded on impact.

Korea and Algeria

The battles in Korea gave the Marines the opportunity to add new names to their roll of honor but in Algeria the Foreign Legion fought a different kind of war that eventually even threatened the Legion's continued embodiment.

In 1950 the United States suddenly found itself embroiled in an unexpected conflict on the Korean Peninsula. To meet the enemy in this theater of action, the country relied heavily on its elite shock troops – the US Marine Corps. During this same period France would have to deal with rebellion in Algeria and the loss of her long hold on Indochina. The French Foreign Legion bore the brunt of these upheavals and was almost destroyed in the process.

US Marines at Inchon and Chosin Reservoir
At the beginning of the Korean war on 10 July 1950, General Douglas MacArthur was having a conference with General Lemuel Shepherd of the Marine Corps. MacArthur happened to mention the New Britain campaign of a few years before and how well the 1st Marine Division had served him at that time. Then he rose and tapped the stem of his corncob pipe at a spot on the map of Korea hanging on the wall – the port of Inchon on the west coast of the country. 'If,' MacArthur said, 'I only had the 1st Marine Division under my command again, I would land them here and

cut the North Korean armies attacking the Pusan perimeter from their logistical support, causing their withdrawal and annihilation.'

'General,' replied Shepherd, 'why don't you ask for the 1st Marine division?'

'Do you think I can get it?' asked MacArthur seriously.

Shepherd said he thought it might be possible and recommended a request to the Joint Chiefs of Staff. The Marine general further said he believed he could have the 1st ready and in Korea by 1 September. After three successive requests by MacArthur, the JCS finally approved. However, the 1st Division had been stripped of many of its best men for the 1st Marine Brigade, which had been flung into Korea weeks before, so Corps Headquarters had to re-form it for MacArthur's brilliant counterstroke. Thus it was not until 5 September that the wholly reconstituted division was in the Korean theater and ready to go. Its 1st Regiment had been put together from reservists and regulars from Marine barracks by Colonel Lewis (Chesty) Puller in just ten days. The 7th Regiment, commanded by Colonel H.L.

Opposite: A Marine sergeant leads his two-man patrol back to UN lines after a scouting mission in December 1951.

Above: Generals Whitney, MacArthur and Almond observe the pre-landing bombardment at Inchon from the headquarters ship *Mount McKinley*.

Opposite: General of the Army Douglas MacArthur poses for the camera while smoking one of his favorite pipes. MacArthur devised the daring plan for the Marine landing at Inchon.

Litzenberg, had been formed simply by redesignating the existing 6th Marines. The 5th Regiment was still intact. For a fourth regiment to complete the full division, the 1st acquired the 1st Korean Marine Corps Regiment.

MacArthur's strategy for the Inchon-Seoul operation involved four phases: to effect an amphibious landing at Inchon; to take Seoul; to cut the communications of the North Korean Army; and, employing his forces in the Inchon-Seoul areas as an anvil, to obliterate the North Korean Army by a stroke from the 8th Army advancing from the south. Inchon was a city about the size of Omaha, separated from Seoul, some twenty miles inland, by the Han River. It was known that the port city's seaward approaches were difficult. There were strong currents in its harbor on the Yellow Sea and its granite-walled shores had no beaches. Further, its tides had the worst fluctuations of any port city in the Orient. From a military standpoint, the harbor was dominated by a rugged, cave-honeycombed island named Wolmi-Do, which was connected to Inchon's dock area by a causeway some 500 yards long. It was known that most of Inchon's defenders – some 2000 men – would be here. Because of the heavy fighting in the south, it was correctly assumed that the North Koreans would not be able to ship large units north to defend Seoul. General Oliver P. Smith, commanding the 1st, considered the securing of Wolmi-Do the key to the whole operation.

As it was finally worked out, the plan was to take Wolmi-Do on the morning tide of 15 September – the one day when there would be sufficient water to land soon after daylight; the next high tide would be just before dusk. The 3rd Battalion, 5th Marines with a tank force

attached, commanded by Colonel R.D. Taplett, would be the force to take Wolmi-Do. Then Smith would have to wait for the evening tide to land the rest of the 1st at Inchon proper – with not much daylight left. The plan then was to have the 5th Regiment land to the left of Wolmi-Do and take most of the city, while the 1st Regiment, coming in wide on the right, would swing around to cut off Inchon from Seoul to the east. The newly formed X Corps, under Major General Edward Almond, was the designated task force of the whole operation. Following the establishment of the Inchon beachhead by the Marines, the X Corps plan was to capture Kimpo Airfield, cross the Han River and finally, according to MacArthur's concept, capture Seoul and the high ground around it. A Marine Air Wing, operating from the small fast carriers *Sicily* and *Badoeng Strait*, was also on hand. A few days later the 7th Infantry Division would land behind the Marines.

On D-Day before daylight, the attack force crept up the channel toward Inchon. MacArthur, General Smith and other assorted brass were aboard the flagship USS *Mount McKinley*. Before the assault battalion shoved off for Wolmi-Do, fire support ships and Marine Corsairs plastered the island with everything they had. A half hour after the 3rd Battalion landed, up went the Marines' flag on top of Radio Hill – the key strongpoint on the island. 'That's it,' commented MacArthur on the flagship. 'Let's get a cup of coffee.' No counterattack materialized against the 3rd Battalion.

Late that afternoon, after the Navy's heavy guns had spent the day working over everything in sight around Inchon, the 1st and 5th Marines took to their boats in the autumn rain and smoke from burning buildings ashore. Using scaling ladders and cargo nets to get over the granite seawalls, the battalions got ashore in the dark. Although opposition was not as heavy as it might have been, the Marines' landing was no piece of cake. They sustained 196 casualties, including 22 killed. Next day the division advanced to the force beachhead line and General Smith established himself ashore to begin the march on Seoul. Two days after D-Day, the division was ready. Colonel Puller was to take the 1st Marine Regiment straight ahead along the highway to Seoul, taking Yongdongpo en route. Colonel R.L. Murray was to lead the 5th Marines to the left and take Kimpo Airfield. Puller would then cross the Han and join up with Murray to capture the capital. The previous night the 5th Regiment had encountered the first North Korean counterattack, mounted with six Russian T-34 tanks and 200 infantrymen. The 5th repelled the attack and wiped out all the tanks.

By dusk of the 17th, the 5th Marines had reached Kimpo Airfield and the next day they took it. The first plane to land there was a chopper with General Shepherd aboard; then Marine Air Group 33 staged in and commenced flying air

supply missions for X Corps. Inside the next 48 hours, the 5th Marines had formed up for their crossing of the Han. On the more direct route to the river, the 1st Regiment ran into more opposition, but by the 19th Puller's outfit was fighting in the suburbs of Yongdongpo, where the enemy had massed for a defense. Repelling night attacks by some 500 North Koreans and five T-34 tanks, Puller's men took the town next morning and pressed on toward Seoul. Meanwhile, the 5th Marines had crossed the Han on the 20th with some opposition and maneuvered to the right along the river to the stretch of hills that marked the outskirts of the capital. This was the enemy's main line of resistance. For four days, supported by Marine air and artillery, the 5th Marines pummeled away at the North Korean line. Colonel Puller had also crossed the Han by now and was fighting in Seoul itself. The newly arrived 7th Marines had crossed the river as well and were wheeling north of the city to cut off enemy reinforcements. At long last General Smith had his entire division engaged in the fight for the capital. The bulk of the bitterest combat for Seoul, through the heart of the city itself, fell to the 1st Regiment. By the 27th the enemy resistance had declined noticeably, and American flags were appearing above the city's major buildings. Colonel Litzenberg was ordered to secure the communications center at Uijongbu ten miles to the north with his 7th Marines, which he did. By 3 October, Seoul belonged to the Marines and the North Korean army was broken and dispersed. The Corps had taken some 2700 prisoners and inflicted over 13,000 casualties. The cost in Marine casualties was 2459, of whom 457 were killed.

Above: Marine LSTs and an LSM are loaded during the evacuation of Hungnam in December 1950 after the Chinese intervened in the war.

Top: To make sure that the marines would be able to clamber over the sea wall the landing craft for the Inchon landing were all equipped with scaling ladders.

The next move after the triumph at Inchon and Seoul was a second amphibious flanking operation – a right hook up the east coast to Wonsan. Thence the Marine forces would attack northwest from the throat of the Korean peninsula toward the Yalu River and the Chinese frontier. Although the 1st Division had the job of assaulting Wonsan, it turned out that an enterprising mine squadron had cleared Wonsan's harbor of mines and an ROK unit was already in the city. On 26 October the 1st was able to land on Kalma-Pando Peninsula and invest Wonsan. The Marines were somewhat chagrined to find that Bob Hope and his USO show had preceded them by air!

Now the 1st Division was assigned to hold a geographical position larger and longer than any ever attempted by a Marine division. It was a zone of activity fully 50 miles wide and 300 miles long – extending from below Wonsan all the way to the Yalu. To the 1st Marines, General Smith gave the task of securing and patrolling the Wonsan area, while the rest of the division advanced by road and train north to Hamhung; from there it would prepare for the push to the Yalu. To Smith, the idea of having his division stretched out so far to the north was alarming, especially when he heard that 8th Army units had been struck hard by Chinese Communist forces well south of the Yalu. But he had his orders: extend the zone of action northwest through lofty mountains past the Chosin Reservoir – a man-made lake some 75 miles inland – and from there push on to the Yalu.

Actually, the only possible route up this zone was a steep mountain road which meandered its way through dangerous passes and along cliffs from Hamhung to the reservoir. Smith's plan was to go forward in a column of regiments – the 7th leading, the 5th next, and the 1st to follow and close up after clearing some trouble spots in the Wonsan area. Aloft, marine Corsairs were to scout ahead. On 2 November the 7th Marines struck out and, brushing aside light resistance with artillery and air support, bivouacked that night in a mountainous perimeter near Sudon below the village of Chinhung-Ni. Here they were hit hard by three regiments of the 124th Communist Chinese Forces (CCF) Division. Quilt-coated Chinese infantrymen, blowing eerie bugle calls and whistles, attacked all night long and infiltrated soft spots in the perimeter. But the Marines held to their hilltops assisted, when morning came, by Marine artillery and Corsairs. The mop-up continued all day, with the enemy sustaining over 1000 dead.

Yet much more fighting was to come in this area. Ahead lay the village of Chinhung-Ni at the mouth of the tortuous Funchilin Pass. Gateway between the coast and the mountain plateaus above, it rose to over 2400 feet along its length of some nine miles. First into and through Chinhung-Ni were the battling 7th Marines under Colonel Litzenberg (known to his men as 'Litz the Blitz'). At the end of their climb up the Pass was Koto-Ri. By 7 November the 124th Chinese Division had exhausted itself, and that night it retired into the hills. On the 10th the 7th

Below: Marine landing craft head for the beach at Inchon while targets ashore burn from the effects of the preliminary bombardment.

Above: Marine
artillerymen fire in
support of the 1st Marine
Division in an action in
September 1952.

Right: Marines of the 1st
Division gather to read
an announcement posted
on one of their M26
Pershing tanks, May
1952.

howled down from Manchuria and the temperature hit a frigid 20 below zero, things began going badly for the Marines at Yudam-Ni and also between Koto-Ri and Hagaru-Ri. Soon the 1st Division was concentrated in four tight perimeters surrounded by a whole Chinese Army group. Realizing the seriousness of his situation, General Smith ordered the 5th Marines to hold up the general attack to the west and the 7th to start clearing the route from Yudam-Ni back to Hagaru-Ri. Next day he ordered the 5th back to Yudam-Ni as well.

It was now necessary to retain control of the Toktong Pass to let the regiments fall back on Hagaru-Ri. For five long days this defense was achieved by a single company in an isolated outpost seven miles from Hagaru. Repeatedly staving off Communist Chinese attacks, Capt. W.E.

Marines had taken Koto-Ri practically unopposed. Three days later they reached Hagaru-Ri at the southern end of Chosin Reservoir. A large town, it had been selected by Smith as the 1st's forward base for the Yalu operations ahead. As Colonel Litzenberg occupied Hagaru-Ri, Smith set about closing up his far-flung division and improving communications. He was still worried, for his left flank was wide open; it was 80 miles southwestward to the nearest 8th Army troops. So far, his MSR (Main Supply Route) had not been molested, yet he did not at all like the prospect of stringing out his division along a single mountain route for some 120 miles from Hamhung. Smith then brought up the 5th Marines from the south and spread their battalions along the MSR as insurance. The 1st Marines, now disengaged from Wonsan, were also moved north.

While the enemy seemed quiescent in the X Corps zone, they were, in fact, massing their forces daily against the 8th Army. Reports were coming in of powerful Chinese columns 150,000 men strong swarming across the Yalu. To help out the 8th Army, MacArthur ordered General Almond to wheel his X Corps attack around left from Chosin and thrust westward against the Chinese left flank and their MSR. This movement placed the Marine division in the van of the new effort. On 24 November the 7th Regiment pressed west of the reservoir, then through Toktong Pass to Yudam-Ni; two days later the 5th Marines joined them there for the push even farther west. Just as Smith had his whole 1st Division poised to jump off from Yudam-Ni, word came that the 8th Army was in deep trouble and falling back. Moreover, he was as yet unaware of even worse news; namely, massing in the hills just west of Yudam-Ni – his present position – were eight Chinese divisions under the veteran commander General Sung Shih-lun. Their orders: 'Destroy the Marine division.'

When the 5th Marines attacked on 27 November they gained only about 2000 yards, for the enemy was holding in strength. As the wind

Barber's Company F, 7th Marines, made a stand at 'Fox Hill' that ranks with any other in Corps history for sheer valor. When the 1st Battalion, 7th Marines – fighting their way back toward Barber – finally arrived and relieved him, they found that 82 unwounded Marines of Company F's 240 men still stood their ground. But Toktong Pass had remained secure, allowing the main elements of the 1st Division to make their way back to Hagaru by 3 December. There were too many walking wounded to ride, so many hopped along as best they could behind jeeps and trucks; those who rode were too weak or wounded or frostbitten to stay on their feet.

This weary column, with its wounded and Chinese prisoners, had marched and battled for almost 80 hours to cover the 14 miles from Yudam-Ni. Except for a few guns and some

Left: A Marine armed with a Browning Automatic Rifle advances while a buddy prepares to give covering fire during a patrol in December 1951. The Korean War was the first conflict in which the US forces fought in integrated units.

trucks that had run out of gas, all that these Marines left behind them was their dead – and they had been decently buried. Meanwhile, three Army battalions of the 7th Infantry Division had been cut off and were disintegrating east of Chosin. Under repeated Chinese attacks, these units became bands of stragglers staggering as best they could across the frozen reservoir to Hagaru. Slightly over 1000 frostbitten soldiers, many of them wounded, made their way back to Hagaru and the Marine perimeter on 2 December.

As the 1st Division was regrouping at Hagaru, its most urgent problem was evacuating more than 4000 casualties of all units who had accumulated from the bitter fighting at Yudam and Hagaru. This seemingly impossible feat was accomplished by Air Force and Marine fliers whose aircraft kept lumbering in and out of a 3000-foot airfield at Hagaru. Not only were all the casualties flown out, but so were 136 Marine dead, extra weapons and even some typewriters – and 500 Marine replacements were flown in! When an alarmed Air Force general arrived and proposed to Smith that an aerial Dunkirk-type evacuation be mounted, the Marine general replied that every Marine fit to fight would stay with the division for a final breakout; only casualties would leave by air. It was also at this juncture that General Smith made his now-famous announcement: 'We are not retreating. We are just attacking in a different direction.'

On 6 December the 7th Regiment led the breakout from Hagaru. First in, they were also first out. Under air support from Marine Corsairs and planes from four fast carriers, the

Marines marched and fought their way south toward Koto-Ri. During the night of the 6th and 7th, the 3rd Battalion, 11th Marines, was struck on the road by over 800 Chinese, whom they managed to beat off. After an 11-mile fighting march, the first phase of the Chosin breakout was complete, with some 14,000 United States and British troops concentrated at Koto-Ri.

Their greatest obstacle, however, lay just ahead of them. This was the push down the treacherous Funchilin Pass, held by fanatical Chinese whose orders were to stop the 1st Division from reaching the sea. Halfway down the Pass, they found that part of a vital one-way bridge had been destroyed by the Chinese. Smith's plan was to have the 7th Regiment, supported by the 5th, attack down the Pass, with

Main picture: Men of a Marine rocket artillery battery wait while helicopters arrive with ammunition in a photograph taken near Panjong-ni in August 1952.

Below: A Bell HTL-4 helicopter of the 1st Marine Air Wing on a training flight in Korea in 1951. This type of helicopter was used for scouting and medical evacuation duties.

A Marine recoilless rifle team fires on an enemy strong point near Chinchon-ni on 16 April 1951.

'Chesty' Puller and his two battalions as the rear guard. Below the Pass and still holding Chinhung-Ni, the 1st Battalion, 1st Marines was to attack up the Pass and capture Hill 1081, a dominating position. To solve the blown bridge difficulty, the division was fortunate in having attached to it an Army engineer company specially trained in building Treadway bridges. Some Air Force 'Flying Boxcars' from Japan were called in to air-drop several sections of the Treadway steel bridging, and the engineers went to work.

On 8 December, as the 7th Regiment thrust south along Funchilin Pass, the 1st Battalion attacked up it and along its ice-covered ridges. When the battalion commander and his artillery forward-observers saw that Hill 1081 and the ridges around it were alive with unsuspecting Chinese soldiers, they called for the whole division artillery to open up. One of the most destructive 'shoots' of the Koran War took place, with hundreds of the enemy slain. All that day, the two attacks, north and south, drew closer to each other. With the mercury at 15 below zero, the 1st Battalion got set for its final thrust at Hill 1081 and took it with a bayonet charge. From its summit they could see the advance guard of the 7th

Regiment coming down Funchilin Pass. Under covering fire from the 7th, the Army engineers trundled the Treadway sections into position to close the blown bridge. It worked – and the Pass was now clear for the division to cross and proceed southward to the sea.

The Chinese made last-ditch efforts to check the division, but the cold was too severe and their harassment soon ceased. The 1st Division and its various attached units finally emerged from the Korean mountains, exhausted, but proud and intact, with its wounded, many of its dead and hundreds of Chinese prisoners. On the night of 11-12 December the 1st entered the staging areas at Hungnam Harbor to embark on waiting transports.

During the Chosin Reservoir campaign, General Smith's division and Marine aviation had sustained 4400 battle casualties, with 730 killed. Many more became casualties due to frostbite. For the Chinese Communists, the campaign was disastrous. They took nearly 38,000 casualties, including some 25,000 slain in combat or by disease and the cold. The three Chinese armies pitted against the 1st Marine Division were shattered at the close of the campaign and disappeared from the enemy order of battle.

Left: A soldier of the 1st Marine Division brings in two North Korean prisoners who had tried to avoid capture by changing into civilian clothes.

Below: Chinese troops are guarded after their surrender to a company of the 7th Marines near Koto-ri on 9 December 1950.

The Foreign Legion in Algeria (1954-62)

On 1 November 1954 the Algerian War commenced, albeit so quietly that the French did not realize they had a major rebellion on their hands. The Fells, as the rebels were now called, carried out several raids in the Aurès Mountains around Biskra, attacking police stations, isolating a French community and killing several French soldiers. The French commander in Algeria, General Paul Cherière, simply assumed that these tribesmen were merely carrying out another local revolt and that his army would soon put them down.

As the months passed, however, French Army and Legion intelligence officers learned that new names were involved in the rebellion. The major organization was called the National Liberation Federation, or FLN, and its military offshoot was the National Liberation Army – ALN. The rebel leaders were men like Ben Bella, Ferhat Abbas and Krim Belkcem, and they had already divided up the country into military districts. Soon what had begun as a few hundred rebels in active revolt would erupt into an all-out war. It would involve hundreds of thousands of French troops, divide France and Frenchmen alike and almost destroy the Foreign Legion.

In 1956 Morocco and Tunisia were promised full independence from France, but the French government had no intention of letting Algeria

Above: Legionnaires inspect a motley collection of arms taken from Algerian Nationalists in 1952 before the full-scale fighting began.

Right: A Foreign Legion unit marches out from the famous headquarters training barracks at Sidi-bel-Abbès.

go. Knowing this, the Algerian nationalists were determined to fight for their freedom, just as the Viets had done so successfully in the decade that ended at Dien Bien Phu. Berber and Tuareg tribesmen were joined by the Arabs of the coastal areas to form a modern army which was dedicated to ousting the hated French.

The FLN operated swiftly and stealthily looting and razing whole villages and slaying pro-French Arabs. Village leaders loyal to France were tortured, mutilated and butchered before their own families. When Legion forces arrived, the frightened villagers would say they had seen and heard nothing. And each FLN strike brought more recruits to its ranks. To stamp out this terrorism, the desperate French undertook a huge census operation and sought to issue every man, woman and child in Algeria ID cards. In 1957 they sealed off the Moroccan and Tunisian borders with electrified wire. The Morice line, stretching from Bône on the Mediterranean to Tebessa, comprised almost 200 miles of wire laced with minefields and bristling with searchlights and blockhouses. With the Legion patrolling this line, FLN infiltration into Algeria was stemmed. Thousands of French troops garrisoned towns and villages to protect the inhabitants. But the hard duty of hunting down the rebel tribesmen in the Kabyle and Aurès Mountains fell to companies and battalions of the Legionnaires and the regular parachute regiments, 20,000 of the 400,000 French troops then in Algeria.

The Legionnaires themselves wondered whether they were soldiers or policemen. Before they could question rebel prisoners, French gendarmes would step in and haul them off for civil trial. Weeks or months later, the Legionnaires might catch the same men again, only to hear them protest that they couldn't be FLN because the police had let them go. Frustrated Legion officers muttered that Algeria was Indochina all over again.

Colonel Pierre Jeanpierre, a survivor of Dien Bien Phu, led the elite 1st Foreign Parachute Regiment. For these dedicated men, the FLN had to be crushed absolutely and the war won – if not for France, then for the Legion. In 1955 the 1st and 2nd *Régiments Étrangers Parachutistes* (REP) had been formed from carefully screened volunteers. Battle-hardened veterans, they would fight to the death for their officers. These paras did not wear the traditional white *kepi*, but a green beret bearing a silver badge with an eagle's wing and a sword. Jeanpierre handpicked his young officers and non-coms – lieutenants like Roger Degueldre and Philippe Durand-Ruel, and Sergeant Major Laszlo Tasnady, perhaps the best stalker in the Legion. Their home base was not Sidi-bel-Abbès, but a town named Zeralda west of Algiers, where they had converted a Nissen-hut camp into a model barracks.

From Zeralda Jeanpierre's troops made their stinging attacks into the Aurès, Ouarsensis and

Kabyle Mountains. The colonel's mobile command post was a helicopter – one of the first to be so used in modern warfare – in which he hovered above his charging sections to direct their movements. His superiors often smiled at Jeanpierre's blunt manner, glowering gaze and rough exterior, but they knew he was a master at liquidating the Fells. Inside six months he and his 1st REP had crushed every major concentration of rebels in the mountain areas. Vanquished in the countryside, the FLN infiltrated the larger towns and eventually began to spread terror in Algiers itself, placing delayed-action bombs in movie houses, cafes, office buildings and athletic stadiums. Their most notorious commanders were Yacef Saadi and his assistant, Ali la Pointe, who made their headquarters somewhere in the vast slums of the famous Casbah, with its myriad hovels and dark confusing alleyways.

Early in 1957 the new French commander-in-chief, General Raoul Salan, ordered the 10th Paratroop Division under General Jacques Massu to clean up the terrorists in Algiers. Massu moved into the Casbah with Legion, marine and army paras, but continued bombings made it necessary to isolate the whole quarter with barbed wire. In September, through clever undercover work by Massu and his men, Saadi's headquarters were found and he was taken. Two weeks later la Pointe's hideout was also discovered, and he and some of his cohorts were blown up by the paras in a tremendous explosion that rocked the whole Casbah.

Men of a Legion parachute unit dismount from their transport helicopter to join a search operation conducted near the town of Bougie in 1954.

Clockwise from top left: Generals Raoul Salan, Edmond Jouhaud, Maurice Challe, and André Zeller who had commanded many of the Legion's operations in Algeria and who led the 1e REP in the April 1961 rebellion against de Gaulle's Algerian policy.

Colonel Jeanpierre, who had been wounded by a grenade tossed by Saadi as he was captured, had become a living legend in Algeria. His 1st REP unit boasted more medals than any other in the Legion. He was practically assured of a higher command in the French Army, but the more he saw of French politics and political generals, the more determined he was to remain a Legionnaire, content with commanding his crack regiment.

On 29 May 1958 Jeanpierre received intelligence that two bands of rebels had been seen in force on some hills near Guelma. When he ordered two companies dropped by helicopter on the twisted scrub of Mermera Hill, they were immediately set upon by the Fells. Although the Legionnaires tried grenade tactics and called in artillery fire and strafing planes, nothing could prise the rebels out of their caves. Shortly after noon, his men saw Jeanpierre's personal helicopter, the *Alouette*, swoop over the well-entrenched

hand on the casket and swore an oath: '*Mon Colonel*, I will die rather than leave Algeria in the hands of the FLN.' That oath and its consequences would play themselves out to a sad conclusion in the Algerian War.

By now most Frenchmen, weary of taxes and the huge cost of the Algerian pacification, were calling for a strong man to take charge of the government. Thus Charles de Gaulle returned as prime minister on 1 June 1958. On 4 June he appeared in Algeria and tried to mollify Salan and other generals disaffected by the handling of the war. De Gaulle left them with the assurance that Algeria would remain French forever, and that he thoroughly approved of stamping out the FLN resistance.

At the end of 1958 General Salan stepped down as commander-in-chief in Algeria and a forceful Air Force officer, General Maurice Challe, took the reins. He immediately started another phase of pacification, which did nothing

Below left: The Legion's opponents, the Algerian guerrillas, in training at a camp near the Algerian–Tunisian border.

Fell positions. Some could hear his voice as he radioed back: 'I'll see how many there are.' As his chopper darted and circled over the caves, the rebels poured sheets of automatic gunfire up at it. Suddenly the racketing sound of the rotors ceased, the motor coughed and the blades whirled silently to a stop. Like a stone, the *Alouette* plunged down into a clump of bushes, a fuel line severed. Dashing to the spot, a few Legionnaires gingerly lifted their colonel from the wreckage and placed him in a truck. Two hours later his shocked men heard him breathe his last. No one could quite believe that the great Jeanpierre was dead. Enraged, they assaulted Mermera Hill again and again until they had killed or captured every last FLN rebel.

Over 30,000 people turned out for the funeral of the legendary colonel – a Legionnaire for a quarter of a century and a survivor of Syria, Mauthausen, Indochina and Suez. General Salan and other high officers paid their tribute to the fallen hero, followed by his officers. Lieutenant Roger Degueldre, whom Jeanpierre had commissioned from sergeant major, placed his

to endear the French to the Algerians; in fact, it caused hundreds more to join the FLN. But the 1st REP kept up the pressure on the rebels. On 13 May 1959 Sergeant Major Laszlo Tasnady's section encountered an ambush in the Bou Zara wadi of the Ouarsensis Mountains. After a fierce grenade and explosive attack on a rebel cave, Tasnady ran forward to help a wounded Legionnaire and took a rebel bullet in the back and another in the neck. So died the most famous non-com in the Foreign Legion. The savage fighting in Indochina had transformed this quiet Hungarian into the Legion's finest guerrilla fighter. A week before, his friend Sergeant-Major Janos Valko of the 5th Battalion REP had been killed; a few days later Tasnady had learned that another friend, Sergeant-Major Istvan Szuts, had been hit and wasn't expected to live. They had all joined the Legion together in 1946 and had gone through Bel-Abbès together as rookies. The three of them had hardly known enough French among them to exchange greetings. All had made sergeant major and had won more combat medals and citations than most of their

Above: Since their withdrawal from Algeria the Legion has trained in many aspects of warfare. Here a Legionnaire fixes an explosive charge on a tank during a 1965 exercise.

officers. Now all were dead within a week of each other. But they passed into Legion legend together as well. Their coffins lay in state at Sidi-bel-Abbès as the 1st Regiment paraded before the Monument aux Morts. A plaque in the Legion museum at Aubagne commemorates the three Hungarians who joined the Legion in their teens and were dead before the age of 33.

Meanwhile the rift between Algiers and Paris was widening. High-ranking officers who had backed de Gaulle's return to power were stunned when the new president, on 16 September 1959,

Legion training remains tough and demanding. Here live ammunition is used during an amphibious warfare exercise.

announced his alternatives for Algeria – independence, complete union with France or self-government under French aegis. Openly critical of de Gaulle for offering self-determination, tough General Massu was relieved of his command early in 1960. Angry Europeans in Algiers, feeling betrayed, barricaded themselves in buildings and openly defied the gendarmes. Dozens on both sides died in these demonstrations and finally the Army paras were called in to restore order in the city. These men, missing their old leader Massu, hardly knew which side to support. But even more confused and divided were the Legionnaires. For six years they had hunted down the FLN rebels in the deserts, mountains and towns, but now that they were finally getting the upper hand, de Gaulle talked of handing over the whole country to them. Most of all, doubt was creeping into their minds about the fate of the Legion itself. Why had men like Jeanpierre and Tasnady died in the war to save Algeria? What of the other Legion dead at Bel-Abbès? The idea of the Legion without Algeria seemed unthinkable.

On 4 November, in a radio and TV broadcast, de Gaulle let the blow fall: 'Having resumed the leadership of France, I have decided in her name to follow the path that leads no longer to Algeria governed by Metropolitan France but to an Algerian Algeria . . . an Algeria which, if the Algerians so wish . . . will have its government, its institutions, and its laws.' As of 1961, the rebels

would have their independence.

This announcement shocked and horrified the Legion, especially the paras of the 1st REP who did not even answer reveille the next morning. 'Why,' asked their officers, 'hunt down the men who will soon take over Algeria?' A month later Lieutenant Roger Degueldre left the regiment and dropped out of sight. Technically, this made him a deserter – but no man in the outfit would have reported him. This resourceful and determined young officer began to lead a clandestine existence, canvassing the younger para officers to find out if they would take part in an attempt to retain Algeria for France. He made many trips in disguise between Algiers and Paris to keep the senior military officers privy to the mood of the army in general – and the Legion in particular. In Paris secret groups of military men were meeting to figure out ways to reverse de Gaulle's Algerian policy. In Algeria, generals like Edmond Jouhaud – and even Maurice Challe himself – were waiting for some propitious moment to countervene the de Gaulle declaration. Many civilian leaders of the FAF (French Algerian Front) fully expected the Legion's paras to take over Algiers.

By mid-April 1961, the secret group of senior military men in Paris had decided to stage a rebellion to take Algeria by force. General Challe himself would lead it, backed by other generals including Jouhaud and André Zeller. They were promised support from the 1st REP, two Legion cavalry regiments and two army para regiments. The putsch would be launched in Algiers on 20 April. The aim was to seize power, finish the war against the FLN and set up a French Algerian state along democratic lines.

When army headquarters fell into their hands on 22 April, the 1st REP had virtually taken over Algiers. Inside two hours they had possession of every key center of power. With 50 officers and 8000 men, Generals Challe, Jouhaud and Zeller congratulated themselves on pulling off a successful coup d'état. Now paras in mottled combat dress and green berets patrolled the streets and guarded the main civil and military buildings in the city. At Constantine and Oran similar coups had been staged. However, a few thousand troops holding three or four towns did not mean that all Algeria was theirs. Where, in fact, was the revolt to go from here? There was talk by some leaders of urging Challe to drop paras on Paris itself before de Gaulle could take countermeasures, but at this wild plan, Challe demurred.

In fact, Legion General Paul Gardy had not been successful in swinging the whole Legion behind the Challe take-over. Generals and colonels who had promised to back the revolt with their units now waited to see what would happen. After three days, de Gaulle denounced the rebellion and ordered every French soldier in Algeria to obey his government. Challe himself and others now lost heart, realizing that the majority of army officers and their men were listening to

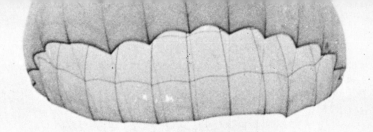

existence some weeks before the army uprising. Its aim was to keep Algeria within the French union and to contest de Gaulle's Algerian policy. Among its members were such dissident generals as Salan and Gardy. At no time did the OAS have more than 3000 members, of whom only 1000 were combatants, but during the next two years its brutal campaign of physical and psychological violence brought Algeria to the verge of civil war, poisoned Franco-Algerian relations and split the country into two camps. Ex-Legion officer Roger Degueldre himself became the strong man of the OAS Action and Operations Bureau. Calling himself by the code-name Delta, he divided up his 100 subversive Legionnaires into commando cells armed with guns, revolvers and plastic explosives which terrorized FLN meeting places and homes. But in the end Algeria achieved its independence, and Degueldre was caught, tried and executed by a firing squad in July 1963.

After Algerian Independence Day in 1962, the Foreign Legion was given four months to pull up stakes and erase all traces of its long presence in Algeria. The French government decided to scatter combat units of the Legion to such places as Madagascar, Djibouti and Corsica. It also designated a new Legion headquarters at Aubagne, just east of Marseilles. In its four-month grace period, the Legion set about shipping to Aubagne the symbols and relics of its long and proud history. Stone by stone they dismantled their Monument aux Morts and erected it anew on the parade ground at Aubagne – facing south toward Africa.

On the evening of 24 October 1963, the 700 remaining Legionnaires stood at attention for their last formal parade in the square at Sidi-bel-Abbès. All carried torches. An officer paid tribute to the dead they were leaving behind them. In the square two black silk flags were spread out; they had been taken from the Chinese during the siege of Tuyan Quang in 1885. In the will of the officer who had captured these flags was a stipulation that should the Legion ever quit Algeria the two flags must never accompany it to France. A Legionnaire lit his torch, knelt and applied the flame to the flags. Then the 700 men also lit their torches and sang 'Le Boudin' as they watched the dwindling flames flicker out in the twilight.

After the Algerian revolt the Legion parachute units were reorganized and paratroop training is still carried out by Legionnaires as in this exercise in the 1960s.

Paris and not Algiers. The next day Challe announced his decision to surrender himself. Except for some Legionnaires like Roger Degueldre, who were determined to fight on for French Algeria, most who had taken part in the coup climbed into their trucks and returned to their barracks. But many wept as they did so. It was not long before the worst offenders, the 1st REP, found their camp at Zeralda ringed with Sherman tanks and gendarmes.

Their officers were told that they must consider themselves prisoners and de Gaulle himself ordered the 1st REP to repair to Bel-Abbès, where it was to be disbanded. The 1st's commanding officer handed over the regiment to the authorities; as officers shook every man's hand, many Legionnaires wrenched off their medals and threw them to the ground. So the 1st Foreign Parachute Regiment was no more. In the summer of 1961, Challe and Zeller stood trial and were sentenced to fifteen years' imprisonment.

More than a dozen Legion officers went underground in Algeria and France to continue fighting for the dream of a French Algeria. Most of these allied themselves with the OAS (Secret Army Organization), which had proclaimed its

The Green Berets

In Vietnam the Green Berets were faced with a new kind of struggle – an ultimately unsuccessful struggle to win hearts and minds and to help uncertain allies to defeat a determined and aggressive enemy.

The United States Army's Green Berets date back to the organization of the First Special Service Force. Formed on 9 July 1942 at Fort William Henry Harrison in Montana, this unit came to be called the 'Devil's Brigade' by its German opponents. A joint American-Canadian unit, it was raised and commanded by Major General Robert Frederick. The force was originally organized for sabotage operations in occupied Norway, but was sent instead to Europe. There one of its most famous operations was a savage six-day battle for Monte La Difensa in the Mount Maggiore hill mass, an important obstacle to the progress of General Mark Clark's 5th US Army up the Italian peninsula from Naples. The 'Devil's Brigade' later saw action in France, where it was subsequently inactivated. The crossed arrows and distinctive unit insignia of the present-day Special Forces was first authorized for the Special Service Force by the Secretary of War on 26 February 1942.

After World War II the US Army Special Forces came into their own again in 1952, when the original 10th Special Forces Group, comman-

ded by Colonel Aaron Bank, was activated at Fort Bragg, North Carolina. Bank was doubtless somewhat disappointed at the size of his new command, which consisted of only one officer, one warrant officer and eight enlisted men; the Army Chief of Staff had authorized 2500 men. Undaunted, Bank moved his sparse unit into the newly formed Psychological Warfare Center at Bragg and began training. Within nine months over 1000 new members had joined his fledgling force. Many of these were former members of the Rangers and the Office of Strategic Services (OSS), looking for an outfit in which they could train for the unconventional kind of warfare that had been used so successfully in World War II and Korea.

These new SFers soon boasted that they were the modern Army elite because they were trained in every aspect of warfare. They knew jungle fighting, underwater operations, demolitions and airborne operations. They also claimed familiarity with just about any foreign weapon. Almost constantly in the field, these soldiers learned to function in every sort of climate and terrain. In

Opposite: A Special Forces officer and one of his men serving as advisers to the South Vietnamese forces near a village called Thoi Binh in 1964.

An American Special Forces adviser and a group of Vietnamese officers discuss plans for a road clearing operation in 1964. Despite the best efforts of the Special Forces men, the Vietnamese forces were often badly led by their officers.

November 1953 the Group was split and half were deployed to Bad Tölz, West Germany, where they moved into Flint Kaserne, a large complex where elite SS troops had once been billeted. These men retained the 10th Special Forces Group designation, while those remaining at Fort Bragg became the 77th Group. This latter unit emphasized the flexibility of Special Forces with their motto 'Anything, any time, any place, anyhow!'

As the 10th Group became well established in Germany, a new item of headgear began to appear among its members – a green beret. These distinctive caps had sometimes been seen on SF soldiers back at Bragg, as indeed had such other unauthorized headgear as cowboy hats, sock hats and hunters' caps – but only in the field. They were never worn with Class A uniform or in public places. But the men of the 10th had adopted the beret with all uniforms – and their Group commander okayed it in 1954. At Bragg Colonel Edson Raff, commander of the Psychological Warfare Center, was also making an effort to turn the green beret into an authorized item, a campaign he waged throughout the Special Forces' early history. He was more successful in getting approval on the distinctive shoulder patch that is still worn today. But the fight for the green beret would not be won until 1961.

In 1956 the PSYWAR Center's name was changed to the Special Warfare Center, with classes in several phases of unconventional warfare. SF soldiers were trained in five basic military occupational specialties: US and foreign weapons, medical techniques, engineering, com-

munications and intelligence operations. Another major SF unit, the 1st Special Forces Group, was activated on 17 June 1957 and stationed at Okinawa to train men for duty in Taiwan, Thailand and later Vietnam and Laos. By 1959 more and more SF soldiers were assigned to Southeast Asia for temporary duty. They worked in advisory roles with the forces of the countries there as the conflicts in the area continued to grow.

Back in the States in June 1960, the old 77th Group was redesignated the 7th Group. At the same time came the activation of the 1st Special Forces as the parent of all existing Groups. This brought the 1st, 7th and 10th Groups into the same command. Before long the new 7th Group was also providing men for duty in Vietnam, as the United States' role there increased. As the Army's Special Forces entered its second decade, it was well prepared for what seemed to be inevitable – open and bitter war in Southeast Asia.

Although it was just beginning to become involved in this fighting in Vietnam, Special Forces had another tussle on its hands back in the US – the hitherto unsuccessful push for authorization of the green beret as standard headgear. It was to be resolved only in the following year, as a result of events in Southeast Asia.

In 1959 and 1960 the insurgents in South Vietnam – known to the South Vietnamese as Viet Cong (a contraction for Vietnamese Communists) – had grown alarmingly in number and in their power to terrorize the people. Thirty Special Forces instructors had been sent from Fort Bragg to South Vietnam in May 1960 to set up a training program for the Vietnamese Army. The following year, on 21 September, President John F. Kennedy announced a program to provide additional military and economic aid to Vietnam and began to show particular interest in the Army's Special Forces. His enthusiasm, based on his conviction that these units had great potential as a counterinsurgency force, led him to become a very powerful advocate. The President himself made a visit to the Special Warfare Center to review the program, and it was by his authorization that the Special Forces troops were finally allowed to wear the green beret, effective September 1961.

Up to 1961 the government of South Vietnam and the US Mission in Saigon, in dealing with the insurgency, had put primary emphasis on developing the regular military forces, which largely excluded the ethnic minority groups of the country. But in late 1961 several programs were initiated to develop the paramilitary potential of some of these groups, primarily the numerous Montagnards who lived in the strategic Central Highlands. Special Forces detachments were assigned to provide training and advisory assistance to these programs, which eventually came to be known collectively as the Civilian Irregular Defense Group (CIDG) program. The develop-

ment of paramilitary forces among these groups became the primary mission of the Special Forces in Vietnam.

Actually, US Special Forces occupied an unusual position vis-à-vis the South Vietnamese Army, the Vietnamese Special Forces and the indigenous population involved in the CIDG program. The rules of engagement specified that the SF troops would serve in a purely advisory capacity to the Vietnamese Special Forces, which was charged with the direct command responsibility for the CIDG Group. Except for special instances, the Americans were there to assist them – not to assume any command. In practice, however, Americans often had to – and did – assume direct command later on. One of the factors involved in this was the mutual mistrust and dislike between the civilian irregulars, especially the Montagnards, and the Vietnamese military men who were commanding them.

The basic structure of the Special Forces Group (Airborne) consisted of a headquarters and headquarters company, three or more line SF companies, a signal company and an aviation detachment. The headquarters units encompassed all the staff sections for command and control, as well as the major portion of the group medical functions and the parachute rigging and

A Special Forces instructor supervises firing practice by a group of Montagnard tribesmen at Plei Yt training center in February 1963.

Left: A sergeant from the 5th Special Forces Group gives instruction in the use of a grenade launcher to a Vietnamese member of the Civilian Irregular Defense Group at Trai Trung Sup in 1967.

Above: A US Special Forces adviser carefully removes a bazooka shell from the firing tube after an inexperienced Vietnamese soldier had rammed it home too far during an engagement with the Viet Cong in January 1964.

Main picture: A Special Forces officer calls in a situation report while on patrol with a Vietnamese unit near An Khe in 1969.

The Special Forces' task was often complicated by poor Vietnamese supply arrangements which meant that Vietnamese troops alienated local support by requisitioning food.

air delivery elements. The line SF company was commanded by a lieutenant colonel and was normally composed of an administrative detachment and an operations detachment C. This C detachment, or team, commanded in turn three operational detachment Bs. Each B, in its turn, commanded four operational detachment As, which were the basic 12-man units of the Special Forces. It was in these small A, B or C teams that the Green Berets conducted their advisory missions. Eventually, the 5th Group had such teams located throughout the whole of South Vietnam, from the wide plain of the Mekong Delta region up to the edge of the Demilitarized Zone (DMZ). In the early years of SF involvement in Vietnam, the philosophy of how best to employ the US forces was implemented and adjusted on a practical basis. Both the US and South Vietnamese governments were dealing with a Communist-inspired insurgency, and for the United States it was a new experience. Many local tactics were

tried on the 'let's-see-what-happens' principle. If something worked, then it became an acceptable counterinsurgency tactic; if it did not, it was simply dropped.

The Special Forces also found itself playing a peculiar role in South Vietnam – one far different from that foreseen for it when it was created in the 1950s. At that time, its troops were trained to wage unconventional war under conventional war conditions. The war in Vietnam, however, never fell neatly into the conventional category. 'Enemy or enemy-controlled territory' was the countryside of South Vietnam itself, the government of which had invited the US military presence. Yet the enemy insurgents – the Viet Cong – were themselves guerrillas. Far from waging guerrilla warfare against conventional forces in enemy territory, the SF soldiers found themselves in the position of trying to put down guerrilla insurgency in 'friendly' territory. At first, the CIDG program was concerned with what was called 'area development.' The aim was to provide a certain area with security from 'VC' influence and terrorism, to help the people to create their own defenses and, if possible, to enlist support for the Vietnamese government from its own outlying citizens. Operations necessarily took an offensive course only because many of the rural areas involved were already controlled by the VC. One of the main reasons for the creation of the CIDG program was that the Montagnards and other minority groups were prime targets for Communist propaganda – partly because of their dissatisfaction with the Vietnamese government – and it was vital to prevent the VC from recruiting them and taking complete control of their large and strategic land holdings.

In 1961 the danger of Viet Cong domination of the whole highlands region of South Vietnam was very real. Vietnamese Army efforts to secure this vast stretch of land, which was a natural buffer zone between north and south, had been ineffective. The Communists, on the other hand, continued to exploit this buffer zone and would eventually use it as a springboard into the more densely populated areas. Not only had the Vietnamese made no attempt to gain the support of the Montagnards and other minority groups like the Nungs, but it had actually antagonized them in the past. Dissatisfaction among the Montagnards reached a point where in 1958 one of the principal tribes, the Rhade (Rah-day), organized a passive protest march. Vietnamese officials reacted by confiscating the tribesmen's crossbows and spears, an action that further alienated the Montagnards. At this time in South Vietnam, there were some thirty of these tribes, numbering some 200,000 people.

With the permission of the Vietnamese government, the US Mission, in the fall of 1961, decided to try to win over these people. It approached the Rhade tribal leaders with a proposition that offered them weapons and training if they would declare for the South Vietnamese government and participate in a village self-defense program. The village of Buon Enao in Darlac Province, with a population of some 400 Rhade, was chosen. Under Green Beret advisors, the villagers erected a fence around Buon Enao as a protection against Viet Cong attackers, and as a visible sign to other tribes that they had chosen to participate in the program. Shelters were dug within the village where women and children could take refuge in case of attack, housing was constructed for a training center and a dispensary was set up to provide much-needed medical aid promised by the US Mission. An intelligence system was established to control movement in and out of the village and provide warning of attacks.

Three weeks later the Buon Enao villagers publicly pledged that no Viet Cong would enter their village or receive assistance of any kind. Meanwhile, fifty volunteers from a nearby village

Rhade that in time they even began recruiting among themselves.

Soon the program was expanded into the rest of Darlac Province, with new centers at Ea Ana, Lac Tien, Buon Tah and other settlements. By August 1962 the CIDG program encompassed 200 villages, and additional Green Berets and Vietnamese Special Forces took part. The Buon Enao program was considered a resounding success, and strike forces accepted the training and weapons enthusiastically; they also became strongly motivated to oppose the Viet Cong, against whom they fought well. Toward the end of 1962, the government declared all of Darlac Province secure. At this time it was decided by American planners to practice what later became known as 'Vietnamization'; that is, the program would be turned over to the Darlac Province chief, who would use his own people thereafter to extend the defense and strike force program to

Below left: Special Forces advisers eat with their Vietnamese unit during a pause while on patrol near Duc Khanh in December 1965.

had been brought in for training as a local security or strike force to protect Buon Enao and its immediate environs. Permission was obtained from the chief of Darlac Province to extend the CIDG program to forty other Rhade villages within a radius of about 15 kilometers. The chiefs and subchiefs of these villages went to Buon Enao for training in village defense, and were told that they too must build barbed-wire fences around their villages and declare their willingness to support the Vietnamese government. With this expansion of the CIDG program, half a Special Forces A detachment (1st Special Forces Group) and several members of the Vietnamese Special Forces were brought in to assist in training village defenders and the full-time strike force. The composition of the Vietnamese Special Forces at Buon Enao was always at least 50 percent Montagnard. By the middle of April 1962, all forty villages were incorporated into the CIDG program. The program became so popular with the

other tribal groups, such as the Jarai and Mnong. During their near decade in Southeast Asia, the Green Berets were to play a Vietnamization role with other groups as well, among them the Numgs and the Cao Dai. The soldiers shared the life of the natives and advised and assisted many innocent victims of fire, flood, famine, disease and poverty.

By the end of 1962, the US Special Forces in Vietnam consisted of one C detachment, three B detachments and 26 A detachments. There was also a headquarters unit in Saigon. About this time the decision was also made to carry out Operation Switchback, in which the Army would assume all responsibility for US participation in the Civilian Irregular Defense Group, including training and operations. It also, of course, included control of all Green Beret units. By December 1963 Special Forces detachments, working through counterpart Vietnamese Special Forces units, had trained and armed 18,000

Above: Two Special Forces sergeants confer with a Vietnamese interpreter during an operation in the Central Plateau area in 1964.

men as strike force troops and over 43,000 as 'hamlet militia,' the new name for village defenders. As part of Operation Switchback, headquarters of the US Army Special Forces (Provisional), was moved to Nha Trang on the coast. This new location, situated halfway between the 17th parallel and the southern tip of the country, was more accessible to Green Beret detachments throughout Vietnam, and it afforded good facilities for unloading supply ships from Okinawa.

By the end of 1964 the Montagnard program was no longer an area development program in the original sense of the term. There was a shift in emphasis from expanding village defense systems to the primary use of CIDG camps or centers as bases for offensive strike-force operations against the VC. Higher headquarters now wanted to supplement the government pacification program with intensified counterguerrilla warfare. Security and camp defense took precedence over civil action, and much stress was laid on the role of CIDG strike forces as 'VC hunters.' A second major shift in mission gave greater importance to border surveillance.

Viet Cong reaction to the expansion of the CIDG program at first took the form of simple harassment or occasional probing fire. But as Operation Switchback was being completed, the VC stepped up their resistance. In 1963 an attack in strength by two reinforced VC ccompanies overran the camp at Plei Mrong. After this there was an increase in camp security everywhere, with secondary defensive systems set up inside the outer perimeter.

In the mid-1960s, however, the turnover or

Vietnamization process was not going as well as had been hoped. The turnover of a CIDG camp to the Vietnamese Special Forces often resulted in the absorption of the irregulars into Vietnamese Army units. The latter often resented this, for there was still mutual suspicion and hostility between the Vietnamese and the Montagnards. For this and other reasons, Montagnard resentment flared into an armed uprising in September 1964. The Montagnards struck in five CIDG camps, killing some Vietnamese Special Service troops. But Special Forces soldiers, acting as intermediaries, succeeded in calming down the Montagnards, and most insurgents returned to their base camps a few days later. The following month such Montagnard demands as representation in the National Assembly were largely granted by the government.

This uprising forced a reevaluation of the CIDG program and placed new emphasis on developing more satisfactory Vietnamization techniques. There were also several developments in the area of combat operations during the period between 1963 and 1965 – just before the extensive buildup of conventional US forces. These were important in that they laid the foundation for the combat operations that would characterize the SF civilian irregulars in the final years of the Vietnam war – 1965 to 1970. A continued emphasis was placed on the offensive role of strike forces in both area development and border-surveillance operations, but the latter were not as effective as the planners had hoped. The Viet Cong were clever enough to avoid contact on the border, where their purposes were

Two Vietnamese members of the CIDG return to the 5th Special Forces camp after a night patrol, Mekong River Delta, 1967.

Below: A member of the 1st Special Forces Group looks out from the unit's hilltop camp in Vietnam.

Right: A map showing the main areas of fighting in Vietnam and the American operational zones.

DONG HOI

NORTH VIETNAM

SOUTH CHINA SEA

KHE SANH   CA LU   DONG HA
                     QUANG TRI

SAVANNAKHET   LANG VEI   **HUE**

L A O S

A SHAU

DA NANG
HOI AN
DUY XUYEN

I

THAILAND

PAKSE

KHAM DUC

QUANG NGAI
DUC PHO

DAK TO

KONTUM

PLEIKU

AN KHE   **QUI NHON**

SOUTH

II

C A M B O D I A

Tonle Sap

KOMPONG
THOM

VIETNAM

BAN ME THUOT

NHA TRANG

KOMPONG
CHAM

DALAT

Cam Ranh Bay

AN LOC

BAO LOC

**PHNOM
PENH**

Mekong

TAY NINH

III

BIEN HOA
XUAN LOC

Bassac

SAIGON

PHAN THIET

CHAU DOC

KAMPOT

LONG XUYEN

SA DEC

MY THO

VUNG TAU

CAN THO

VINH
LONG

BEN TRE

Mekong
Delta

IV

CA MAU

	AREAS IN SOUTH VIETNAM SPARSELY POPULATED
	AREAS IN SOUTH VIETNAM WITH MORE THAN 150 PEOPLE PER SQUARE MILE
	MAIN GUERRILLA ACTIONS
	AREAS OF PROLONGED CONFRONTATION
I	CORPS TACTICAL ZONES

0   MILES   150
0   KILOMETERS   250

© Richard Natkiel, 1982

Above: An American adviser rests while Vietnamese units up ahead check that no ambush has been set on the road.

Right: A Special Forces instructor of the 5th Special Forces Group teaches hand-to-hand combat to Vietnamese CIDG members.

served if their main force units, replacements and supply columns could simply cross undetected.

There were also command problems. Vietnamese Special Forces men normally served as strike-force commanders both in the CIDG camps and on active missions in the field. On patrol, however, the VSF often bungled or renounced this role, with command then going to a Green Beret officer or non-com by default. In some instances, the good rapport that readily developed between the Special Forces and the strike-force troops tended to diminish the authority of the VSF to the vanishing point in the chain of command.

To remedy these and other tactical deficiencies, new programs were initiated by Saigon authorities in mid-1964. The first of these was Project Leaping Lena, under which SF A detachments trained VSF and CIDG troops in techniques of long-range reconnaissance patrolling. In time Leaping Lena became Project Delta, the first of the special operations that would come to be the most powerful and effective combat operations of the Vietnam War. A project force was organized into a reconnaissance element and a reaction force, the latter being the equivalent of a battalion with three or more companies. Another special operations force created at this time was the mobile strike force. It consisted of highly

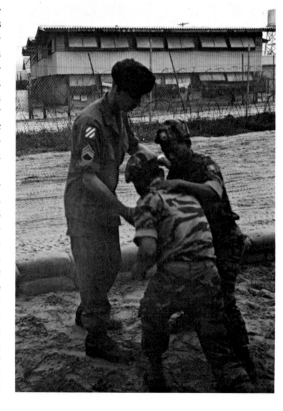

trained CIDG units organized into separate companies at Special Forces company and base levels for use as reserve and reinforcement elements to CIDG camps threatened or under attack by superior numbers of the enemy. Mobile strike forces were also capable of conducting raids, ambushes, combat patrols and other small-scale combat operations. They were also airborne qualified. Mobile strike forces were always flexible in their organization, but a typical company would have a headquarters element, three rifle platoons, a weapon platoon and a recon platoon. From the mobile strike force concept, during the period 1966-67, would evolve Projects Sigma and Omega, which had good success in carrying the guerrilla war to the enemy.

Meanwhile, through 1964 and 1965, VC operations in the vicinity of CIDG camps continued at a high level of intensity. Due to careless security and VC infiltration, camps at Hiep Hoa and Polei Krong were overrun in the early summer of 1964. Then the Viet Cong attempted a similar raid on the 300-member strike force at Nam Dong on 6 July with a reinforced battalion of several hundred men. It opened with a mortar barrage followed by three savage ground assaults. The VC had approached across a river and an airstrip, and surprise had been complete. As the shattering barrage lifted, the first VC attack rolled over the outer perimeter. Strike troops within – many of them Nungs – fought well, manning machine guns and defending communications trenches. The VC had crept up to breach the lines of barbed wire through the tall grass, so that they could toss grenades into a heavy mortar emplacement. This emplacement was the scene of heroic action when the Green Beret commander, Captain Roger Donlon, himself wounded, repeatedly attempted to rescue a wounded team member. For his gallantry Donlon was awarded the first Medal of Honor since the Korean War, conferred on him by President Lyndon Johnson some months later. The defenders at Nam Dong cut down many of the enemy as they attempted to breach the barbed wire of the camp's inner perimeter; their ammunition was almost gone when the VC finally withdrew at daylight. Close examination of the enemy dead suggested that the attacking force had been beefed up by special shock troops comprised of well-set-up and muscular young men.

In the early years, the CIDG program was essentially a defensive effort aimed at strengthening indigenous minorities and winning their allegiance so they would not fall to the Communists. The mission was to control the Viet Cong, through either area development or border surveillance or both. The civilian irregulars and Green Berets were not hunting the VC in the beginning. However, with the massive American commitment to, and buildup of, conventional forces in South Vietnam in 1965, all this changed. It opened the door to the next stage in the evolution of the Special Forces CIDG program – one in

which they would find themselves cast in a distinctly offensive role. They were now to become the hunters, with the mission of searching out and destroying the Viet Cong and the North Vietnamese Army.

Of course, the conventional US forces were also there to defeat the enemy, but American soldiers arriving in Vietnam found themselves in an environment entirely different from anything they had ever experienced. They were not used to the tropical rain, heat and jungles, nor did they know much about the Vietnamese people. Most importantly, they did not know who or where the enemy was, or how to search him out. By contrast, the Special Forces soldiers and their irregular troops were accustomed to the jungle and the climate, could communicate with the people and were familiar with their culture. Participation by SF men in tribal and ceremonial functions was not at all uncommon, and many a Green Beret wore the Montagnard bracelet presented to him by the tribe with which he worked as a token of its respect. This is where the Special Forces men took on an added responsibility – familiarizing and guiding the conventional forces in a land new to them and a concept of war foreign to them. They and their irregulars were by now trained guerrillas themselves, capable of meeting the enemy on their own terms.

By mid-1965 the Green Berets of the 5th Group had assumed wide-ranging tasks. These included assistance to civilian agencies in dredging canals in enemy-controlled villages and in building schools, hospitals and meeting halls. But fighting

Vietnamese volunteers are instructed in the use of hand grenades at the 1st Special Forces Group camp at Nui Ba Den in 1964.

Above: The modern Special Forces soldier trains for covert operations behind enemy lines. Shown are men of the 18th Special Forces Group practicing cross-country ski operations.

Opposite: A soldier of the 11th Special Forces Group camouflaged and equipped for jungle warfare.

was now their main mission, and many attacks like the one at Nam Dong were repelled at Dong Xoai, Plei Me and several other camps. For heroism at Dong Xoai, Lieutenant Charles Williams received the 5th Group's second Medal of Honor. But the year 1965 was also one of many casualties.

Combat actions during the period 1965-68 fell into three main categories. First, there were the actions connected with the opening, closing or defending of CIDG camps, especially those along the border. Battles were fought at camps A Shau, Lang Vie, Con Thien, Thuong Thoi and Bu Dop. These ran to a pattern: when a camp became a real nuisance to the enemy, he was likely to attack it in great strength in an attempt to destroy it. Otherwise the camps were left alone, and any contacts were the result of sending out patrols from the camp.

Second, there were combat actions that grew out of larger special operations, including Project Delta operations in I Corps; Blackjack 33 operations in III Corps under Project Sigma – the first action in which mobile guerrilla forces were employed in conjunction with a project force; Blackjack 41, in which two mobile strike-force companies conducted a parachute assault in the Seven Mountains area of IV Corps; and a mobile strike-force action carried out in III Corps area around Soui Da, in which the force was credited with rendering the VC ineffective. The latter eventually developed into Operation Attleboro.

Finally, the third type of action took place when CIDG troops were used in tandem with conventional forces in conventional combat operations. Among these were Operation Nathan Hale, jointly conducted by CIDG forces, the 1st Cavalry Division and the 101st Airborne Division; Operations Henry Clay and Thayer; Operation Rio Blanco in I Corps, involving CIDG troops, Vietnam Army and Ranger troops, Korean Marines and US Marines; and Operation Sam Houston in II Corps, conducted by the 4th Infantry Division and CIDG troops. In addition, CIDG troops and Special Forces soldiers played a vital part in the defeat of the 1968 Tet Offensive. The border surveillance camps, with their strike forces cutting severely into enemy infiltration and supply routes, bore the brunt of these attacks. At Camp Ben Het, especially, the CIDG troops encountered one of the heaviest attacks of the offensive.

While a strong effort was made to increase the number of these operations, command emphasis during this period centered on improving techniques in three chief ways – and these efforts were to pay off handsomely. First, it was hoped to increase pressure on the enemy with solid intelligence rather than random search methods. Via a new procedure adopted by the 5th Special Forces Group, a map-plot of all enemy sightings within each camp's area of activity was kept. Superimposed over this plot was a second plot of all company search-and-destroy operations conducted by the camp. At the end of each month, an analysis of these plots soon revealed whether the camps were in fact operating properly. Second, an effort was made to conduct operations over a greater range of territory and to sustain them longer; special long-range recon platoons were developed for this purpose. Third, both the Vietnamese Special Forces and 5th Group headquarters directed that in all cases operations were to begin and, where feasible, end during the hours of darkness – a tactic long employed by the enemy. The only exceptions were those heliborne, reaction and other special operations that had to be carried out during daylight periods. By the spring of 1967 well over 90 percent of the actions conducted by units subordinate to, and advised by, the 5th SF Group began at night.

This new program effected a marked increase in the number of enemy contacts developed by the CIDG, a decrease in the number of enemy attacks on installations and a growing confidence

on the part of VSFs and irregulars in their own ability to operate at night. The increase in the number of enemy killed – by actual body counts – and the comparative decrease in Special Forces and CIDG losses were directly attributable to the improved techniques. By carrying the fight to the enemy instead of waiting for him to pick his own situation, the Green Berets and irregulars were able to use their supporting fire effectively against an often surprised and unprepared opponent.

The rapid reaction capability of the mobile strike forces in camp defense was no better illustrated than in the action at Bu Dop in 1967. From January through March of that year, repeated contact with the North Vietnamese forces was made in this vicinity in the Phuoc Long Province of III Corps. On 14 January one CIDG company from Bu Dop, accompanied by two Green Berets and two Vietnamese Special Forces men, left the camp with the mission of conducting a search-and-destroy operation nearby. This strike force

A Special Forces adviser watches a Vietnamese machine-gun team fire on Viet Cong positions near Ben Cat during a Vietnamese search and destroy operation in November 1964.

moved out through terrain consisting of rubber trees, bamboo thickets, dense undergrowth and savannah grass into an area where a Bu Dop recon patrol had had a brush with the enemy a few weeks before. At the sound of firing, the company immediately deployed into three files to search the area. Then the point squad took fire and suffered one killed and one wounded. Next, firing broke out all around the company, and Green Beret advisers Sergeant First Class R. Williams and Staff Sergeant J. Boorman made radio contact with a forward air controller who in turn requested air strikes. Under heavy fire from its right flank, the company lost nine more effectives – two killed and seven wounded. Williams and Boorman advised an assault from the right flank to prevent encirclement, and a momentary lull in the enemy fire enabled the company to follow this tactic.

The CIDG company then assaulted and over-ran the enemy positions, with cumulative casualties of three killed and eleven wounded. When their requested air strikes showed up, they withdrew to the west to locate a landing zone for medical evacuation. Eight hours into the mission, the air strike was made on the retreating enemy. The CIDG company then continued the assault, finding the bodies of 25 North Vietnam Army soldiers in the enemy positions. While waiting for the helicopters, the men had collected and assembled all enemy equipment and documents captured. From the east the company was still taking small-arms fire, so additional air strikes were made in that direction. With the landing zone located and secured, the medical evacuation went forward.

In his search of the area, Captain Chester Garrett found that sixteen more North Vietnam Army soldiers had been slain, and additional maps and drawings indicated that plans were afoot to attack Camp Bu Dop and the Bo Duc Subsector. Inside two hours the mobile strike force at Nha Trang had been airlifted to Bu Dop to defend the camp.

Unconventional operations were also carried out by mobile guerrilla-force units, which had essentially the same characteristics as the mobile strike forces. But they were also highly responsive to the needs of the SF companies in each of the four Corps zones, in that operational control rested with the SF company commander for the guerrilla force in his area. The troops of these mobile guerrilla forces would infiltrate an area to cut enemy supply routes, conduct surveillance, seek out enemy forces and installations and collect intelligence. VC base camps were found, watched and, if possible, raided – or at least harassed, if the enemy proved to be too strong. They also cut lines of communication by ambushes and raids and planted them with mines and booby traps.

A mobile guerrilla force was inserted into its assigned area of operations by the most unobtrusive means possible. Once there, the unit became a true guerrilla force in every respect except that of living solely off the land. Resupply items were delivered by air. The force operated from mobile bases, and its troops were capable of remaining and operating in a particular area for thirty to sixty days. Such a force also required complete freedom of action within its area in order to achieve success. For this reason, once an area was designated for conducting an operation, the mobile guerrilla 'owned' that area – including control of area support. Blackjack 33, a typical unconventional operation, was carried out between 27 April and 25 May 1967 in the III Corps area. It was the first operation in which a mobile guerrilla force was used in conjunction with the long-range reconnaissance capability of a project force – in this case, Project Sigma. This operation was highly effective, with 320 of the enemy killed.

Infiltration by helicopter in Vietnam was best accomplished at last light, when the pilots could still see well enough to insert a guerrilla force and have a few minutes to slip away from the landing zone as both force and helicopters were enveloped by darkness. Since the enemy was familiar with this method of infiltration, it was necessary to deceive him as to the exact point of landing. The helicopters often set down briefly at three or more points in the vicinity of the landing zone to create uncertainty in the enemy's mind as to the exact point of insertion. However, the VC adopted simple but often effective countermeasures against helicopter infiltration. Chief among these was planting long bamboo poles upright in jungle clearings potentially useful as landing zones. Or they would densely cover such clearings with punji stakes. Under some circumstances, infiltration of guerrilla forces was best accomplished on foot. Roadrunner and recon teams were quite easily inserted into a reconnaissance zone from a base camp under cover of darkness, or even during daylight hours if the camp was known to dispatch small patrols in random directions as a matter of routine.

The chief task of the Special Forces during the last two and a half years of the 5th Group's stay in South Vietnam was to complete the turnover of the Civilian Irregular Defense Group program to the Vietnamese. The Vietnamese Special Forces, however, had been slow to develop soldiers of high professional skill, partly because the introduction of large US regular military forces had made the war a more conventional conflict. Still, the 5th SF Group continued to place strong emphasis on delegating responsibility to the Vietnamese. While the aim of conventional forces was to win the war, the goal of the Special Forces was to help the South Vietnamese win what was really their war – and that goal was never forgotten. The increased tempo of the war after the 1968 Tet Offensive did not permit the Vietnamese armed forces to take over border surveillance until 1970. But even before that it was apparent to both the Military Assistance Command, Vietnam, and the Vietnamese Joint

General Staff that the Army of Vietnam had reached a level of competence that would enable it to take over the CIDG program, with its missions of border surveillance and interdiction of the enemy.

As for the US Special Forces troops they were in combat right up to the day they left the country. New camps were built and old ones were fortified and strengthened in preparation for the Vietnamese takeover. Then, on 14 January 1971, the 5th Special Forces Group received its official notification for stand-down and redeployment to the United States. As roll-up operations were carried out, Vietnamization of all CIDG units proceeded simultaneously. On 1 March the 5th Special Forces honor guard left the Nha Trang air base, with the rest of the Green Beret units soon to follow. In a ceremony conducted at the Green Beret Statue at the John F. Kennedy Center on 5 March, the 5th Group returned its colors after nearly a decade of combat.

Although their mission had ended in Vietnam, the Berets soon demonstrated that they could be an important asset to the nation during peacetime. After their return to Fort Bragg, they launched a campaign of intensified civic action programs. The program was called SPARTAN, an acronym for Special Proficiency at Rugged Training and Nation-Building. The 5th and 7th Groups worked with Indian tribes in Florida, Arizona and Montana to improve their living conditions and built roads and medical facilities for them.

Special Forces active duty units today include the 5th and 7th Groups at Fort Bragg; the 10th Group at Fort Devens, Massachusetts; and a detachment in West Germany. Still maintaining their rigorous training programs and high standards through devotion to duty, the Green Berets remain professionals in the business of helping others in peace and war.

Special Forces troopers are trained for a range of unconventional operations. Here a frogman comes ashore after an underwater demolition exercise in 1981.

The Special
Air Service

The modern elite force must be able to raid behind enemy lines, fight a counter-revolutionary war and rescue terrorists' hostages. The SAS has performed all these roles in its short history with an enviable record of success.

The idea for the Special Air Service originated with Lieutenant David Stirling, a British commando officer, early in World War II. When his own commando unit was disbanded in North Africa, Stirling and a few brother officers began to think of other ways to hit Germany's extended supply lines in the Western Desert. Since one approach would be by dropping small teams of parachutists well behind enemy lines, Stirling and his friends appropriated a consignment of parachutes to make some practice jumps. On his very first drop, Stirling's chute snagged and ripped on the trailing plane, accelerating his fall. He crashed on the hard desert terrain and severely injured his back and legs.

While he was recuperating in hospital, Stirling began writing down his ideas on how strategic raids that penetrated deeply behind enemy lines could be made by small, select forces. Such raiding forces would not require the huge naval back-up entailed by full-blown commando assault units. Rather, Stirling proposed using parachute saboteurs who would be trained to inflict a level of damage to Nazi airfields equivalent to that of a

commando force twenty times greater. Further, Stirling foresaw that the number of men in such a team would ideally be four. In such small numbers, the men would tend to buddy up into two pairs, so that no one would emerge as a leader in the orthodox sense. Each man in this module would have at least one special area of expertise, as well as a knowledge of the others' fields. In an operation – often carried out in pitch darkness – each man would exercise his own individual judgment and ingenuity for the success of the mission. Only the best, most professional type of soldier would be selected for this Special Air Service, as Stirling named it. It would eventually grow to be of regimental size, but the four-man modules would not be subdivided into the usual infantry battalions but – as befitted an air service outfit – into small Squadrons. Moreover, the four-man groups would be taught to forget all sense of class and even rank. As the two-buddy pairs emerged, they would learn to share their lives like a small family – often for months on end under conditions of isolation.

When Stirling, still on crutches, left the hospit-

THE SPECIAL AIR SERVICE

Main picture: A Long Range Desert Group unit sets out on patrol in May 1942. Their vehicles are US-made Chevrolet trucks armed with an assortment of machine guns.

Below: The Italians and Germans made various efforts to intercept LRDG attacks. An Italian patrol is seen in southern Tunisia, 1942-43.

al, he was determined to 'sell' his idea to no less a personage than the Commander-in-Chief, Middle East, General Sir Claude Auchinleck. Through the latter's sympathetic deputy C-in-C, General Neil Ritchie, who saw the ingenuity of the idea, Stirling finally obtained an audience with Auchinleck. The general was enthusiastic about the scheme. Promoted to captain, Stirling was authorized to recruit some 60 men from his old commando outfit. The imposing if inaccurate title of Special Air Service Brigade was bestowed on the unit to confuse the enemy about its true size. In one of its early successful operations, an SAS unit of only a handful of men, in cooperation with the Long Range Desert Group, destroyed

more than 100 Luftwaffe planes on the ground within a few weeks. In August 1942 the SAS was expanded by the addition of a unit of French paratroops and attained regimental status as the 1st SAS Regiment. Before the war in the Western Desert was over, it had destroyed almost 400 planes and vast quantities of other war material. So successful were these soldiers that Adolf Hitler himself issued a proclamation stating: 'These men are dangerous. They must be hunted down and destroyed at all costs.'

As for Stirling, he had the misfortune to be captured in Tunisia and sat out the rest of the war in the Colditz prisoner-of-war camp. However, his brother, William, commanded a second SAS

regiment in raids on Sicily and the Italian coast, preparing the way for the Allied invasion. Later it was engaged in raiding activities throughout the Aegean, Greece and the Adriatic. In March 1944 both regular SAS regiments were brought back to England and augmented by Free French and Belgian squadrons, plus a long-distance communications unit. This combined force was designated 1 SAS Brigade. It was then decided to use the SAS to train and supply the Resistance movement in occupied France by parachuting in small reconnaissance parties. Soon after D-Day some 40 SAS bases had been established from the Channel to the Vosges, from which small modules, mostly of Stirling's four-man type, were sent out to harass enemy communications in any way they could. Railroads were blown up, highways were mined and convoys were ambushed; in addition, invaluable information on bombing targets was passed along to the RAF. Military experts later agreed that the successful SAS effort at disrupting German resistance in depth was largely responsible for Pattons 3rd Army's quick seizure of Paris. In the Low Countries and Germany, the SAS regiments were actively engaged until the end of the war. In October 1945, after a brief operation in Norway to disarm thousands of German soldiers, the wartime SAS regiments were disbanded.

Top right: Colonel Roger Keyes VC, killed in an abortive raid on Rommel's desert HQ in November 1941.

Right: German transport aircraft destroyed on their airfield. Enemy airfields were a favorite target for LRDG raids.

A British instructor works with Malayan members of a 'Ferret' unit in 1948. Trained in jungle fighting, many of the British members of Ferret units were soon absorbed into the revived SAS.

But, a few years after the war, there was a new need for the SAS. While Britain had left India and Burma, she had reoccupied the Malay Peninsula and in 1948 established its nine states as the Federation of Malaya. Soon afterward there followed a revolt by Communist guerrillas, most of whom were Chinese and inspired by the successes of Mao Tse Tung in China. Some 1200 of these guerrillas, who had managed to lay their hands on a bonanza of approximately 4000 British and captured Japanese weapons, took to the Malayan jungles and openly declared war against the 'imperialist' British. Then began a reign of terror, with executions of British and other European planters. After these raids the guerrillas melted back into the mountainous jungle which, with its miles of bamboo stands, great trees and swampy valleys, was ideal for long periods of concealment. Although the British scraped together some Gurkha battalions and other forces and wiped out a few guerrilla camps, by mid-1950 the Communist Terrorists, or CTs, as they were known, clearly had the upper hand in the war and had killed over 1300 civilians, police and soldiers.

Worried, the British finally came up with the Briggs Plan, after General Sir Harold Briggs, who put it into effect in Malaya. Essentially, the plan called for the inhabitants of over 400 villages to move to new, fortified villages. Further, it called for measures to keep food supplies from the guerrillas by every possible means. A third phase of the plan proposed to create a special military force to live in the jungle for the purpose of harassing the bandits – and denying them any sanctuary or rest by keeping pressure on them. Much of the Briggs Plan was the brainchild of an ex-World War II SAS commander named J.M. 'Mike' Calvert, and it was he who was directed to

create the special force to operate in Malaya. He called it the Malayan Scouts (SAS). After much trouble Calvert, who had called for volunteers from all units of the Army, finally got his regiment together. It was composed variously of SAS reservists, territorials, Gurkhas and even some deserters from the Foreign Legion. With its A, B and C Squadrons, the regiment's first base was Johore just north of Singapore; here they began two months' intensive training in jungle warfare. Simultaneously, Calvert chose as his first operational area the large village of Ipoh, 300 miles north of Johore. His strategy was to penetrate deep into the jungle with patrols of up to 14 men, heavily laden with supplies, and establish strong forward bases equipped with radios. From these, smaller teams of three or four men could fan out and become thoroughly familiar with large sections of jungle where ambushes could be set and bandit food-supply lanes cut.

When Mike Calvert, exhausted from his organizational efforts and also suffering from fever, was invalided home to England, the regiment was taken over by Lieutenant Colonel John Sloane in late 1951. Thanks to Calvert's recruiting program, the SAS now had four squadrons in Malaya and a headquarters section. In February 1952 an extensive parachute operation by the SAS and other units was pulled off with great success. Its objective was food denial to the guerrillas. In some jungle areas, the CTs were already feeling the effects of the Briggs Plan and had begun to grow their own crops. To accomplish this in the jungle, however, they had to clear trees from large areas to admit sunlight. To the British advantage, these clearings could be easily seen from the air and made good targets. The principal one chosen for attack was at a place called Belum Valley near the Thai frontier. As planned, two squadrons of SAS, Gurkha units, some Royal Marine commandos and Malayan police would advance on Belum Valley on foot, while an SAS squadron of 54 men would parachute into a drop zone near the area.

For the SAS parachutists involved, it was their first experience with what became known as 'tree-jumping' – which in Malaya soon became an SAS specialty. It was foreseen that some of the men would be hung up in the trees, so they were issued a hundred feet of rope which they could secure to branches or chute straps to let themselves down to the ground. They also knew that if they landed in bamboo it could splinter and cut them, and that a landing in spiked or dead trees could break their bones or necks. While there were no casualties on the Belum Valley drop, there were on almost every subsequent mission.

The effect of this and other successful raids, with the Briggs Plan of food denial, was to force the CTs even deeper into the jungles of central Malaya. Obliged to hunt the enemy in these steaming, murky regions, the SAS had another opportunity to prove its value. SAS soldiers armed with shotguns and new Patchett carbines spearheaded these operations in Pahang and Kelantan Provinces, dropping into place via parachute or helicopter. They also made their first contact with the aboriginal interior tribes, the Seman and the Sakai, who were at the mercy of the Communist terrorists. SAS teams began to win over these tribesmen, turned their villages into tiny fortresses and built landing strips for resupply. Much depended on these isolated SAS modules, whose members were often weeks and months in the jungles working with the tribesmen and selling them on the idea of self-defense.

Representative of operations from 1954 on, when the CTs were becoming concentrated in certain specific areas, was Operation Termite in the Ipoh region. Lasting from July to November, it commenced with heavy bombing of the jungle by the RAF. Two SAS squadrons were then parachuted into the clearings made by the bombs. In this and subsequent operations, several 'tree-jumping' casualties occurred. While Termite yielded the capture, death or surrender of only 15 of the enemy, its real value lay in the conversion

An instructor demonstrates how to immobilize a communist suspect at a jungle warfare training camp in Malaya.

Above: General Briggs
(in civilian clothes) who
formed the British plan of
operations arrives in
Malaya in 1950 to be met
by General Harding,
then commanding the
British Land Forces in
the Far East.

of many aborigines into firm allies. By 1956 the SAS had five squadrons – one a Parachute Regiment Squadron – totaling 560 men operating in the jungles of Malaya. The tide of the war had now changed markedly. Terrorist killings had fallen off to only a few per month and their bases were increasingly remote.

The SAS's next chance to prove itself came in late 1962, when Indonesian-fomented guerrilla attacks were launched against government installations in the Sultanate of Brunei on Borneo. Brunei, with the adjoining colonies of North Borneo and Sarawak, was a British dependency in northern Borneo. While these territories were large, they still represented only a quarter of the whole island. The other three-quarters belonged to Indonesia, whose head of state, President Sukarno, had the goal of unifying under his leadership all of Southeast Asia. The British responded to the Brunei uprising by throwing together a hasty force of Royal Marine Commandos, Gurkhas and Highlanders from Singapore. In a few weeks, order was restored in the coastal towns and hostages taken by the rebels were released. Nevertheless, it was clear that a new jungle war was about to begin.

Sensing a new job for 22 SAS, its commanding officer, Colonel John Woodhouse, offered its services in northern Borneo. General Sir Walter Walker, commanding the Borneo forces, gladly accepted the offer of an SAS squadron with the idea of using it for a mobile reserve infantry unit. Woodhouse had to explain to Walker that the SAS was not trained to fight as conventional infantry. Its particular value in Borneo would be that SAS soldiers could operate in pairs, or if necessary alone, speaking Malay which was understood on the island, to provide an intelligence and communications network in the vast jungle area. Walker agreed, and soon 22 SAS soldiers were emplaning for Borneo.

By January 1963 Sukarno had made it obvious that the campaign would not be confined to the Brunei area alone. On the contrary, Indonesian subversion would make it necessary for British forces to protect a wild and mountainous frontier some hundreds of miles long; enemy raiders could strike without warning across any vulnerable point. Teams of between two and four men from A Squadron were deployed out across a 700-mile front. Each of these teams was responsible for a front of some seven miles, so patrolled

Main picture: Parachute drops into the jungle were probably the most hazardous new technique learned by the SAS in Malaya.

Bottom: A Chinese woman places an answered questionnaire in a sealed box while British soldiers look on. Attempts to gain information about communist activity were aided if informers could expect anonimity. The SAS were particularly adept at gaining the confidence of the local population in their operational areas.

that it could block most of the natural approaches northward from Kalimantan, as Indonesian Borneo was called. Needless to say, it was impossible for these tiny teams to cover such a large area. The trick was to make friends with the jungle tribes so that they would act as scouts for the SAS men, who in turn would report back any activity by the enemy over their radios. Any such activity could then be dealt with by helicopter assault teams. Even a day-old track or a piece of equipment dropped by an enemy soldier was valuable information. Through tact, charm and courtesy, the SAS men made themselves welcome to most of these tribespeople and the system began to work well. Nearer the mountainous border, the SAS men moved into key villages and, dispensing portable radios, medical aid and other favors, made themselves part of the native community and often lived there for a number of months. Helicopter landing zones were carved out of the jungle, so that a radio message could quickly bring in a 'step-up' party of Gurkhas or Royal Marines. The villagers were trained by the SAS

men to help themselves by staying alert to any signs in the surrounding jungle, particularly the mark of a rubber-soled boot known to be worn by the enemy.

Inevitably, the British had to bring more troops and helicopters to Borneo. A search of towns in Sarawak yielded plans for the Clandestine Communist Organization (CCO) to resort to terrorist tactics, and police began confiscating shotguns in the Chinese community. On the border some cross-frontier raids were occurring from Indonesian Borneo. However, the SAS's success with the cooperative intelligence network motivated General Walker to form and train the Border Scouts. Unfortunately, they tended to function as conventional infantry rather than as intelligence gatherers, which made them vulnerable to surprise attacks. More SAS men were needed to train the scouts in preventing such raids through effective intelligence work.

In 1964 the SAS Regiment, reinforced by new men from England and Australia, began to launch its first cross-frontier recon missions between Indonesia and Brunei. The success of these patrols into Kalimantan, which marked the turning point of the war in Britain's favor, led to more ambitious operations in which the SAS found the exact river routes by which the Indonesians moved men and equipment up to the frontier. These deep-penetration teams were equipped with new, light and very powerful Armalite rifles. They were taught never to leave anything in enemy territory to betray the presence of British troops – no cigarette butts, no cartridge cases, never photos or letters from the UK – not even the heel print of a standard-issue boot.

In mid-1964, faced by increasingly bold attacks from the Indonesians, General Walker initiated what were code-named Claret operations. These were more powerful counterstrikes, first by artillery, then by 'killer' teams drawn from the best infantry battalions and led by SAS guides. Initially penetration into enemy territory was stipulated at 5000 yards, but this was increased fourfold to allow the Claret teams to forestall likely buildups or attacks, to harass the Indonesians by ambush and to force them to shift their camps back from the frontier. Inevitably, some SAS recon teams were ambushed by the enemy despite all precautions. As one SAS veteran put it, 'The man who is stationary in the jungle has the tactical advantage. We sometimes found it necessary to spend as much as twenty minutes in any half-hour period sitting and listening, and only ten minutes on the move.'

The last Indonesian invasion, by 50 enemy troops into a Sarawak area near Brunei, ended in disaster for them. It was an enemy coffee-can label that put a Gurkha battalion on their track. The war ended in the fall of 1966 after Indonesia signed a peace agreement with Malaysia. British casualties were 19 killed and 44 wounded; the Gurkhas lost 40 killed and 83 wounded. The enemy's dead alone numbered 2000.

An officer on watch at an observation post near the border of Brunei with Indonesia in 1965.

In 1964 the government set 1968 as the year British forces would leave the Aden colony and turn the country over to the South Arabian Federation, and Britain found herself committed to fighting a lost cause until that date arrived. For one thing, Britain was to retain her bases in Aden, which she would need as staging posts to maintain her global commitments east of Suez. Yet until independence came, she was obligated not to abandon the tribal rulers with whom she had had treaties of protection since the previous century. Late in 1963 trouble flared up when a grenade was hurled at the British High Commissioner and some Federal ministers as they prepared to fly to London for a conference, The forces pitted against Britain were those of the new Republican government in Yemen, to the north of Aden. It had already called on its 'brothers in the Occupied South' – Aden and the Federation – 'to be ready for a revolution and join the battle we shall wage against colonialism.' A strange war began to take shape, with Britain on one side and Yemeni nationalists backed by both Egypt and the Soviet Union on the other. The frontier was ill-defined, and the Adeni, Egyptian and Yemeni nationalists were bringing weapons across it. Further, the fierce border tribesmen had no love for the British or Aden's Federal Regular Army (FRA). For them, guerrilla warfare was a way of life, and they were supplied with money and rifles by the Yemen Republic. The battle was on for control of the blistering, roadless, well-nigh waterless Radfan Mountains a few miles to the north of Aden Colony.

In April 1964, when the SAS A Squadron was sent to Aden, the scope and strength of the opposition in the Radfan Mountains was not yet comprehended by the British. Although some battalions of the FRA and a few Britons did manage to occupy the mountains for a few weeks, they were forced to withdraw to guard key frontier points. The tribesmen promptly reinstalled themselves in their positions and began attacking traffic on the Dhala Road between Aden and Yemen. So began the long Radfan campaign, with the British determined to re-enter and con-

A RAF Belvedere helicopter brings supplies to a paratroop formation fighting in support of an SAS detachment near Hajib, South Arabia, in May 1964.

Above: Marines carry water to their position on 'Cap Badge' hill in the Radfan Mountains in 1964. The hill had been captured in an operation involving paratroop and SAS men as well as the Marines.

Right: A heavily laden patrol moves forward in search of a rebel unit in the Wadi Tayn area of the Radfan.

trol the mountains. Besides the SAS, the newly improvised group consisted of two battalions of FRA infantry, elements of 45 Royal Marine Commando, a troop of Royal Engineers, a battery of Royal Artillery and a Royal Tank Regiment unit.

The initial plan was to seize two key hill positions code-named 'Rice Bowl' and 'Cap Badge', since they commanded the camel routes from Yemen. The Marines were to march several miles into hostile territory along the Dhala Road and then ascend to take the more northerly position – Rice Bowl – while a para company was to be dropped near the foot of Cap Badge. It had to be a night operation, for both groups knew that to be caught in the valley after daybreak – with the guerrillas in strong positions above them – meant certain annihilation. Equally suicidal would be an attempt to land the paras in an undefended and unmarked drop zone. Normally, the paras' own pathfinder company would advance and set up such a zone, but this time the job was given to a nine-man SAS team commanded by Captain Robin Edwards. It would have to cover eight miles to reach its objective, with only some 24 hours to establish the drop zone. This brave team of men, the so-called Edwards Patrol, was ill-fated. Discovered early by the Arabs and forced to fight a fierce running battle in the hills, only

seven survived, and two of these were badly wounded. Edwards and his radioman were killed and decapitated by the guerrillas, and their heads were displayed publicly in Yemen.

After this, the overly ambitious main operation to seize key Radfan hills was scaled down to more modest targets. Instead of heavy strikes, 45 RMC and para units climbed and fought their way forward peak by peak, taking nearly six weeks to subdue the mountainous region and scatter the tenacious tribesmen. After that SAS squadrons were rotated between stints in Aden and the Borneo War until the latter ended in 1966. These sporadic clashes in Aden did not amount to a continuous campaign, but they served to build up the SAS's technical war experience, which would earmark the Regiment for usefulness in the coming Dhofar war in Oman in the 1970s and counterterrorism in Europe. Meanwhile, SAS soldiers continued their guerrilla operations in the Radfan hills, with the war smoldering on until the British withdrawal in 1967.

By 1969 the SAS was eking out a day-to-day living testing new equipment and doing such jobs as providing bodyguards for foreign heads of state. Just as rumours were beginning to circulate that the SAS had outlived its usefulness and might be disbanded, new problems surfaced in both Oman and Northern Ireland that demanded their presence.

Soon after the breakdown of law and order in Northern Ireland in 1969, SAS men of D Squadron were sent to quarters in Newtownards, near Belfast. The situation in Ulster Province had now grown potentially violent between civil rights demonstrators and the Royal Ulster Constabulary. Many Protestants were convinced that the civil war they had feared for decades was ready to erupt, while the Catholic communities were equally afraid that they were to be persecuted. After a tragic armored-car incident in which Royal Ulster Constabulary (RUC) officers, attempting to quiet a Catholic area in Belfast, inadvertently fired into a block and killed a child, Ulster did teeter on the brink of real civil war, and British soldiers were sent in to control the situation. The SAS, concerned at this time with possible Protestant gun-running, patrolled the countryside between the Mourne mountains and

the glens of Antrim. Although they searched everywhere, including incoming fishing boats on the coast, they found no caches of arms. By the spring of 1971, after the hard-nosed Provisional Irish Republican Army (IRA) surfaced to launch bombing campaigns, the authorities were determined to penetrate and destroy this network.

In the spring of 1972, SAS men – mainly officers and non-coms – became part of the military intelligence system in Ulster. Some were attached to units already in the province; however, they were only part of a much larger and constantly increasing network of intelligence specialists which, in the end, became overly complex and often counterproductive. In 1974, in an effort to impose greater order on the intelligence mess in Northern Ireland, more SAS officers were brought in to manipulate agents in the field. That year also saw the first use of an orthodox SAS squadron in Ulster, brought in despite the political resistance to such a deployment in London and Belfast at a time when clandestine negotiations with the IRA were going on. Later it was agreed at Prime Minister level that additional SAS soldiers should be sent to Northern Ireland, but without attendant publicity and often in plain clothes, to carry out assignments.

In January 1976, Prime Minister Harold Wilson, alarmed at increased IRA guerrilla warfare in the wild border country of South Armagh, announced that the SAS was to be formally committed to this area. Here the terrorists had had great success in raids on northern objectives, leapfrogging back and forth across the maze of

British Army soldiers on watch near a road block in the 'bandit country' of South Armagh in which the SAS operated so successfully.

British troops patrol alongside the Dublin-Belfast rail line in 1976.

frontier roads linking them to the friendly territory of the Irish Republic. Once back across the border, they could not be pursued by British forces. At the time of the SAS commitment, British Army border casualties stood at 49 dead, while the IRA had suffered no fatalities. Furthermore, in the South Armagh region many blow-for-blow retaliatory killings of Catholics and Protestants were occurring. Prime Minister Wilson, hoping to make a psychological impact on the IRA capitalizing on their reputation, made a public announcement that the SAS would enter the fray.

The SAS strength in South Armagh was gradually increased to squadron size, and by 1977 it had reportedly doubled. Their mission was to apprehend ten of the most powerful Provisional IRA leaders in the area. Less than a year after their commitment, the SAS had arrested three of them and killed a fourth who had tried to grab one soldier's rifle away from him. The other six were chased back to the south. Early in January 1977, at a spot in South Armagh where a young British Army corporal had been shot dead in an ambush, an SAS patrol pulled an ambush of its own. Tipped off by local civilians that there was a suspicious-looking car in the vicinity, an SAS patrol surprised an armed IRA party; after a fierce fire-fight, one of the terrorists lay dead. These and other SAS ambushes on IRA raiders from the south had a distinct deterrent effect. While British soldiers and Royal Ulster Constabulary men continued to be shot elsewhere in Northern Ireland, the IRA raids in South Armagh all but ceased during the SAS presence.

The SAS in Ulster, however, found themselves hamstrung in many of their efforts against the IRA. The latter, committed to a war of liberation against the forces of Britain, could claim the protection of the law in the Irish Republic – whose government it did not recognize – as well as in Northern Ireland. Further, the SAS often met covert hostility from elements in the police forces on both sides of the border, although theoretically they were all trying to put down a common antagonist. Not only could they not legally pursue the IRA across the frontier, the SAS was subject to the civil laws if they returned unprovoked gunfire; like any civilian, they could be charged with possession of firearms with intent to endanger life. On one occasion eight members of an SAS motor patrol, which had inadvertently crossed the border into the Republic and become lost, were taken into custody and actually made to stand trial in Dublin. Had they been convicted of possessing arms with intent to put life in jeopardy, the SAS troopers could have been imprisoned for twenty years. Fortunately, they were not.

Thus the SAS had to play its assigned role in Ulster with the utmost delicacy and discretion. As one cynical SAS soldier put it: 'Letting the opposition shoot first is what we call the "Irish Dimension."' Even so, SAS units today continue their missions in troubled Northern Ireland. Together with other British forces, the SAS's record of terrorist apprehensions and weapons hauls without bloodshed in Ulster is undoubtedly one of the finest accomplishments in a distinguished regimental history.

In May 1980 the SAS was instrumental in resolving a ticklish international crisis, and after years as political outcasts, its soldiers became heroes overnight. On this occasion the SAS anti-terrorist Counter Revolutionary Warfare Team (CRWT) went into action in England itself for the first time. Several years of planning, critiqueing and rehearsing were put to the test in eleven action-packed minutes in the Iranian Embassy in London.

The incident began after the body of the Iranian press attaché, Abbas Lavasani, was thrown from the besieged embassy onto the steps at Princes Gate. The terrorist leader, whose name was Own, declared that unless his demands for negotiations with three Arab ambassadors in London were met, he would murder another hostage every half hour. He also demanded a guarantee of safe conduct out of England for his men and their hostages. Meanwhile, negotiators from the London police sustained the discussions while the SAS CRW team swung in on special ropes from the roof of the building to the balconies. The embassy building itself had 50 rooms. In all there were now 20 hostages. Fifteen of them were men, who were all in Room 10, which was the telex room overlooking the streets on the second floor, guarded by three of the terrorists. In Room 9 on the far side of the building, there were five embassy staff women hostages who were in the charge of one terrorist. In addition, there were two new hostages – Police Constable Trevor Lock, who had been taken prisoner in the terrorists' assault on the embassy, and a British Broadcasting Corporation man named Sim Harris. These two men were near the telephone booth on the first floor; they had been with Own as he talked with the police negotiators just seconds before the first assault commenced.

At the front of the embassy, the only plausible point of attack was across a balcony on the first floor level. However, this route had the obstacle of a window made of armor-plated glass which would have to be blown in with explosives. But, in order to take full advantage of the element of surprise, an SAS team at the rear of the building would have to enter as soon as they heard the frontal team's charge go off.

Unfortunately this plan never worked out. Some four pairs of SAS soldiers on the embassy roof began their descent on two ropes down the rear of the building. Another team, carrying charges of plastic explosive to deal with the front window, was ready to go on to a nearby balcony. As the frontal team started down, one of the two men inadvertently swung against an upper storey room's window and broke it with his boot. When this happened the terrorist chief, Own, laid down the telephone he was using and went to see what was the matter. Constable Lock followed him; unbeknownst to Own he had managed to conceal his service revolver under his uniform. As for the rear assault team, they had learned of the frontal team's difficulties and decided to make their own attack now instead of waiting for the explosion.

The first pair of SAS men dropped quickly to the ground at the back of the embassy. As they got set to blast their way into the building, the second two-man team had already made the first-floor balcony. Immediately they began hacking away at the window and tossed in the first 'flash-bang,' or concussion grenade, which was meant to stun any terrorist within. Meanwhile, a man in the third team was in trouble; he had gotten tangled in his abseil rope and could move neither up nor down. This presented a problem for the team on the ground floor, who were now ready with their explosive charge. To have set it off would surely have killed the man trapped in his rope above. Instead, they too commenced hacking away at their window, throwing in flash-bangs as they went in. Inside the embassy, Own was now preparing to fire at one of the SAS men who had broken into the rear of the building. Seeing this, Constable Lock made a flying tackle and brought down the terrorist chief. There now ensued a savage struggle between the two men, during which the constable drew his concealed pistol. Just then the SAS man cried out, 'Trevor, leave off!' Own then rolled over and was about to shoot Lock when slugs from the SAS soldier's submachine gun ripped with deadly impact into his body.

As this was going on, two SAS men at the front of the building were rigging up the plastic charge to the armor-plated window. When the ten-second fuze was activated, the pair dashed for cover to a nearby balcony. Seconds later the explosion rocked the embassy, as the armored window shattered into shards. Afterward SAS men burst into the embassy through the smoke and rushed up the stairs. Sim Harris, the BBC man, was just feeling his way out through a win-

Overleaf: British Broadcasting Corporation employee Sim Harris leaps across the balcony to safety as the SAS attack on the Iranian Embassy begins. Harris was unfortunate enough to be in the Embassy applying for a visa for an assignment to Iran when the terrorist occupation began.

Below: A masked SAS man prepares to charge into the Iranian Embassy after detonating an explosive charge to blow in an armored glass window.

dow when an SAS soldier brushed by him, barking, 'Get down!' Harris complied and the team darted past him after tossing more concussion grenades. Outside, other SAS men of the CRW team fired a gas cartridge into a front room at the top of the embassy where a sixth terrorist was concealed. Around the back of the embassy, the soldier who was still enmeshed in his abseil rope was getting singed each time he swung against the window opposite him – for a fire had broken out inside and was consuming the heavy drapery. Seeing this, his mates had no choice but to cut his rope and drop him to the ground. Picking himself up, he followed the others inside the embassy where, spotting an armed terrorist, he got off the first burst and killed the man.

In Room 10, the three terrorist guards had decided to kill their hostages upon hearing the first sounds of fighting. They did kill the assistant press attaché, Samad-Zadeh, and then tried to murder the chargé d'affaires, Gholam-Ali-Afrouz, who was shot in the face and legs. A third hostage escaped death only because a terrorist's slug was blocked by a large coin in his pocket. At this point, hearing the SAS soldiers approaching, they resorted to a common terrorist ploy: they pretended to be hostages themselves. A few instants before the SAS burst into Room 10, they cast their weapons aside and threw themselves onto the floor among the hostages. The SAS soldiers had a single primary mission – to retrieve the hostages alive. As they surveyed the people on the floor in Room 10, they had no clue as to which ones were the terrorists; they gave no sign of surrender. Recently arrived from Ireland, the soldiers were very wary of booby traps, and they fully suspected the terrorists to be carrying concealed explosives, perhaps grenades, with which they could do further damage. The SAS men had little choice except to kill the terrorists. One hostage pointed them out and they were shot one by one. In Room 9 the single young terrorist hid among the women hostages where it was a simple matter to identify and apprehend him.

A final terrorist was shot in the upstairs room in which he had taken refuge. The only one to survive was the boy who had guarded the women. Since the upper floor of the embassy was now burning furiously and the fire threatened to spread downward, the hostages were removed to the rear lawn of the embassy grounds. But firing still echoed through the building as SAS continued to shoot away locks to search other rooms. In the SAS tactical headquarters near the embassy, it was discovered that their only casualties were one soldier burned and another who had had his thumb nearly shot away. And the Home Secretary, William Whitelaw, who had urged the Prime Minister earlier that day to employ the SAS in this sensitive mission, was there to thank and congratulate them. That same evening, Prime Minister Margaret Thatcher herself joined the soldiers at SAS headquarters to watch the television film of the memorable rescue.

The publishers would like to thank Design 23 who
designed this book and Ron Watson who compiled
the index. The following agencies and individuals
kindly supplied the illustrations.

Arromanches Museum (via MARS): p 81
Michael Badrocke: pp 54, 55
Bison Picture Library: pp 1, 29, 38 bottom, 84, 86 lower, 88,
  89, 92, 93, 96 both, 176 top, 177 bottom
Chaz Bowyer: pp 50, 52, 53, 55 upper, 56, 57
Ann Brown Collection, Brown University: pp 6, 10, 11 both,
  12, 13, 15 all three, 32, 33, 34-35 all three
Bundesarchiv: pp 26 top, 86 top, 95 bottom
Bundesarchiv (via Robert Hunt): p 99
Library of Congress: pp 22-23
ECPA: pp 30-31
Carina Dvorak: pp 90, 91, 94 both, 97, 98 both, 100, 101
Robert Hunt Library: pp 28 lower, 87 top, 95 upper
Imperial War Museum, London: pp 26-27, 108 top left, 114
  top right, 176-177
Imperial War Museum (via Robert Hunt): p 87 bottom
Imperial War Museum (via MARS): pp 66, 68, 70, 70-71, 72,
  73, 74, 75 all three, 76-77 both, 79, 80, 82
Imperial War Museum (via Jennifer Moore Personality
  Picture Library): pp 69, 177 top
Peter Newark's Historical Pictures: pp 8, 9 both, 17, 28 top,
  31, 155 right, 156, 157
National Archives, Washington DC: pp 20, 27 top, 42, 44, 45,
  47, 48, 104 upper, 105, 110-111 both
Maps © Richard Natkiel: pp 27, 167
Paul A Rockwell Collection: p 61 bottom
US Air Force: pp 58-59 both, 60, 61 top, 62, 63, 64, 65, 116,
  124, 126, 130 bottom right, 132 both, 133
US Air Force (via Carina Dvorak): pp 128-129 both, 130
  bottom left, 131 bottom
US Air Force (via Robert Hunt): pp 130-131
US Army: pp 38 top, 102, 104 bottom, 106, 106-107, 107 top
  right, 108 top right, 109 both, 112, 117 both, 118 both, 120,
  121, 122, 125, 142, 143, 158, 160, 161, 162-163 all three,
  164, 165 both, 166, 167, 168 both, 169, 170, 171, 172, 173
US Army (via MARS): pp 71, 107 top left
US Marine Corps: pp 2-3, 4-5, 19 both, 21 both, 22 top, 23
  top, 24, 36-37 both, 39, 40-41, 49, 114-115, 140, 144 top,
  144-145, 146-147 all three, 148-149 both, 150-151 all three,
  front cover
US Navy: p 134
US Navy (via MARS): pp 138 top, 139
Wide World Photos: pp 152-153 all three, 154, 155 left, 174,
  178, 179, 180-181 all three, 182, 183, 184 both, 185, 186,
  187, 189